"This is a book of many virtues. It undertakes the conversation that the later Heidegger was too haughty and the mature Marcuse too disappointed to initiate. In light of this conversation, both Heidegger and Marcuse scholars will be provoked to take a deeper and more fruitful approach to these two giants of twentieth century philosophy. More important still, the book's brilliant readings of Plato, Aristotle, Heidegger, and Marcuse give new resonance to Feenberg's own work and open up new avenues for his extraordinarily circumspect and incisive social philosophy."

—Albert Borgmann, University of Montana

"The Heidegger and Marcuse controversy over technology is an exciting story, not yet told, and Feenberg is clearly the one to do it."

—Douglas Kellner, University of California at Los Angeles

"It is well known that Marcuse was a student of Heidegger, and it is clear that the theme of technology's deep transformation of our experience is quite prominent in both. But there has been little serious, detailed, philosophically informed treatment of this common issue in both thinkers.

"Feenberg's book admirably fills that gap and more, illuminating each philosopher by comparison and contrast with the other, and finally offering an extremely well-informed and original perspective on the issue. (Modern technological pessimism rarely admits the possibility of the 'redemption' announced in the subtitle.) This is certainly the most philosophically ambitious and thoughtful treatment of Marcuse yet published, and is in its own right a sophisticated, compelling meditation on critical theory and our technological fate."

—Robert Pippin, University of Chicago

Heidegger
and Marcuse

The Catastrophe and Redemption of History

Andrew Feenberg

Routledge

New York • London

Published in 2005 by
Routledge
270 Madison Avenue
New York, NY 10016
www.routledge-ny.com

Published in Great Britain by
Routledge
2 Park Square
Milton Park, Abingdon
Oxon OX14 4RN U.K.
www.routledge.co.uk

Routledge is an imprint of the Taylor & Francis Group.

Printed in the United States of America on acid free paper.
Typesetting: Jack Donner, BookType.

Library of Congress Cataloging-in-Publication Data

Feenberg, Andrew.
Heidegger and Marcuse : the catastrophe and redemption of history / Andrew Feenberg.
    p. cm.
  Includes bibliographical references.
  ISBN 0-415-94177-6 (hardcover : alk. paper) - ISBN 0-415-94178-4 (pbk. : alk. paper)
  1. Heidegger, Martin, 1889-1976. 2. Marcuse, Herbert, 1898–
3. Technology-Philosophy-History-20th century. I. Title.
B3279.H49F387 2004
193–dc22
                                                                      2004019355

10 9 8 7 6 5 4 3 2 1

Contents

Acknowledgments

Like most authors, I owe thanks to many people, most especially Junichi Murata, Shunsuke Kadowaki, and Yasuo Kobayashi for inviting me to the University of Tokyo Center for Philosophy to lecture on the themes in this book. Gernot Böhme also generously included me in his conference on Critical Theory of Nature where I presented an early version of my argument. Richard Polt and Albert Borgmann encouraged me at an early stage. Robert Pippin was an insightful interlocutor. Debates with Iain Thomson and Jerry Doppelt have enabled me to sharpen many of my ideas. Jeffrey Kochan, Dana Belu, Jessica Thompson, and John Abromeit sent me useful comments. Anne-Marie Feenberg has once again been the faithful reader of too many drafts to count.

Preface

I arrived in La Jolla, California in the fall of 1965 as a graduate student in philosophy. One of my reasons for coming was what I had heard of Herbert Marcuse. He was not yet famous but he was well known and what was known about him intrigued me. I was interested in phenomenology, but a philosopher wild enough to synthesize Marx and Freud was wild enough for a young graduate student looking for an alternative to the dry as dust positivism then dominating American philosophy.

At the first opportunity I asked Professor Marcuse to help me study Martin Heidegger's *Being and Time*. He accepted my proposal and we spent many Tuesday afternoons debating the meaning of obscure passages in this book which, unbeknownst to me, had inspired Marcuse to leave Berlin for Freiburg 38 years before.

One afternoon as we left Marcuse's office a magnificent sunset appeared before us. Standing on the balcony of the Humanities Building dazzled by the spectacle of nature, Marcuse turned to me and said, in his deep, heavily accented voice, "Make me a phenomenological reduction of this!" I was unable to reply. I remember feeling the demand to be unfair, sarcastic.

Zen Buddhists are supposed to achieve sudden enlightenment meditating on an unsolvable problem called a *koan*. Phenomenology seemed to collapse in the face of Marcuse's stunning *koan,* but sudden enlightenment did not follow. It could not possibly have occurred to me then that the rejection of a phenomenological reduction that late afternoon confirmed yet again Marcuse's decision to abandon Heidegger's mentorship in 1933. He had found another way to understand beauty and its promise of happiness.

A few months later, my fellow graduate students and I created a magazine to publicize our anti-war views. Recall that this was early on in the Vietnam War and the American public was still supportive. Dissent was the act of a small minority to which we belonged. We asked Marcuse for an article to start us off. He contributed "The Individual in the Great Society" (Marcuse 1966a). This article described the suppression of individuality under the impact of technological advance. It ends with a convoluted passage I want to quote here as it offers a clue to my *koan* and the agenda of Marcuse's later work which I try to understand in this book.

> Under both aspects, the traditional concept of the individual, in its classic-liberal as well as Marxist form seems to be untenable—canceled (*aufgehoben*) by the historical development of productivity.... Authentic individuality would remain the distinction of the creative artist, writer, or musician. The idea of making this creative potential general among the population at large militates against the very function and truth of the artistic creation as a form of expression ... because it [art] implies dissociation from, and negation of, common sense and common values: ingression of a qualitatively different reality in the established one. In the case of the second alternative (fundamental transformation of the society), individuality would refer to an entirely new existential dimension: to a domain of play, experiment, and imagination which is outside the reaches of any policy and program today. (Marcuse 2001, 80)

This article was composed in 1965. It accurately foresaw the shipwreck of Lyndon Johnson's Great Society on the rock of Vietnam. What it did not, could not foresee was the rise of the New Left and the counter-culture. At that time demonstrations against the war in Vietnam on most campuses, including ours, attracted students by the dozens, not the thousands, who would soon be mobilized by the anti-war movement.

Marcuse believed that the elimination of true individuality in "one-dimensional society" explained the absence of opposition. Individuality requires mental independence and a standard, a vision of a better world. The arts have always represented such an alternative. (Our magazine was called *Alternatives*.) In modern times a limited form of individuality became widely available. The Enlightenment opened a public sphere within which political ideals sustained a critical stance. Now the space of public debate was closing down. Once again individuality was to be found primarily in the aesthetic realm. For it to emerge from behind its old artistic borders, Marcuse claimed, it would have to take a far more radical form than in the past. The new individuals would realize the negative, critical content of art in the real world, overthrowing its common sense, and devaluing its values.

Aesthetics as the form of a new consciousness and sensibility! The generalization of the oppositional force of beauty as social critique! What strange notions! I had no idea that in 1918 Marcuse participated in the German Revolution as a member of the Berlin Soldiers' Council and shortly afterward wrote a thesis on novels featuring artists in conflict with society. For him the unity of political and aesthetic opposition was no mere fantasy. But I also recall this personal detail from my student days: on the wall of his dining room in California, he had a large print of Breughel's *Fall of Icarus* which he kept as a permanent warning against romantic idealism.[1]

The full implications of Marcuse's ideas on individuality unfolded finally with the rise of the New Left. In France the May Events of 1968 demanded "All Power to the Imagination," a slogan that refuted his gloomy prognostication in the passage quoted above. He was only too happy to be refuted. We witnessed the beginnings of the movement together in Paris. Returning to his hotel in the Latin Quarter he was accosted by a group of students who had just occupied the *Ecole des Beaux Arts*. They recognized him from his picture in the newspapers where he was celebrated as the "Guru of the Students in Revolt."

We entered the *Ecole* and Marcuse addressed the hundred or more young artists gathered in the main assembly hall. It is easy to imagine the excitement of the author of a thesis on aesthetic resistance at the podium of this monument to "affirmative culture."[2] He was warmly received. French students celebrated the grandfathers of the revolution in preference to their fathers whom they blamed for social ills. Marcuse made a short speech in French, greeting the students in the name of the American student movement and congratulating them on challenging "consumer society." They seemed impressed by this echo from the depths of history, although the Maoists in the audience were visibly puzzled by the reference to consumption.

When *An Essay on Liberation* appeared a year later it was dedicated to the French "militants," the students and young workers in revolt. "The radical utopian character of their demands," he wrote in the preface, "far surpasses the hypotheses of my essay" (Marcuse 1969a, ix). That book explored in some detail the generalization of aesthetic resistance that the earlier article had dismissed. The boundaries of art had burst and aesthetics had become a new kind of politics with the transformation of the technical base of society as its goal. The young resisted not merely because they disagreed with government policy but because their sensibility rebelled at the waste and violence of the society around them.

An Essay on Liberation and the several books that followed attempted to explain the new forms of opposition emerging in one-dimensional society. Although this was a topic that fascinated me during this same period, I was never fully convinced by Marcuse's approach. The emphasis on aesthetics did not quite correspond with my experience of the movement. I would have said its core impulse was revulsion at the conformist pressures of the culture of the 1950s in which we had all grown up rather than an aesthetic vision of the future. In any case, what I took from Marcuse was his critique of technology which I have developed further in my own books over the last 15 years. My doubts about the aesthetic interpretation of the New Left were widely shared. Marcuse's last writings had diminishing impact and eventually contributed to the decline of his reputation.

Now, looking back on Marcuse's work, I am still not convinced. But I see his thought in a very different light today. When Marcuse left Heidegger he rescinded the phenomenological reduction for all situations and occasions (sunsets included). But rereading him, I find the traces of Heidegger's thought everywhere in his writings and in the most surprising places. And I miss reference to Heidegger there, too, in the most problematic of Marcuse's speculations where phenomenology might have been helpful.

Those speculations are a development of ideas already present in his earliest publications under Heidegger's tutelage. These early works constitute a unique philosophical position that has been called "*Heidegger-Marxismus*." Marcuse arrived at this position by a twofold path: on the one hand he concretized the concept of authenticity in *Being and Time*; on the other hand he developed a new interpretation of the Hegelian and Marxian dialectics of "real possibility" or "potentiality." Marcuse did not quite follow these paths to the point of intersection but we can project a likely unification of his thought at which he would no doubt have arrived had he remained under Heidegger's influence for a few more years.

Heidegger's concept of authenticity continues a philosophical tradition that begins with Rousseau and Kant. In their thought the essence of the human being is freedom. This marks a break with substantive notions of human nature such as Aristotle's that define the human in terms of definite qualities and virtues. Human nature, insofar as there is such a thing for a philosophy of freedom, consists of formal properties of the subject rather than a repertoire of attributes. But the logic of freedom in Rousseau and Kant is bound to a notion of rationality that ends up determining the *telos* of human development much as had earlier substantive theories of human nature.

For existentialists—and despite his denial Heidegger is a kind of existentialist—freedom is illusory unless it escapes every rationalistic conception of its end. This Heidegger accomplishes by defining human "*Dasein*" as a self-questioning and self-making being "thrown" into a world without rhyme or reason and destined to discover its own meanings there. But inauthentic existence, average everyday existence, consists in conformism and refusal of self-responsibility. The insight into freedom represented by Heidegger's philosophy is too hard a lesson to be commonly lived. To be fully human—authentic—is to acknowledge the groundlessness of human existence and nevertheless to act resolutely. By resoluteness Heidegger does not mean arbitrary decisions but rather "precisely the disclosive projection and determination of what is factically possible at the time," that is, the response called for by the situation (Heidegger 1962, 345). In resoluteness the human being intervenes actively in shaping its world and defining itself, as opposed to inauthentic conformism. Unfortunately, Heidegger's philosophy offers no means for determining criteria of what is "factically possible" and so leaves the question of action in the air.

Marcuse took over this theory unreservedly in his early writings, but he rejected Heidegger's abstract formulations. What is this "situation" in which the human being is "thrown," and what are these "possibilities" so vaguely invoked by Heidegger in *Being and Time*? The emptiness of such categories invites revision. Heidegger himself filled in the blanks with Nazi ideology for a time, although one wonders how he made the leap from the heights of philosophical abstraction to the lower depths of nationalism and racism. Marcuse turned in the opposite direction toward Marxism. The self is thrown into a capitalist society where the alienation of production is the source of the inauthenticity that must be overcome. Now authenticity becomes the "radical act" of revolutionary refusal of the existing society.

In Heidegger making and self-making are intimately connected in the concept of being-in-the-world developed in the first chapters of *Being and Time*. Dasein's answer to the question of its being is bound up with the technical practices through which it gives meaning to and acts in its world. But, strangely, production drops out when Heidegger explains authenticity in the second division of his master work. This ambiguity disappears as Heidegger develops his later critique of technology. Technical practice ends up *unmaking* worlds and the reference to self-making, and with it the whole problematic of authenticity, simply disappears from Heidegger's discourse.

Marcuse resolves the ambiguity differently. He first introduces the Marxist idea of revolution in a two-sided formulation that encompasses the transformation of both individual and society. As he describes it, the central concern of "the Marxist fundamental situation ... is with the historical possibility of the radical act—of an act that should liberate a new and necessary reality as it brings about the actualization of the whole person" (Marcuse 1987c, 350).[3] Marcuse soon turns to the Hegelian idea of labor as an objectification of the human spirit to join Heidegger's phenomenological analysis of production with his abstract conception of human self-making. Labor is an engagement with possibilities actualized through struggle with nature, possibilities which belong to the human being as well as the object. The "possibility" required by the "situation" is thus neither the determined outcome of objective processes as orthodox Marxists supposed, nor an ineffable intuition with dubious results as in Heidegger himself, but a free appropriation of the human essence in a socially concrete form through the liberation of labor.

Marcuse never articulated the relation between his theories of authenticity and possibility quite as clearly as this. The radical act and the dialectical interpretation of history are the two sides of an arch awaiting the keystone to join them. I will argue in this book that that keystone is the later critique of technology through which Marcuse returned to these themes in disguised forms. In the process, he again encountered Heidegger's thought which in the interim had become a critical philosophy of technology.

Like Heidegger the later Marcuse saw technology as more than technical, as more even than political; it is the form of modern experience itself, the principal way in which the world is revealed. For both philosophers "technology" thus extends its reach far beyond actual devices. It signifies a way of thinking and a style of practice, indeed, a quasi-transcendental structuring of reality as an object of technical control (Marcuse 1964, 218–219). Release from this form of experience can only come through another form of experience, an aesthetic form. In Heideggerian terms, as Hubert Dreyfus explains them, Marcuse calls for a new disclosure of being through a transformation of basic practices (Dreyfus, 1995; Marcuse 1964, 231).[4] Marcuse's aesthetics does not just introduce a criterion of beauty into radical political judgments, but describes the a priori form of a new type of experience belonging to a new social order.

While Heidegger no longer calls for resoluteness in the face of the inauthentic world of technology, Marcuse remains committed to "authentic individuality," as we have seen. In his last works an authentic human existence is to be achieved at the level of society as a whole through the aestheticization of technology, that is, through its transformation into an instrument for realizing the highest possibilities of human beings and things. Marcuse realizes now that this cannot be achieved on the basis of the existing capitalist technology regardless of the prevailing property and political relations. The very general notions of labor and possibility with which he worked in his early writings covered over the awful gap between making and self-making in a world organized around modern technology. A further concretization is necessary to distinguish the type of technology that can join them. But *Heidegger-Marxismus* long since abandoned, Marcuse lacked the theoretical means to articulate his new position coherently and persuasively. His last works are inspiring gestures at a theory he no more than hints at. How then are we to understand his turn to aesthetics and his concept of a new science and technology?

A possible solution to the enigma of Marcuse's later thought came to me two years ago when reading Heidegger's 1931 lectures on Aristotle's *Metaphysics*. These lectures present a strange reading of Aristotle. In Heidegger's account, Aristotle's conception of being in general is derived from the Greek practice of technical making, from *techné*. In its role as an ontological model, *techné* is not treated objectively as an event in the world, but phenomenologically described from within on its own terms, anticipating Heidegger's own thought in *Being and Time*. Exaggerating only slightly, one could say that Heidegger presents Aristotle as a phenomenological philosopher of technology. *Techné*, understood in this manner, reappears in Heidegger's later critique of technology as a contrasting mode of revealing that is respectful of human beings and nature. *Techné* realizes the inherent potentialities of things rather than violating them as does modern technology. Thus here in the early Heidegger there is already an analysis of an emancipatory technology. Although Heidegger himself never proposed a revival of *techné*, this suggests a new way of understanding the connection between Marcuse and his teacher.

In 1969, Heidegger met with a group of friends in Le Thor, Provence. The record of their discussions has been published in a volume entitled *Four Seminars*. Here we find the only reference to Marcuse in Heidegger's published writings. He notes that production is defining for the "world" in Marx, and further, that production is a type of *praxis*. "Reversing Hegel's idealism in his own way, Marx requires that being be given precedence over consciousness. Since there is no consciousness in *Being and Time*, one could believe that there is something Heideggerian to be read here [in Marx]! At least Marcuse had understood *Being and Time* in this way" (Heidegger 2003, 52).

What is Heidegger saying in this derisive remark about his former student? Marx claimed that the fundamental relation to being is not consciousness but *praxis*. *Being and Time* similarly describes the human relation to the world as fundamentally practical. In his student days, Marcuse noted the parallel and read *Being and Time* as the key to Marx. But Heidegger himself goes on to dismiss productionist metaphysics. Being, he argues in his later work, cannot be understood through the model of technical making. This is the stance consistently maintained by the later Heidegger which he projected back onto his early work.

The Aristotle course gives the lie to this self-representation. Heidegger was not a consistent critic of productionism. In fact much of *Being and Time* was inspired by Aristotle's account of *techné*. He told his class in 1931: "We have to clarify for ourselves what it signifies that man has a relation to the works that he produces. It is for this reason that a certain book called *Sein und Zeit* discusses dealings with equipment; and not in order to correct Marx, nor to organize a new political economy, nor out of a primitive understanding of the world" (Heidegger 1995a, 117, trans. modified). Thus, Marcuse was not mistaken in interpreting *Being and Time* as a productionist text, and hence also in finding Heidegger relevant to the early Marx. Marcuse remained true at some level to an earlier Heidegger the later Heidegger rejected and concealed.[5]

As we will see, Marcuse's aesthetic radicalism in his own later work is intricately intertwined with these repressed themes in Heidegger. In my view, there remains much in Marcuse that is theoretically incomplete precisely because he refused either to drop central phenomenological themes or to develop them phenomenologically. Marcuse's aesthetics of technology introduces a fatal ambiguity in his thought. At first it seems that he follows the usual Marxist formulations in which potentialities are objective properties of society. But in the late Marcuse potentialities are revealed aesthetically, that is, to an attuned subject. Such a subject, technically engaged with the potentialities of its objects, is analyzed for the first time not in Marx but in Heidegger's phenomenological interpretation of Aristotle. Only a phenomenological account of values in action can make sense of the notion that aesthetics provides the normative basis for the reconstruction of technological rationality. And when Marcuse imagines aesthetics incorporated into everyday sensation as a critical force, his hypothesis implies a phenomenological conception of experience. It is not unreasonable to suppose that such a conception of experience could be reconciled with the sort of objective considerations brought forward in Marcuse's social theory. But he does not pursue this line and falls between the two alternative interpretations of potentiality, an existential-aesthetic interpretation and a Marxist notion based on an evaluation of social forces.

On this I am in partial disagreement with Douglas Kellner's excellent intellectual biography of Marcuse. Kellner explores Heidegger's influence on the early Marcuse in some detail and notes that traces of Heideggerian thought remain till the end. But Kellner emphasizes the fundamentally Marxist, i.e., non–Heideggerian character of Marcuse's work after his discovery of Marx's *Manuscripts* of 1844 and claims that even earlier Marcuse's "fundamental project is the reconstruction of Marxism" (Kellner 1984, 77–78, 389–90; see also Abromeit, 2004). This evaluation is intended to counter dismissive attacks on Marcuse from more or less orthodox Marxists. I do agree with Kellner that the superficial similarities between Marcuse and Heidegger fall away quite early. But I will argue that there is considerable continuity at the deepest philosophical level. This continuity is never quite made explicit but it is tantalizingly present in Marcuse's work and particularly clear after 1968. As Reinhart Maurer remarks, "Heidegger's and Marcuse's later writings circle around the same philosophical-historical problems, and the solutions for which they hope exhibit a similar structure" (Maurer 1970, 241). To identify that structure one must enter into the details of some of the most abstract early texts of Heidegger and Marcuse.

Why did Marcuse fail to explain the links between his early work under Heidegger's influence and his later work? He could not go back to his existential roots after the "Fall of the Titans of German philosophy" (Marcuse 1968, 42).[6] Heidegger's betrayal stood as an absolute barrier between Marcuse as a Marxist and the other great trend of 20th century European thought, phenomenology and existentialism. The split between these trends now appears less significant than it did before they were both overshadowed by postmodernism and poststructurialism. Perhaps they were not opposites but *frères ennemis* with too much in common not to be in rivalry. Sartre's later work represents the one great failed attempt to synthesize the contending trends in the framework of a philosophy of consciousness. In this book I argue that philosophy of technology could have offered another possible synthesis that was never developed to its logical conclusion. I attempt to break through the barrier between these trends and make explicit a remarkable theory of *techné* initiated by Heidegger, continued by Marcuse, and suppressed in the end by both.

February 2004   Vancouver, British Columbia

CHAPTER 1

Techné

Prologue with Plato and Aristotle

Heidegger and Marcuse

We are several hundred years into the project of Enlightenment, initiated in the 18th century by thinkers who believed in progress. We are the heirs of that project, which freed science and technology for the adventure of modernity. This has made all the difference. No doubt human nature remains much the same—at least the level of aggression remains disturbingly high—but the means at our disposal are now more powerful than in the past. Quantity has changed into quality as technology alters the basic parameters of human action. New dilemmas emerge in a society reconstructed around these new technical means.

Two philosophers have reflected most deeply on this situation. Martin Heidegger invites us to study technology as the decisive philosophical issue of our time. Most philosophers either celebrate technical progress or worry about its unintended consequences; they conceive society as separate from technology, which holds either a promise or a threat. Heidegger, on the contrary, defines modernity itself as the prevalence of technology. Particular technical achievements and failures are unimportant since our very dependence on technology gives rise to general catastrophe. Heidegger's student, Herbert Marcuse, reformulated the philosophy of technology in the framework of a radical social theory and projected an alternative to the desperate situation Heidegger described. For Marcuse technology is not a fixed destiny as it is for Heidegger. The promise of Enlightenment remains to be fulfilled in the future through a deep transformation of technology. Together, these two philosophers offer the deepest insight into the danger of technology and the possibilities of redemption.

Heidegger's philosophy of technology is a puzzling combination of romantic nostalgia for an idealized image of antiquity and deep insight into modernity. His originality lies in treating technique not merely as a functional means but as a mode of "revealing" through which a "world" is shaped. "World" in Heidegger refers not to the sum of existent things but to an ordered and meaningful structure of experience. Such structures depend on basic practices characterizing societies and whole historical eras. These constitute an "opening" in which "being" is revealed, that is to say, in which experience takes place. Human being, called "*Dasein*" by Heidegger, can only be understood as always already involved in a world in this sense. As such, it is "being-in-the-world." The things of the world are "revealed" to *Dasein* as they are encountered in use and so Heidegger calls them "equipment" (*Zeug*).

Heidegger's language sounds mysterious. We will return to the reason for his peculiar locutions in a later chapter. Here it is enough to consider what he is saying at the simplest level. He is not claiming that things exist because we use them but rather that their meaning is tied up with our existence as experiencing, active beings. As such we encounter them as this or that particular object available for this or that role in our lives. A thing that was in principle out of any possible contact with a being such as ourselves, would not "make sense" but would be a bare existence, its infinite potentials a meaningless blur. It is we who order experience into recognizable objects. Without us, chairs and tables would not be the sort of things one calls chairs and tables (e.g., things to sit on, to eat at, to set and stack and clean, and so on). Mountains and stars too would be empty of meaning out of the context of a world in which such things have a place even if it be purely aesthetic, imaginary, or scientific. The difficult point is that without a finite being-in-the-world to encounter them, things are literally meaningless, non-sense, without distinction, boundaries, or definiteness. It is absurd to talk about "things" on this hypothesis. What we normally call "objective reality" is perfectly real, but it falls under this finite horizon we cannot coherently think our way around, behind, or beyond.

This picture of *Dasein*'s active and engaged being-in-the-world is obscured in modern times by technological thinking which treats everything as essentially an object of cognition, a simple matter of fact, including human beings themselves. Heidegger argues that this objectivistic outlook is not innocent. It goes along with the fundamental restructuring of the world by technoscience. Eventually human beings as well as things become mere components in the technical system. The modern world is a place of total mobilization for ends that remain obscure. It is this apparent "value freedom" or "neutrality" of technology that Heidegger and later, Marcuse, identify as the source of the uniqueness and the tragedy of modernity. This is what allows technology to destroy both man and nature. A world "enframed" by technology is radically alien and hostile. The danger is not merely nuclear weapons or some similar threat to survival, but the obliteration of humanity's special status and dignity as the being through which the world takes on intelligibility and meaning; for human beings have become mere raw materials like the nature they pretend to dominate (Heidegger 1977).

Both Marcuse and Heidegger are controversial figures. Marcuse is remembered as the guru of the New Left, the darling of 1968, a drastic foreshortening of a career that extended over more than fifty years of intense philosophical activity. Heidegger, of course, is the philosopher who betrayed his calling by becoming a Nazi and recognizing Hitler as his "*Führer*," never renouncing his error publicly even after World War II. And Heidegger is also, in the view of many, the greatest philosopher of the 20th century.

Here there will not be much discussion of these contentious issues. Others have explored every aspect of the Heidegger case. The conclusion I have reached from studying their views is that while Heidegger's thought could be accommodated to certain aspects of Nazism, especially to its eschatological mood and elitist spirit, only an astonishing insensitivity could have blinded him to even more important incompatibilities. Apparently, he found excuses for Hitler's biological racism and the persecution of his Jewish neighbors, students, colleagues, and teacher. But then he was hardly alone in combining academic brilliance and moral blindness (Sluga 1993). In any case, I do not dismiss Heidegger's philosophy as Nazi ideology, and thus continue to study it for its contributions to our understanding of technology.

Marcuse shared that view in the period of his apprenticeship to Heidegger. Like Heidegger's other Jewish students, who included Hannah Arendt, Hans Jonas, and Karl Löwith, Marcuse never noticed Heidegger's political leanings until the surprise announcement that he was to become the first Nazi rector of the University of Freiburg.[1] To the end of his life Marcuse praised Heidegger as a great reader of classic philosophical texts, and that is exactly what will interest us here. Not only did Marcuse admire Heidegger's teaching, he drew quite openly on Heidegger's critique of modern technology in *One-Dimensional Man* (Marcuse 1964, 153–54). A history of philosophical influence remains to be unraveled.

Despite my intention to focus on philosophical issues, my position is bound to annoy some scholars. In the tradition of Frankfurt School Critical theory, Heidegger is the very devil. Theodor Adorno could think of nothing worse to say of Marcuse than that he was a secret Heideggerian, and Jürgen Habermas articulated his deep uneasiness at the extreme negativity of Adorno's negative dialectics by hinting that its conclusions resembled Heidegger's. On the other side of the fence there are few Heideggerians who have shown an interest in Critical Theory. In that tradition the problems of political and economic domination that concern these Marxist philosophers are generally dismissed as merely "ontic."

I intend to forge ahead despite these controversies. In any case, I am interested in other aspects of the thought of Heidegger and Marcuse. My approach is based on Heidegger's distinction between the Greek notion of *techné* and the modern idea of technology. Where the ancient craftsman built his world in making the product of his craft, modern technology destroys the world to the extent of its technological success. Greek philosophy analyzed being on the model of *techné*, and, Heidegger argues, technology is the model for understanding being in modern times (Lovitt, 1980). Heidegger sees no way back to the world of the

Greeks, no way to recover ancient *techné* in a modern context. His late speculations on what he called the "new beginning" are much celebrated by postmodern
commentators. But these speculations on what might follow the passage through
modernity are so vague and abstract the commentators cannot agree on what they
mean, much less make a convincing case for sharing Heidegger's hopes.

Marcuse left Heidegger behind in 1933 and joined the Frankfurt School in
exile. Yet in the background of his thought there is an analysis of Greek philosophy
that can have no other source than his teacher. But Marcuse was never interested
in the secularized eschatology that today seems to fascinate postmodern students
of Heidegger. Instead of plunging forward into these mysteries, Marcuse looks
back to the Heidegger of his own early studies, the Heidegger whose interpretation of the technical model of being can be read to imply a very different
redemption. In this peculiar reading, the task of a post–Heideggerian philosophy
is to conceive a technology based on respect for nature and incorporating life-
affirming values in its very structure, the machines themselves. I understand this
utopian demand as an implicit recovery of the idea of *techné* in a modern context,
freed from the limitations of ancient Greek thought and available as a basis for a
reconstructed modernity.

This is the hypothesis which I will work out in this and the following chapters.
I begin with a reconsideration of the place of Plato, Aristotle, and Hegel in the
thought of Heidegger and Marcuse. I do not agree with the commonplace view
according to which Marcuse dropped Heidegger to take up with Hegel and Marx.
This view is contradicted by the fact that in 1930 Marcuse presented Heidegger
with a doctoral thesis on *Hegel's Ontology*, which is couched in Heideggerian terms.
How can this be explained? Aristotle is the missing link between Hegel and
Heidegger on the one hand and Marcuse on the other.

Those of us who remember Aristotle from college days as dull reading, too
close to common sense to generate much excitement, will be surprised to learn that
his thought was absolutely crucial for all three thinkers. Heidegger's admiration
for Aristotle is frequently noted but rarely analyzed in the detail it requires.[2] This
is an admiration Heidegger shared with Hegel, whose interpretation of Aristotle
he regarded as a landmark in the development of modern thought. But
Heidegger's Aristotle is practically unrecognizable: the Greek philosopher is transformed into an existential ontologist *avant la lettre*.

In 1923, Heidegger gave a lecture entitled "Phenomenological Interpretations
in Connection with Aristotle" (Heidegger 2002, 111ff).[3] Aristotle's greatest
achievement according to this lecture is his analysis of *kinesis*, movement, but
movement in a sense no earlier interpreter of Aristotle had ever conceived. It is the
movement of "factical life," later called "*Dasein*," that Aristotle is supposed to
have grasped for the first time. This movement consists in practical engagements
with the world and these are interpreted in Aristotle's theory of *techné*. *Techné* is
the model of "revealing" for the Greeks, that is, the form of Greek experience of
the world. The study of *kinesis* leads directly to the problems of ontology, the very

problems with which Heidegger is most concerned. In this interpretation Aristotle appears to anticipate Heidegger's own theory in *Being and Time* according to which everyday instrumental activity offers the basic access to reality. Theodore Kisiel sums up Heidegger's view at this early stage in the development of his thought: "The field of objects which yields the original sense of being is that of the *produced* object accessible in the course of usage. Accordingly, it is not the field of things in their theoretical reification but rather the world encountered in going about our producing, making, and using which is the basis, the according-to-which and toward-which of the original experience of being. . . . Being means *being produced*, and as produced, begin accessible for use and disposable, meaningful in regard to one particular way of getting around" (Kisiel 1993, 264).[4]

However, as he develops his critique of technology, Heidegger begins to argue that the production model is the remote source of modern technological thinking and therefore fundamentally misguided. Already in the period when he is actually writing *Being and Time,* he begins to retreat from the position sketched in the early Aristotle lecture. He still approves the Greeks' focus on production but he claims they grasped it inauthentically as an object in the world and not as the original disclosure of a world (Heidegger 1982, 110–11). In some of his later works the Greek concept of production is redefined by Heidegger as a purely ideal process of manifesting entities. Production is cut loose from its common sense roots in the making of artifacts and becomes a synonym for revealing (Heidegger 1998, 222). By 1939, Heidegger is denying that *techné* is at all helpful in understanding *physis*, precisely the opposite position from that of his earlier works (Heidegger 1998, 223). In the 1950 lecture on "The Thing," Plato and Aristotle are dismissed for having confused the essence of the thing with the *eidos* mobilized in the *techné* of its making (Heidegger 1971, 168). Salvation will come from a domain beyond production. Interpreters often project this later negative attitude toward production back on the early work, with confusing results since Heidegger never entirely breaks with his own phenomenological account of it. In fact, his technology critique still implies the earlier approach in complicated ways we will explore in later chapters.

Marcuse had left by the time Heidegger made this "turn." His thought continues the early Heidegger's production-centered analysis of being. The model of *techné* influences him profoundly although its presence in his thought is soon masked by the influence of the early Marx. Marcuse's innovative reinterpretation of Hegel is a study of this very same problematic of movement central to Heidegger's own early philosophy. I will argue that Marcuse's turn to Hegel is not a turning away from Heidegger but an attempt to work out the implications of Heidegger's early Aristotle interpretation for Hegel's dialectic which, Marcuse asserts, is itself based on Aristotle. The dialectic describes the internally contradictory character of existence Marcuse interprets as a theory of revealing in something like Heidegger's sense.

The central chapters of this book develop this background in detail. Once this task is accomplished I will turn to Marcuse's later work which appears now in a rather different light. Many things that have puzzled and sometimes outraged commentators since the 1960s come into focus as reflections of continuing Heideggerian influences. It would be too much to say that Marcuse is a crypto-Heideggerian, but he is indeed addressing questions posed by Heidegger and offering an alternative response. This is especially apparent in the existential demands of Marcuse's politics, his "two-dimensional" ontology, and his approach to art and technology. These issues will be discussed in the concluding chapters of this book.

Techné and the Good

We are well aware that we are a technological society, and not just because we use so many devices but also in our spirit and our way of life. But only recently has this awareness reached the humanistic disciplines. It is strange that the 20th century, the century of astonishingly rapid technical advance, should have produced relatively little philosophical reflection on technology. John Dewey is the only figure of the stature of Heidegger to concern himself extensively with this theme (Hickman 1990). When Heidegger and Marcuse wrote about technology, it was still possible and indeed more than possible—intellectually respectable— to ignore it. Their path breaking reflections went beyond the boundaries of conformist thought in philosophy and other humanistic fields. Now all that is slowly changing; indeed, it *must* change for these fields to retain any significance.

Surprisingly, these modern resistances to the question concerning technology, particularly strong in philosophy, were not shared by the Greeks. Of course the Greeks, at least Plato and Aristotle among them, shared their society's aristocratic prejudice against work and admired pure contemplation above all else. But this did not prevent them from reflecting on the ontological significance of technical activity which Heidegger later reinterprets as the "question of being." How did they pose the question?

Philosophy begins by interpreting the world in terms of the fundamental fact that humanity is a laboring animal constantly at work transforming nature. This fundamental fact shapes the basic distinctions that prevail throughout the tradition of Western philosophy. The first of these is the distinction between what the Greeks called *physis* and *poiésis*.[5] *Physis* is usually translated as nature. The Greeks understood nature to be that which creates itself, that which emerges from out of itself. *Poiésis* is the practical activity of making in which human beings engage when they produce something. We call these created beings artifacts and include among them the products of art, craft, and social convention.

The word *techné* is at the origin of the modern words for technique and technology in every Western language, although these have a somewhat different meaning as we will see. In ancient Greece it signifies the knowledge or discipline associated with a form of *poiésis*. For example, medicine is a *techné* that aims at healing the sick; carpentry is a *techné* that aims at building from wood. Note that for the Greeks, *technai* show the "right way" to do things in a very strong, even an objective sense. Although artifacts depend on human activity, the knowledge contained in the *technai* is no matter of opinion or subjective intention. Even the purposes of things made share in this objectivity insofar as they are defined by the *technai*.

The second fundamental philosophical distinction is that between existence and essence. Existence answers the question whether something is or is not. Essence answers the question what the thing is. *That* it is and *what* it is appear to be two independent dimensions of being in the Western philosophical tradition. But existence is a rather hazy concept, difficult to define. Apart from St. Thomas Aquinas' attempts to understand existence as an "act," it has failed to interest mainstream philosophy. Most of the attention is given to essence and its successor concepts as developed by the sciences because this is the content of knowledge.

These two distinctions are self-evident. They form the basis of all philosophical thought in the West. But the relation between them is not obvious, is in fact puzzling. The source of the puzzle is the Greeks' understanding of *techné*, the ancestor of modern technology. Strange though it seems, they conceived nature, *physis*, on the model of the artifacts produced by their own poiétic activity.[6]

With artifacts the distinction between existence and essence is real and obvious. The artifact exists first as an idea and only later comes into existence through human making. But note that for the Greeks the idea of the artifact is not arbitrary or subjective but rather belongs to a *techné*. Each *techné* contains the essence of the thing to be made prior to the act of making. The idea, the essence of the thing is thus a reality independent of the thing itself and of its maker. What is more, as we have seen, the purpose of the thing made is included in its idea. In sum, although humans make artifacts, they do so according to a plan and for a purpose that is an objective aspect of the world.

In nature, on the other hand, the distinction between existence and essence is not obvious. The thing and its essence emerge together and the essence does not have a separate existence. The flower grows along with what makes it a flower: that it is and what it is "happen," in a sense, simultaneously. We can later construct a concept of the essence of the flower, but this is our doing, not something required by the very existence of nature as it is for artifacts. Unlike *techné*, which is essential to the manufacture of artifacts, *epistémé*, knowledge of nature, appears to be a purely human doing to which nature itself would be indifferent. Or is it? Here is where the story gets interesting.

This difference between the relation of essence to *physis* and *poiésis* is important for an understanding of Greek philosophy and the later tradition precisely because philosophers have tried so hard to surpass it. Plato's theory of ideas is the foundation of this tradition. For Plato the concept of the thing exists in an ideal realm prior to the thing itself and allows us to know the thing. Note how similar this theory is to our analysis of *techné* in which the idea is also independent of the thing. But Plato does not reserve this theory for artifacts; rather, it is applied to all being. He relies on the structure of *techné* to explain not only artifacts, but nature as well.

Plato understands nature as divided into existence and essence just as artifacts are and this becomes the basis for Greek ontology. This has many important consequences. There is no radical discontinuity between technical making and natural self-production because they both share the same structure. *Techné* includes a purpose and a meaning. The Greeks import this understanding of artifacts into the realm of nature which they then interpret teleologically. The world is thus a place full of meaning and intention. This conception of the world calls for a corresponding conception of human being. We humans are not the masters of nature but work with its potentials to bring an ordered world to fruition. Neither our knowledge of that world nor our action in it is arbitrary but rather they expose and complete what lies hidden in nature.

What conclusion do we draw from these historical considerations on ancient Greek philosophy? I will be provocative and say that the philosophy of technology begins with the Greeks and is in fact the foundation of all Western philosophy. After all, the Greeks interpret being as such through the concept of technical making. This is ironic. Technology has a low status in high culture but it was actually there at the origin of that culture and, if we believe the Greeks, contains the key to the understanding of being as a whole.

If we now turn to the ethical consequences of this "technical" theory of being, we will begin to understand the basis for the later critique of technology in Heidegger and Marcuse. We can uncover the Greek outlook by reviewing Plato's original discussion of *techné* in one of his greatest dialogues, the *Gorgias*. It is worth spending some time with this text since it offers a kind of template of all the basic issues which will concern us. The argument appears remarkably modern at first, pitting Socrates against an instrumentalist who sharply distinguishes means from ends and considers ends subjective. If we recognize the typical prejudices of our times in Socrates' adversary, in Socrates we find an alternative worldview so charmingly expressed we can almost believe it.[7] As we will see, in some complicated sense Heidegger does believe it, or at least he attempts to give it a philosophical weight it has not had for centuries.

The *Gorgias* is the first text in the Western tradition to treat the relation of technique to values as a problem. In this dialogue, Socrates debates the nature of the *techné*, or "art," of rhetoric. He distinguishes between true arts that are based on a *logos*, and what the English translation calls mere knacks, *empeiriae* in Greek, that is, rules of thumb based on experience but without an underlying rationale (Dodds 1959, 225).

For Plato, a rationale or *logos* necessarily includes a reference to the good served by the art. Knowledge of the *logos* of the art thus involves a teleological conception of its objects, a normative idea of their "essence" conceived as the fulfillment of their potentialities. If the art is shipbuilding, its *logos* will not only instruct the builder in putting together boards in some sort of arrangement, but will also guide him in making a ship that is strong and safe. The doctor's art includes not only various notions about herbs but also a curative mission that governs their use. In this, these arts differ from a mere knack of combining pieces of wood or herbs without an underlying order and purpose.

Technical logic and objective finalities are joined in true arts, while knacks serve merely subjective purposes. But because we are prone to accept appearances for reality and pursue pleasure instead of the good, for each art there is some knack that imitates its effects and misleads its clients. Cosmetics substitutes for gymnastics, giving the appearance of health without the reality. Rhetoric, the power to substitute appearance for reality in language, is the supreme and most dangerous knack. In a debate on shipbuilding or medicine, the orator will silence the expert every time. Means triumph over ends. The only way to protect oneself is through knowledge which distinguishes appearance from reality and identifies the *logos* of each art. Knowledge is thus essential to the pursuit of the good.

Callicles is the most articulate advocate of the knack of rhetoric in the *Gorgias*. He has an unlimited appetite for power and pleasure which he serves through his mastery of the tricks of language. That such ambition was not merely a personal idiosyncrasy is clear from a reading of Aristophanes, Thucydides, and other contemporary authors, all of whom denounced the moral degeneration and egoism of the imperialistic Athens of the 5th century. In external affairs, the Athenians oppressed their own allies. Internally, the assembly became a battlefield of power hungry orators. Plato's version of the question of his age was thus, quite simply, does might make right? His answer to this question is the basis of rational ethical thought in the West.

I will briefly review the argument with Callicles as Socrates' refutation of his views sets the stage for modern debates over technology and values. Callicles intervenes in the middle of the dialogue. He argues that the justice Socrates makes so much of is more useful to the weak than the strong. The strong can impose their will without the help of law. As a mere special interest of the weak, justice has no claim on them. Natural justice consists quite simply in the rule of the stronger over the weaker and is diametrically opposed to conventional justice.

Callicles analyzes the earlier debates on these terms. In all of them Socrates has caught the defenders of rhetoric in contradictions. These victories, Callicles asserts, were due to a trick, namely, playing fast and loose on both sides of the line between the natural goals rhetoric can achieve, such as power and pleasure, and the merely conventional values of ethics and aesthetics.

Callicles' analysis is astute. For example, Polus asserts both that it is better to do injustice than to suffer it, and also that doing injustice is uglier than suffering it. He thus finds himself claiming that one and the same thing, unjust action, is better, i.e., less painful and worse, aesthetically. But, Callicles argues, pain belongs to nature and beauty to convention. Any argument that mixes the two realms will be inconsistent. And so Callicles demands that Socrates answer according to nature, giving up any direct appeal to ethical or aesthetic values.

Callicles then defends a hedonistic doctrine according to which the good is the purely subjective sensation of pleasure, a natural value. On these terms there is no gap between the appearance of the good and its reality. No science of the good is required to "know" that one is having a good time! But without a distinction between appearance and reality, the Socratic distinction between *techné* and *empeiria* collapses: rationality, the *logos,* is irrelevant to the pursuit of the good defined as a mere feeling each can verify for himself.

The following chart sums up Callicles' analysis with, in brackets, a fourth good added by Socrates in the course of the discussion:

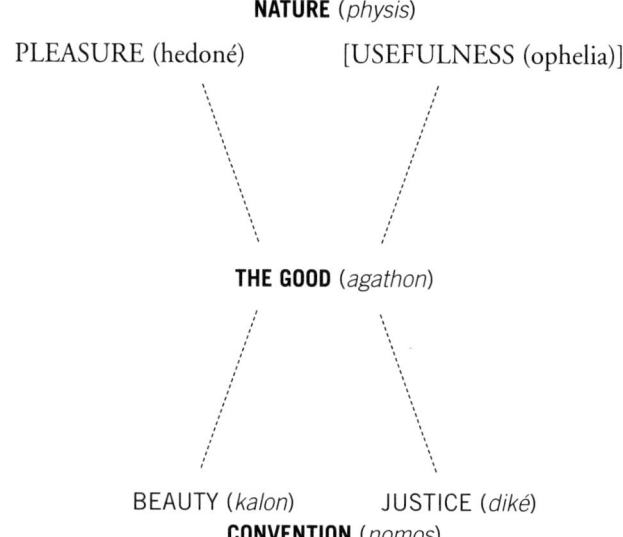

NATURE (*physis*)

PLEASURE (hedoné)   [USEFULNESS (ophelia)]

THE GOOD (*agathon*)

BEAUTY (*kalon*)   JUSTICE (*diké*)
CONVENTION (*nomos*)

Socrates agrees to Callicles' strictures and quickly gets Callicles to admit that the unrestrained pursuit of pleasure leads to harm, for example, ill health. Pleasure is thus not the highest value but is pursued "for the sake of the good" (Plato 1952, 72). In this passage Plato identifies the good with *"ophelia,"* usefulness, another natural value, and so the contradiction into which Callicles now falls—affirming that pleasure both is and is not the good—cannot be blamed on any tricky play on the difference between nature and convention.

After this decisive refutation, Socrates returns from natural goods to the ethical and aesthetic values temporarily bracketed at Callicles' request. In the famous myth that concludes the text, Socrates dismantles Callicles' distinction between nature and convention. Rhadamanthys judges the dead and punishes each soul that suffers from "distortion and hideousness by reason of the irresponsibility and licentiousness, the insolence and intemperance of its acts" (Plato 1952, 104). Divine justice is meted out according to aesthetic criteria—"distortion and hideousness"—but there is no question of conventional appearances prejudicing the eye of the judge. The aesthetic reference is ontological; it measures the "naked" soul's actual reality. Such an ontological conception of aesthetics was perhaps more accessible to the Greeks than to us as they commonly referred to persons and their actions as beautiful or ugly for their moral qualities (Dodds 1959, 249–50). The aesthetic in this sense refers to how the individuals *define* themselves through their actions (as virtuous, a thief, generous, a liar, etc.). What one does is not accidental to one's being, but stamps it with a particular character that others can evaluate according to objective criteria. The act of self-definition is a function of rational self-control (or the lack of it) in terms of ethical and aesthetic standards.

The Tyranny of Reason

Modern readers have difficulty taking the conclusion of Plato's dialogue seriously. The earlier shift in the argument from ethics and aesthetics to the conflict between hedonistic and functional goods appears to place it on a purely rational plane we can more easily accept. Since such things as health are counted among functional goods, there is plenty for *techné* to do even without guidance from contentious ethical and aesthetic standards.

But just how modern is even this phase of Plato's argument? In one sense his idea of *techné* seems obvious. Technologies are in fact subordinated to purposes which appear in the technical disciplines as a guide to resources and procedures. Many of these purposes derive from considerations such as health and safety that have an objective rationale. A software engineer working for Rolls-Royce Aircraft explained to me that 10 percent of his time was spent writing software and 90 percent was spent testing it for safety. Plato would no doubt approve: the *logos* is at work at Rolls-Royce.

Yet we moderns can no longer generalize from such examples as Plato did.[8] For every benevolent aircraft designer, there is a bomb builder somewhere. We can still relate to Plato's emphasis on the need for a rationale, a *logos*, but we're not so sure it necessarily includes an idea of the good. In fact we think of technologies as normless, as serving subjective purposes very much as did Plato's knacks. What has happened to disconnect technology and value in modern times?

The founders of modern thought, Descartes and Francis Bacon, wrote at a time when technology resembled far more closely the plows and spears of Plato's Athens than the automobiles and Internet of today. Nevertheless, Descartes had the temerity to promise that we would soon become "the masters and possessors of nature" through the cultivation of the sciences, and Bacon famously claimed that "Knowledge is power." Clearly, these early modern thinkers are, at least in intention, in a different world from the Greeks—our world. Nevertheless, they share with the Greeks the fundamental distinctions between nature and artifacts, essence and existence. But Descartes' and Bacon's understanding of these distinctions is different from that of the Greeks. This is especially true of the concept of essence. For them as for us, what Aristotle took for essences are conventional rather than real. The meaning and purpose of things is something we create, not something we discover. The gap between human being and world widens accordingly. We are not at home in the world, we conquer the world. This difference is related to our basic ontology, our concept of nature. The question we address to being is not *what* it is but *how* it works. Science answers this question rather than revealing essences in the Greek sense of the term.

Note that technology is still the model of being in this modern conception. This was particularly clear in the 18th century Enlightenment, when philosophers and scientists challenged the medieval successors to Greek science with the new mechanistic worldview. These thinkers explored the machinery of being. They identified the workings of the universe with a clockwork mechanism, a device. Strange though it may seem, the underlying structure of Greek ontology survived the defeat of one of its chief principles, its concept of essence.

In the modern context technology does not realize objective essences inscribed in the nature of the universe, as does *techné*. It now appears as purely instrumental, as value free. It does not respond to inherent purposes, but is merely a means serving subjective goals. For modern common sense, means and ends are independent of each other. Technology is "neutral" in the sense that it has no preference as between the various possible uses to which it can be put. This is the instrumentalist philosophy of technology that is a spontaneous product of our civilization, assumed unreflectively by most people.

Technology in this scheme of things encounters nature as raw materials, not as a world that emerges out of itself, a *physis*, but rather as stuff awaiting transformation into whatever we desire. This world is understood mechanistically not teleologically. It is there to be used without any inner purpose. The West has made enormous technical advances on the basis of this understanding of reality. Nothing restrains us in our exploitation of the world. Everything is exposed to an analytic intelligence that decomposes it into usable parts. In the 19th century it became commonplace to view modernity as an unending progress.

But for what ends? The goals of our society can no longer be specified in a knowledge of some sort, a *techné*, as they were for the Greeks. They remain purely subjective, arbitrary choices, and no essences guide us. Reason now concerns only means, not ends. This has led to a crisis of civilization from which there seems no escape: we know how to get there but we do not know why we are going or even where. The Greeks lived in harmony with the world whereas we are alienated from it by our very freedom to define our purposes as we wish. So long as no great harm could be attributed to technology, this situation did not lead to serious doubts beyond the usual literary protests against modernization. But the 20th century, with its world wars, atom bombs, concentration camps, and environmental catastrophes, has made it more and more difficult to ignore the strange aimlessness of modernity. Because we are at such a loss to know where we are going and why, philosophy of technology has emerged in our time as a critique of modernity.

The most important forerunner of this critique is Max Weber (Weber 1949; Schluchter 1979). Weber distinguishes between "substantive" and "formal" rationality in a way that corresponds in one significant respect to Plato's distinction between *techné* and knack. Substantive rationality, like *techné*, begins by positing a good and then selects means to achieve it. Many public institutions are substantively rational in Weber's sense: universal education is a good that determines appropriate means such as classrooms and teachers. Formal rationality is concerned uniquely with the efficiency of means and contains no intrinsic reference to a good. It is thus value neutral, like the Platonic *empeiria*. Modernization consists in the triumph of formal rationality over a more or less substantively rational order inherited from the past. The market is the primary instrument of this transformation, substituting the cash nexus for the planned pursuit of values. Bureaucracy and management are other domains in which formal rationality eventually prevails.

The knack in Plato is subservient to the power drive of the individual, Callicles, for example. Because an individual will can establish no overall order in society, Callicles' triumph could only lead to tyranny and the anarchic reaction that follows. Value neutrality in Weber implies a similarly subjective purpose; however, market and political processes do establish an order of some sort. The question is what is that order? Weber himself was rather pessimistic. He foresaw an iron cage of bureaucracy closing in on Western civilization. The logic of the technical means employed in Western society had prevailed over Enlightenment values of freedom and individuality. An order was emerging that lacked any higher purpose or significance, but that was, at least, an order.

In modern times, the terms of Plato's distinction between *techné* and *empeiria* are broken apart and recombined. Where Plato had associated orientation toward the good with rationally elaborated means, now the pursuit of power and pleasure has its own logic as a system of means institutionalized in markets and bureaucracies, and that logic imposes itself independent of human will and any conception of the good. This is the difference between the individual tyranny Plato feared, and the tyranny of rational means that haunted Weber.

Weber's pessimism about modernity reaches its paroxysm with the Frankfurt School and Heidegger who substitute technology for markets and bureaucracies as the main instrument of rationalization. Theodor Adorno and Max Horkheimer's classic, *Dialectic of Enlightenment,* had a profound influence on Marcuse's approach to technology. According to this book the struggle to control outer nature requires the sacrifice and suppression of inner nature. The distorted human beings who emerge from the process of civilization are full of aggression and violence which discharges itself in racism and wars (Adorno and Horkheimer 1972). The reduction of reason to a mere instrument underlies this disastrous outcome. The "objective reason" that thought it knew the nature of the universe and could derive rules of conduct from that insight, is replaced by a merely "subjective reason," a truncated vestige of the old metaphysics good only for control and domination (Horkheimer 1947, 11ff). Callicles triumphs over Socrates in the end. Here Weber's distinction between formal and substantive rationality is radicalized in a dialectic of Enlightenment. Enlightenment turns out to undermine its own basis while exposing nature and human beings to untrammeled power. Adorno and Horkheimer conclude, "The fully enlightened earth radiates disaster triumphant" (Adorno and Horkheimer 1972, 3).

Heidegger proposes a parallel argument. As noted above, his approach is based on the contrast between ancient *techné* and modern technology. *Techné* describes the traditional value-charged craft practice of all premodern societies. Craftsmen serve functional needs while also conforming to the broader ethical and aesthetic values of their society. In ancient Greece craft obeys the *logos* in bringing out the objective meanings, or "forms," of its products and materials. The Greeks lived in a world of self-sustaining things confronting human beings with a rich variety of useful potentialities awaiting realization through skillful manipulation. Artistic practice resembles craft and belongs to this Greek *techné* as well.

By contrast, modern technology has freed itself in large measure from the valuative commitments of its society. Heidegger's version of the iron cage is a system of research and development, a technoscience. He argues that reality is fundamentally restructured by this technoscience in a way that strips it completely of its intrinsic potentialities and exposes it to domination. Even the modern Callicles is caught in the system he thinks he masters. Technoscience is more dangerous than rhetoric or markets. The danger is not merely nuclear weapons or some similar threat to survival, but the obliteration of humanity's special status and dignity as the being through whom the world takes on intelligibility and meaning.

Plato would not have been altogether surprised by these diagnoses although the shift in accent, from the abuse of *empeiria* by its users to the inherent destructiveness of technology itself, is peculiarly modern. This shift results from the fact that technology does not merely manipulate appearances but systematizes reality. In Adorno, Horkheimer, and Heidegger, the question Plato addressed is therefore reformulated. Today we are less concerned with the justification of power than with the sheer challenge of its sublime presence as technology. Our question is: Can we live with technology, i.e., with power in its modern form? The ethical problem of right and might is superseded by the ontological problem of the destructive transformation technology operates on both its users and its objects. We are less worried about whether Callicles' descendants have the right to rule us than with whether the world they dominate can survive the means set in motion by their vaulting ambition.

At this point, we seem to have come full circle. Value neutral technology turns out to contain a value in itself after all. As Heidegger expresses it: "The outstanding feature of modern technology lies in the fact that it is not at all any longer merely 'means' and no longer merely stands in 'service' for others, but instead . . . unfolds a specific character of domination" (quoted in Zimmerman 1990, 214). This paradox is already implied in Plato's account of *empeiria*. Recall that "knacks" are not oriented toward a good but are "neutral" in themselves. Gorgias says as much early in the dialogue when he explains that the teacher of rhetoric no more than the boxing coach is responsible for the use his students make of their art (Plato 1952, 15–16). But when Socrates describes knacks such as cookery or cosmetics, it turns out that they are essentially bound up with appearances and hence with various types of seduction and manipulation (Plato 1952, 26). The knack of rhetoric in particular serves domination as does technology in Adorno, Horkheimer, and Heidegger.

While Plato based his hope on *techné,* our modern thinkers despair. They have no faith in *techné* because modern technology has incorporated both *logos,* rationality, and *ophelia,* the useful, into a normless system that everywhere prevails over all competing practices. The modern Callicles is in power, and our thinkers, whether they be conservatives like Heidegger or radicals like Adorno and Horkheimer, can only appeal to a vague future in which his reign might somehow end.

Modes of Revealing

Techné as Revealing

Heidegger's diagnosis of our time is basically different from that of the Adorno, Horkheimer, and Weber. They accept the common sense distinction between substantive and formal rationality. Weber in particular assumed the ultimate subjectivity of goals, as we all tend to in a modern society where there is no universal rational consensus on meaning and value. For Weber, as for us, modern society is right to rely only on facts. The Greek faith in an objective *logos* has long since been refuted by modern science. The nostalgia for the *logos* apparent in Adorno and Horkheimer remains just that, nostalgia. The redemption of Enlightenment they imagined would come not from a recovery of the *logos,* but from a reflective awareness of natural and human limits and needs.

Heidegger too believed that the triumph of value neutral technical means over goal-oriented thinking is the necessary consequence of our modern condition. But he saw this condition as itself historically relative. Our inability to take meaning and value seriously, our prejudice in favor of factual knowledge, is precisely the mark of that relativity. It is this which makes us overlook the ontologically fundamental character of being-in-the-world. As a result, we see Greek *techné* as prescientific. But can we find a way of understanding it that is not internal to modernity? This is the task Heidegger sets himself and he believes it can be accomplished with a phenomenology of everyday human existence.

Heidegger's account of *techné* is quite different from the Weberian approach sketched above. He starts out from the assumption that the world is initially revealed through *techné* and does not preexist it in the form of a collection of present-at-hand things taken up by human technical activity in a contingent manner, for example, on this or that occasion to fulfill this or that passing need.

Every aspect of being he uncovers in the study of *techné* is thus originally posited by *techné*. This even includes the raw materials of technical work. These materials are understood from being out of their place in production rather than as preexisting objects.

There is something like a phenomenological reduction at work here. The "natural attitude," in which things are given objectively, is suspended to allow them to appear as they are originally revealed to human activity. *Techné* itself is considered ontologically, as a relation of *Dasein* to world, rather than as a causal interaction with things. Although this reverses our usual perspective, it is not arbitrary. After all, every human society known to us, with the exception of our own, has notions equivalent to the Greek idea of *techné*—notions that describe the meaning of things in objective terms on the basis of the practices underlying the society's relation to its world. Of course each society assigns these meanings without a scientific basis in our modern sense. But they all do assign meanings; that is the important fact that we overlook in our enthusiasm for the objective scientific view. Something is going on in the traditional relationship of society and world we conceive as arbitrary and subjective but which Heidegger takes for the founding act in which worlds are revealed. There must then be some equivalent founding of our modern world too, and indeed Heidegger identifies this equivalent with modern technology. But for reasons we will explore later, we moderns are uniquely ignorant of the very idea of "world" as it appears to all other peoples and is theorized by the Greeks.

Considered as a phenomenology in this sense, Aristotle's *techné* analysis displays an original unity underlying the dichotomies of objectivistic thinking. In fact it anticipates Heidegger's own analysis of being-in-the-world. This explains why Heidegger's "The Question Concerning Technology" begins with an Aristotelian account of *techné*. The essay is based on the idea that the modern interpretation of technology as instrumental is inadequate, that something deeper underlies our usual assumption that technology is a mere means. As Heidegger puts it, "the essence of technology is by no means anything technological" (Heidegger 1977, 4). What is it then? He initially promises that the essence of technology will be disclosed by an investigation of Aristotle's four causes. Heidegger claims that the Greek word translated as "cause," *aition*, really means to be "indebted." The four causes signify ways in which a thing is indebted for its existence (Heidegger 1977, 8).

Heidegger's example, a silver chalice, is indebted

- to matter, the silver from which it is made
- to the eidos or essence, that is, the idea of how the chalice should look when finished
- to the end or telos, which limits the possible meanings and uses of the chalice to a single way of being
- and finally to the craftsman who "considers carefully and gathers together the three aforementioned ways of being responsible and indebted"

The craftsman is not the cause of the chalice in our sense at all, but a co-responsible agent in bringing the chalice into appearance. The craftsman takes his place in *poiésis* through a specific type of knowledge called *techné* that allows him to gather the other causes and bring the work to completion. *Techné* is thus a mode of revealing insofar as it places the finished work before us, making it present. This Greek mode of revealing Heidegger calls a "bringing forth," a "*Hervor-bringen*" (Heidegger 1977, 10). The Greeks' understanding of being is modeled on the structure of craft production, *techné*, and its type of revealing.

These reflections are actually a sketch of much more elaborate analyses Heidegger developed in his early lectures on Aristotle. The next chapter will explain Heidegger's interpretation of the basic categories of Aristotle's metaphysics, such as *eidos*, form and potentiality, in terms of the concept of *techné*.

Marcuse's Concept of Essence

Heidegger's theory of revealing suggests a way back to a concept of essence, but it specifies no content to that concept. Much as we might like to revive the ancient concept of essence, it rests on an outdated ontology with socially conformist implications. The standards in terms of which potentialities were assigned to things in antiquity were community standards, accepted uncritically by philosophers. For example, Heidegger's chalice has a predetermined form laid down in the culture and accepted uncritically as essential by the craftsman and the community. Greek philosophy betrayed an unconscious fidelity to historically surpassable limitations of its society in treating conventions as essences (Marcuse 1964, 134–35). Modern philosophy cannot proceed in this naïve fashion but demands universal and verifiable grounds

Marcuse accepts the modern view that essences can neither be based on tradition and community standards nor speculatively derived in an *a priori* metaphysics of some sort. But what he calls "one-dimensional thinking" plays out that modern skepticism by rejecting the idea of essence altogether and remaining at the empirical level. It thereby avoids tradition-bound conformism and outdated metaphysics but only by treating the logic of technology as an ontological principle. Today we can design our technological "chalices" any way we wish and this seems a liberation. But liberation has a price: one-dimensional thinking cannot recognize inherent potentialities and so can offer no guidance to social reform. To what can we appeal for criteria? What, for example, are the grounds for preferring respect for nature to exploitation of nature, freedom to domination?

The core of the problem is once again the concept of essence. Like Heidegger, Marcuse dismisses any return to Greek metaphysics. But unlike Heidegger, he refuses to reduce all essential thinking to the contemplation of the process of revealing. Instead, he seeks to reconstruct the concept of essence historically. This involves him in astonishing encounters with Hegel, Freud, and the artistic avant gardes of the early 20th century.

Ancient philosophy joined *logos* to *eros,* theoretical abstraction to striving toward the good. But it lacked historical self-consciousness. The temporal dynamic it found in things was specific to an individual or species. Each type of thing had its own essence, and, although these essences were objects of striving, they themselves did not exist in time. Hence ancient philosophy arrived at a static conception eternal ideas. The fixed nature of its essences corresponds to its own lack of historical self-consciousness, its inability to conceive of *becoming* as the fundamental ontological determination.

Today such an unhistorical conception of essence is unacceptable. We have learned that human beings make themselves and their world in the course of history. Not just individual things are caught up in time, but essences as well. If we are to revive the language of essence today, its conceptualization must therefore be historical. Accordingly, Marcuse reconstructed both *logos* and *eros* as historical categories, reinterpreting the observable tensions in reality as part of a larger historical process.

Marcusian historicism is rooted in the materialism of the Marxist tradition. Dialectics, as a logic of the interconnections and contexts revealed in historical strife, offers an alternative to ancient dogmatism and modern positivism. Its regulative concepts, such as freedom and justice, are not ideals in the traditional sense because they have no fixed meaning. The content of universals such as these derives from tensions in reality rather than from a preconceived speculative notion or an uncritically accepted social consensus. They are not exhausted by any particular institutional arrangement, but always point beyond toward as yet unrealized potentials (Marcuse 1964, 133ff). The function of philosophy as knowledge transcending the given, is now fulfilled by these critical or "substantive" universals.[9]

Hegel's dialectic is in fact an attempt to achieve the very reconstruction of essence Marcuse requires. Hegel's *Logic* dissolves the traditional distinction between essence and appearance in the dynamics of their relation. Things do not have fixed essences separate from their manifestations because things are not themselves stable and fixed. Rather, they belong to a field of interactions which establishes their inner coherence and their boundaries. These interactions are a source of tensions that drive things forward toward their developmental potentialities. For Hegel, potentialities are inscribed in things but do not constitute them as independent Aristotelian substances. Instead, something in the constellation of their present connections gives a direction to their development. But what is this something? Why is development development rather than mere random change?

This question, so far as it concerns Hegel, is usually answered by reference to the "absolute," which is supposed to be the end toward which all things tend. This is a theological Hegel of no conceivable use to Marcuse. In his early work, Marcuse rejected this interpretation and turned to Hegel's concept of life for a radically future-oriented ontology that owes as much to Heidegger as to Hegel.

Heidegger's *Being and Time* describes *Dasein*, human being, as fundamentally engaged with the question of its own being. This question cannot be answered by reference to objective facts or metaphysical notions of human nature, but must be resolved through choices and actions in the world. Heidegger's existential account of the human substitutes time and movement for the atemporal essences that haunted philosophical speculation from Plato on, hence the title of his book.

The analytic of *Dasein* influences Marcuse's interpretation of Hegel's *Lebensphilosophie*, obscured in the *Logic* by the emphasis on the absolute. Life in Hegel's early work is a process of movement, negating and accommodating an environment. The choice of life as a fundamental ontological theme makes sense of the emphasis on interconnectedness and process in the dialectics of development. The life process has a direction: life seeks to preserve and further itself. Yet it is not confined by a predetermined end but invents its future as it moves. This is of course eminently true of modern human beings and their society. There is no longer a prior essence that defines what it is to be human. Human beings now must make themselves. In Marcuse's reading, Hegelian life, like Heideggerian *Dasein*, discovers its meaning ahead of itself as a conditioned choice, an appropriation, not behind as a determining cause. It is negative, not positive.

Once Marcuse joins the Frankfurt School, this original Heideggerian Hegelianism is overlaid with a messianic concept of the future derived ultimately from Walter Benjamin. Now the future is not simply a human creation but a redemptive possibility interrupting the continuity of history. The essential potentialities, while remaining rationally grounded in social analysis and critique, delineate this redemption, revealing the world in its truth. As Adorno writes, "The only philosophy which can be responsibly practiced in face of despair is the attempt to contemplate all things as they would present themselves from the standpoint of redemption. . . . Perspectives must be fashioned that displace and estrange the world, reveal it to be, with its rifts and crevices, as indigent and distorted as it will appear one day in the messianic light. . . . Consummate negativity, once squarely face, delineates the mirror image of its opposite" (Adorno 1974, 247).

All this determines the shape of Marcuse's later critique of technology. He is neither hostile nor indifferent to modern technology but calls for its radical reconstruction. Marcuse remarks that in a liberated society "certain lost qualities of artisan work may well reappear on the new technological base" (Marcuse 1972, 60). And he refers to "The Greek notion of the affinity between art and technics" to illustrate his thesis that technology can be redeemed by the imagination (Marcuse 1964, 238). Although Marcuse does not use the term, the idea of *techné* now reappears as the basis for a new type of world relation, grounded in a life affirming "sensibility," or existential project. This project would instill technology with the mission of realizing the potentialities of human beings and things. Reason itself would be transformed, recovering the progressive promise of the Enlightenment against the present catastrophe. Thus redeemed, reason would transcend the opposition of technique and values, just as does *techné*.

Marcuse's thinking about what I am calling a new *techné* goes through two stages. In a first phase, which lasts until the late 1960s, he interprets the concept of essence through a Hegelian–Marxist concept of potentiality. In Marcuse's Hegelian interpretation, Marxism describes a dynamic of forces through which human potential is realized. The definition of that potential is ultimately the task of those who struggle for its realization, but it is anticipated in the imaginative constructions of art and philosophy. Potentialities emerge from history and are not bound by the given form of things.

In a second phase, under the influence of the New Left, Marcuse identifies a "new sensibility" that engages with the world aesthetically. What theory had identified as potentiality in the earlier argument now appears in sensation itself, as a new kind of sensitivity to things and their possibilities. Criteria for the reform of technology will now emerge in experience itself. Values will once again be found in the world rather than imposed willfully in defiance of all human and natural limits. These values, values of life, cannot of course appear in the form of scientifically verifiable hypotheses or "eternal truths." But they are not merely subjective. What then are values and how do they relate to technology? Like Socrates, Marcuse can only answer this question by relativizing the opposition of nature and culture which underlies this alternative. I will return to his answer in the conclusion of this book.

CHAPTER 2

The Question Concerning *Techné*

Heidegger's Aristotle

The Question

The Saving Power

The main line of Heidegger's critique of technology is familiar from his 1954 essay, "The Question Concerning Technology." I will not belabor it here. Being is "enframed" by the calculative thinking of modern man. We measure, plan, and control ceaselessly, reducing everything, including ourselves, to resources and system components. Nature is "challenged" to deliver up its wealth for arbitrary human ends. It is transformed into a source of energy to be extracted and delivered. But even as human beings take themselves for the masters of being, being "challenges" them to challenge beings. Modernity is the total mobilization of the world by humans who are themselves mobilized in the process. This "*Gestell,*" this "enframing" within which human being and being are ordered, is now the way in which Being reveals itself. It dissolves all traditions, the linguistic heritage, the fixed meanings on the basis of which people have engaged with the world in the past. Being becomes the object of pure will and the meaning of things derives from their place in the technological system rather than from an *eidos.*

Yet somehow a "saving power" is said to appear out of this nightmare. What is this saving power and what does it promise? Unfortunately, in answering this question, the essay makes the most arbitrary and confusing leaps from theme to theme, often proceeding by punning on words rather than logical argument. The passage in which it is introduced is positively dizzying. I will try to summarize it here.

Heidegger begins with a quotation from Hölderlin which authorizes his initial leap from the idea that the technological enframing is "the danger" to the obscurely connected idea that with the danger a "saving power" grows. "Saving," we are told, means revealing something in its essence and so, if Hölderlin is right, we ought to be approaching an understanding of the essence of technology. But what is essence? In the case of enframing, it is not a genus under which particular devices would fall. Rather, enframing, like the "bringing forth" of the Greeks, is a revealing. We are "destined" to this technological revealing in a way that blocks the earlier Greek revealing and indeed all understanding of revealing.

This shows up in the collapse of the Greek concept of essence as the permanently enduring, the *eidos*. "It can never in any way be established that enduring is based solely on what Plato thinks as *idea* and Aristotle thinks as *to ti en einai* (that which any particular thing has always been), or what metaphysics in its most varied interpretations thinks as *essentia*" (Heidegger 1977, 30).[1] For the "permanently enduring" we should substitute Goethe's lexically related phrase, the "permanently granting." "That which endures primally out of the earliest beginning is what grants" (Heidegger 1977, 31). This mysterious formula means that the revealing itself, as the granting of a world to man, is the ultimate essence from out of which we must think the enframing. The enframing is a revealing and so "grants" man something he could not himself invent, namely, beings. The very extremity of the threat implied in this enframing can lead us to a fuller understanding of the process of revealing if only we "pay heed to the coming to presence of technology" (Heidegger 1977, 32).

Never has such a succession of non sequiturs played such an important role in the history of philosophy! Is Heidegger dismissing the Greek concept of essence and substituting a different concept, and if so, what justifies such a radical revision of one of the foundations of Western philosophy? Surely not a vague etymological argument inspired by Goethe! Why is "revealing," as a "granting," now supposed to occupy the conceptual place philosophy has always attributed to "essence" as what endures through change? How can technology, the revealing which precisely blocks awareness of revealing, itself be the bridge to that very awareness? And what is the logical connection between all these themes?

The Language of Being

The questions I have posed in these introductory comments indicate one of the major difficulties of Heidegger's thought. The language in which he expresses himself seems strangely twisted. This is not arbitrary but results from his method. He is attempting to think the Western metaphysical tradition as a whole without being limited to the terms of its latest stage, the stage in which, of course, he himself is situated. How is this possible? By a strict abstention from the forms of thought and language of the tradition. As Richard Polt puts it, Heidegger "embraces the strenuous project of finding the words to describe experience in a way that steers clear of both modern and ancient prejudices" (Polt 2001, 39). Thus, Heidegger must write *under constraint*. In the background of his thought there is always the unexpressed jousting with the tradition from which he is struggling to free himself. The difficulty for us, his readers, arises where the constraint under which he is writing forbids explaining the outcome of that struggle.

Consider terms such as "revealing" and "concealing." Clearly, they are substitutes for traditional concepts such as consciousness and experience which Heidegger rejects as loaded with unacceptable baggage. The concepts of the tradition, such as subject and object, value and fact, can no longer supply the explanations but have become the explananda. But to explain these concepts other concepts are required that do not prejudge all the ontological issues in modern terms. The new conceptual apparatus cannot be an arbitrary personal invention. Instead, Heidegger finds the concepts he requires in the beginning of the tradition as its lost origin. The outcome is the vocabulary of revealing and concealing based on the Greek concepts of *alétheia, physis*, and *poiésis*. This new vocabulary is now supposed to provide a transhistorical framework from out of the very history it explains.

Heidegger could have helped us by saying, "I would like to talk about this or that as you ordinarily understand it, but I can't use your vocabulary without inheriting the very metaphysical assumptions I must escape. Therefore, I have rephrased the familiar problem in this new way." We would have been grateful to this imaginary Heidegger, so solicitous of our need for understanding. Unfortunately, this is not the real Heidegger, an unsympathetic fellow who rather self-indulgently plunges us into the cold water of his thought without any support—there, it's sink or swim!

Many commentators respect his self-limitation and so sink, or at least sink their readers. An account operating under the constraints Heidegger imposed is unlikely to shed much new light on his meaning. We need to permit ourselves what he did not permit himself, a free movement back and forth across the line dividing his language from that of the tradition. This will enable us to understand some things that remain obscure. Of course there is the risk that Heidegger's thought will be reduced to metaphysics, the very thing he attempted to escape. But the other risk is that his thought will end up as a scholastic play with language of interest mainly to a narrow circle of dedicated players.

With this in mind, consider again the breakdown of the traditional concept of essence that leads to the saving power. It would be more natural to express Heidegger's point by saying that today we know that meanings are culturally relative and that this knowledge poses for us the problem of what is ultimately real beyond the bounds of any particular culture. We are infected by history and hence distanced from our own culture sufficiently not to take essences for granted as did the Greeks. This starting point suggests a way of reformulating Heidegger's position.

Let us look more closely at this idea of culture. It appears that we moderns both know and do not know the source of the *eidos*, the essences of things. We know it lies in culture because we know it differs from one time and place to another. Culture, as we moderns understand it, is a human creation. Hence the essences that open up worlds and give meaning to things must also be human creations. This insight goes back to Kant but is now common sense in this nontranscendental cultural formulation. And as in Kant, meaning and reality, value and fact are split apart forever by the discovery of the creativity of the subject.

But this is precisely where the argument breaks down. Kant's transcendental formulation applied to all possible experience and so was safe from self-refutation, but our cultural version is itself part of a specific culture and so undermines itself. It is we moderns who, within the confines of our specific culture, assert the cultural relativity of essences. In so doing we beg the question. We must be right—the facts are obvious—yet we cannot be right—we cannot judge reality as such on the terms of our particular culture.

There is a problem here. If being is revealed *only* in culturally specific forms, then culture is more than culture and cannot be explained as a merely subjective human creation overlaying nature or a thing-in-itself. The very idea of a culture-free nature or thing in itself is itself posited by the culture that conceived culture. This culture is technological: it understands the world on the model of raw materials invested by a subjective plan. But if there is nothing but culture, then there simply is no coherent way to conceive these raw materials as an independent reality in the background of the various cultural dispensations. Furthermore, the origin of culture is incommensurate with the usual concept of human agency. Like language, culture has no authors to whom we can point, yet it does exist each time only in a specific local form rooted in a human community.

But how then can we think this "culture" that seems to have taken on the role of transcendental source of all meaning, including the meaning of the very concept we use to signify it? Heidegger calls this ultimate source "being." We do not create meaning and impose it on preexisting and meaningless things in themselves. On the contrary, we are granted meaning by something that lies beyond all human power. Being reveals itself in our encounter with our world and thus we are indeed implicated in the granting but not as the creating subject that commands a passive reality. Being reveals itself similarly in each dispensation and this alone makes what we call culture possible.

Here we reach the point where we can recognize the "saving power," the way in which our very nihilism can liberate us. With this realization we can free ourselves from the specifically modern culture that overtakes us in the technological outlook. Instead of seeing our world as mere raw materials and system components, we can see it as a particular way in which being appears. But this way, like all others, is partial, incomplete. Being conceals its other possibilities in revealing one of them. Our common sense cultural relativism is the expression of this truth of being in the language of technology. Only in the very different language of Heidegger's "history of being" can we grasp the nature of revealing itself and so free ourselves from the limitations of our own time. This history begins with the Greeks. To understand Heidegger's thought we must therefore return to his interpretation of Greek philosophy, specifically the philosophy of Aristotle.

Posing the Question

"The Question Concerning Technology" condenses and synthesizes a range of Heideggerian concerns over the preceding thirty-five years. Much can be learned about this enigmatic essay by expanding brief remarks which often are little more than hints of previous work. This is particularly true of the beginning of the essay, which in the space of a few pages introduces the ancient Greek concept of *techné*, defines it, and moves on to discuss modern technology. Heidegger maintains and emphasizes the contrast between ancient *techné* and modern technology throughout this essay and others such as "The Origin of the Work of Art." These are the two chief forms of making and, correspondingly, the two chief modes of revealing. Yet from these widely known essays, one cannot really gauge the depth of Heidegger's analysis of *techné* nor understand fully how *techné* differs from modern technology.

The "Question" to which the essay's title refers concerns the essence of technology. The question seems simple but in reality it is shrouded in obscurity and the essay does little to dispel the darkness. In fact, its principal merit is to cast doubt on the obvious answer to the question. Heidegger begins by denying that the essence of technology is technological. With this provocative statement, he distinguishes an instrumental account of technology from an ontological account. The former concerns the function of technology in fulfilling human desires, while the latter focuses on the role of the technological revealing in structuring a world in terms of the exigencies of planning and control. The instrumental account is not wrong, but it is internal to modernity and cannot explain why its promise has gone awry. Only an ontological account illuminates the nature of modernity and its catastrophic outcome. But this conclusion raises further questions.

The ontological account explains technology as a mode of revealing distinct from ancient *techné*. But what does it mean to say that the Greeks or we ourselves have a world revealed through one or another kind of technical activity? How can making artifacts, a particular way of relating to things, take on the ontological task of defining worlds? Furthermore, if *techné* as *poiésis* was such a great thing, why not return to it? Why are we stuck at the end of the essay wondering how we will be "saved" from the technological catastrophe when it seems Heidegger has the answer all along? Why, if not, are we bothering with the Greeks at this late date?

These are no doubt naïve questions, but they are reasonable questions. Since it fails to answer them the essay is incomplete, like a few strands of melody that recall a whole piece heard on another occasion but which are scarcely musical to the uninitiated. The only way to get a clearer understanding of Heidegger's answer to the question of technology is to take these naïve questions seriously and attempt to fill in the gaps in his argument that give rise to them. I have read quite a few accounts of Heidegger's views on technology, but this is rarely attempted. Instead, many commentators emulate Heidegger's agility in leaping over the weak spots in his argument. The uncritical use of Heidegger's terminology, often with bizarre neologisms in translation, is the most annoying aspect of these accounts. Going over the same ground, they arrive at the same point, the point at which the questioning must really begin. That point is Heidegger's early interpretation of Aristotle, specifically, Aristotle's account of *techné*, which is briefly sketched at the start of the essay.

"With Aristotle," Heidegger remarks, "the greatest philosophical knowledge of antiquity is expressed, a knowledge which even today remains unappreciated and misunderstood in philosophy" (Heidegger 1995a, 188). From 1921 to 1939, Aristotle is one of Heidegger's major preoccupations to whom he devotes lecture courses and essays. These early writings on Aristotle are peculiar for doing two apparently incompatible things. On the one hand, they offer extremely careful, even brilliant, readings of the finest details of Aristotelian texts. On the other hand, they continually demonstrate the many ways in which Aristotle anticipated Heidegger's own philosophy. Indeed Hans-Georg Gadamer, who was studying with Heidegger at the time of his 1923 lecture on "Phenomenological Interpretations in Connection with Aristotle," asserts without qualification that for the early Heidegger "in the care of the human being for itself and for its being, there resides that which, as the question of the concept of being, already found its comprehensive response in Aristotle's *Metaphysics*" (Gadamer 1992, 13, my translation). One is left wondering how it is that Heidegger sees Aristotle when he looks in the mirror. In this early anticipation of the analytic of *Dasein*, Aristotle is implausibly attributed a philosophical anthropology based on a phenomenological ontology.

This approach is perhaps entirely true only of the 1923 lecture on Aristotle which Heidegger's intellectual biographer, Theodore Kisiel, claims is the "the "zero-point of the specific project of BT [*Being and Time*]" (Kisiel 1993, 250). This lecture is far more puzzling considered as Aristotle exegesis than as a first draft of Heidegger's own position. To a lesser extent this will hold true of the more rigorous 1931 lecture course on Aristotle's *Metaphysics*. A brief sketch of *Being and Time* is therefore helpful as a preliminary to an exposition of these texts.

Being and Time claims to revive the "question of being," abandoned under the influence of neo–Kantianism in the preceding decades, by studying human being. Heidegger finds it remarkable that human beings not only exist as things, but that they have a relation to their own being. Unlike a rock or a tree, we humans do not merely have objective qualities such as weight and height but must give these qualities meaning in our lives. The being of each human being is "in question" in the sense that one must decide what and how to be the person one is. As a consequence of this self-relation, each person can be said to "have" themselves in a unique kind of self-possession. I not only have a profession, a home, a country, but I must "live" these qualities, assume them, and give them a specific and always contingent significance in a life that is mine and mine alone amidst a world I share with others in my own way. This questionableness and belonging of human being makes of it a very special kind of being Heidegger calls "factical life" in his earliest reflections and "*Dasein*" in *Being and Time*.

Heidegger argues that the analysis of *Dasein*'s way of being can unravel the mystery of being itself. *Being and Time* therefore unfolds as an existential ontology. Heidegger shows that we first encounter the real in the form of a "world," that is, an orderly system of entities with which we interact in use, rather than as a collection of isolated objects of knowledge we "invest" with value and take up subsequently in action. The process of revealing involves the assignment of purpose and meaning to things in relation to *Dasein*'s self-understanding. *Dasein* does not have a stable and definite being but strives to construct itself through its engagements with things and other people. It engages with its world out of concern with its own future. Hence the title of the book, *Being and Time*.

Why is this ontology rather than a psychological account of how human beings experience an objective world of which they are simply a part? Why is an explanation of *Dasein*'s being-in-the-world an account of being itself? The answer to these questions has to do with the significance of phenomenology for Heidegger. Phenomenology offers a first person account of how *Dasein* encounters the world in everyday experience. This account establishes the temporal priority of "worldhood" over objectivity, the fact that we engage with things practically before we contemplate them in knowledge. The objective conception of things is the result of a subsequent constructive process in which knowledge in the usual sense consists. Heidegger argues that the products of that process cannot turn around and explain their origin, for example, reducing the world revealed to *Dasein* to a combination of sense data and feelings. No objectivistic explanation from the third person standpoint of a scientific observer can offer a more fundamental account of being than the phenomenological account. The encounter with being in instrumental activity, very broadly construed, is thus not just the earliest, but also the deepest encounter (Heidegger 1962, 130–33).

This original practical relation to a world is described repeatedly in *Being and Time* in terms of the use of elementary hand tools. However, Heidegger does not say much about the relation between the analysis of worldhood and his concurrent research on Aristotle. In his 1931 lecture course on Aristotle's *Metaphysics*, the connection is made explicit (Heidegger 1995a, 117). The several lecture courses on Aristotle from the early 1920s to the early 1930s serve as a background to understanding the ontology of practice in *Being and Time*. In these courses, the Greek idea of being is interpreted on the model of *techné*. This model is formative for the Greek experience of the world. Aristotle's detailed explanation of it is the core of his thought and the highpoint of Greek philosophy. Heidegger continues, "Not only did the Greeks, Plato and Aristotle, carry out the interpretation of this phenomenon of production, but the basic concepts of philosophy have grown out of and with this interpretation" (Heidegger 1995a, 117; compare Heidegger 1982, 115–16).

In Heidegger's terms, this means that the human activity of making, a specific "comportment" toward the world, is the primordial revealing of being. To put it in the terms of *Being and Time*, a fact about human being, namely, that it possesses a specific "understanding of the Being of all entities of a character other than its own" is ontologically significant (Heidegger 1962, 34). *Dasein* is, again in Heidegger's terminology, "ontic-ontological" insofar as its comportment as a particular being in the world reveals the world, that is, creates an "opening" or "clearing" within which beings come to appearance. And this comportment was initially analyzed by the Greeks as the activity of making artifacts. Their intuition about the nature of being therefore conformed in its essential structure with Heidegger's *Dasein* analysis—and vice versa.

By the mid-1930s, when Heidegger takes up technology as his principal theme, his views have undergone two important shifts. He comes to believe that the revealing of being is not adequately modeled by notions such as equipment and *techné*. On the contrary, the modern technological picture of the world is a kind of degeneration product of the initial ontological overburdening of *techné* by the Greeks. The results of his research into the Greeks are recast as a historical stage in a process that cannot be fully understood from his own earlier standpoint. Heidegger now claims that modes of revealing are historical and that ontology must be pursued as the "history of being." This second shift motivates the contrast between *techné* and technology as historically specific modes of revealing. With this in mind, we begin to see why "The Question Concerning Technology" ignores the issues we normally associate with technology to focus instead on ontology. The next section will explore the key concepts of this ontology as they were first formulated by Aristotle.

Ten Key Concepts

Kinesis

For Heidegger, Aristotle's greatness lies in having placed movement, *kinesis,* at the center of philosophical reflection. Movement in Aristotle's sense refers not just to change of place, but more generally to any kind of change from one state to another. Aristotle's accomplishment was to address the nature of movement in this broad sense of the term, and to understand it as the essence of being. To signify movement in this sense Heidegger introduces the rather recondite German word "*Bewegtheit,*" variously translated into English as "movement," "movedness," and "motility." In Heidegger's view, following Aristotle, *Bewegtheit* is not something that happens to being; it is constitutive of being. "It was Aristotle who first attained—and thus, first created—that level of questioning where (movement is not considered as something merely given along with other things, but rather where) *being-moved* is explicitly questioned and understood as the fundamental mode of being" (Heidegger 1998, 187).

Aristotle understands *kinesis* primarily as the shaping of things as they develop or are made, in other words, as what Heidegger calls their "bringing forth" or "coming to presence." This is, to be sure, an unusual sense of the word movement but that should not prevent us from understanding Heidegger's meaning, which may possibly be the correct interpretation of Aristotle. In any case, Heidegger's explanation of both *physis* and *techné*, nature and art, depends on *kinesis* in this specific sense.

In some of his earliest writings, Heidegger relates Aristotle's conception of movement to human activity in general. Human beings are involved in movement of a special kind which proceeds from their care or concern with the problems of "factical life." Aristotle's concept of *phronesis* is interpreted as an anticipation of Heidegger's own concept of circumspection (*Umsicht*), the form of practical intelligence associated with the movement of factical life.

This approach to Aristotle is concretized fruitfully by identifying the inner structure of Aristotelian *kinesis* with production. Heidegger analyzes this structure in several dimensions, including its relation to the capacities of the producer and to the form and product of the activity of production. Heidegger interprets Aristotle's term "*entelechy*" to signify the moment in which movement gathers itself together and comes to rest in the fully realized product. He claims that the Aristotelian concept of movement is derived from the notion of rest as completion, as the standing still in which movement terminates. The term "*energeia*," usually translated as "actuality," has a similar meaning, Heidegger claims, signifying the "*ergon*," or finished work that stands before us in its completion.

Although movement is interpreted through its terminus, the completed work must not be isolated from the process of its emergence. The unfolding of that process is implied in its end. Movement is understood through rest, but rest itself is a kind of zero point of movement and as such a form of movement. This dialectic of movement and rest conforms with our common sense understanding of animal behavior. For the animal, immobility is a special kind of movement requiring a specific effort rather than a state of indifference, as it seems to be for a rock or other inanimate thing. But as Heidegger interprets it, Aristotle's ontology does not make this common sense distinction quite as we do: not just animals, but all that stands there stably in itself must be comprehended from out of the movement by which it reached that state and holds itself steady.

This interpretation of *kinesis* clarifies some of the most obscure aspects of Aristotle's *Physics,* which, Heidegger says, "is the hidden, and therefore never adequately studied, foundational book of Western philosophy" (Heidegger 1998, 185). For example, we have seen that movement is animated by a "final cause," but the goal of movement is not for Aristotle something merely external to the moving being, an idea or representation in the mind. It is the "*arché*" of movement, an origin that sets in motion that which moves. Hence Aristotle does not share our idea of movement as a contingent interaction between a mutually indifferent cause and its effect. Instead he understands movement through the concept of "*eros*," the desire which draws the moved being toward its object and in which it comes to rest. The dialectic of rest and movement also illuminates the discredited notion of "natural place" in Aristotle which, astonishingly, Heidegger claims "is not in the least refuted, in fact not even grasped" (Heidegger 1995a, 67). Since the Aristotelian thing is drawn to the end point of its own development, if that end point implies a specific spatial location it will come to rest there as it is fulfilled.

Physis

Physis is usually translated as "nature," but once again Heidegger objects. What is lost in the concept of nature is the dynamic character of *physis*, which refers to the movement in which the thing brings itself forth into appearance. In this Heideggerian usage, "appearance" is ambiguous, referring at one and same time to what we call "existence" and "appearing." *Physis* must therefore be understood outside the framework of such distinctions as that between essence and existence, subject and object.

The emergence of the thing out of itself is most obvious in the case of plants and animals. They are in some sense the archetype of *physis* insofar as their existence *can only* be grasped as a process. The plant, Heidegger says, has its *arché* in its rootedness in the earth from out of which it emerges. It stands forth from the earth by going back into the earth, sinking its roots in its source. This double movement—standing forth and going back—characterizes the specific motility of living things.

In a modern context it is tempting to consider *physis* as a kind of mechanical self-making. Biological science considers the organism as a multiplicity of interacting physico-chemical machines, causes. But Heidegger argues that this modern conception is completely un-Greek. From the Greek standpoint, the important point is the form and direction of the process of emergence, not its cause in our sense. This process brings the thing forth in its "truth," in the form it was destined to take, for example, as such and such a plant or animal, and this bringing forth is directed at human witnessing. There is no concern with causality here at all.

Techné

This approach is developed further in Heidegger's reflections on the meaning of *techné*. But he has two rather different accounts. *Techné*, he sometimes claims, does not mean technology or even craft. The term refers rather to know-how in general. Know-how in this sense is what is involved in bringing beings forth as themselves, that is, in recognizing them under this or that category as useful in this or that context or activity (Heidegger 1998, 192–93, 222). Heidegger's point is that things cannot be understood as just there, pure objects before a detached subject of knowledge. Rather, things enter a world through their interpretation in terms of a meaning and a use. This incorporation of things into humanly organized worlds can be understood through the concept of the "*eidos*," or essence, which Heidegger associates closely with *techné*. We will return to this enlarged sense of *techné* later, but for the moment we need to focus on a narrower interpretation that conforms more closely with the usual understanding of the term.

According to the Greeks, things exist either by *physis* or by *techné*. The things of *physis* have their *arché* in themselves. They are self-originating. The things of *techné* have their *arché* in another. They are made or at least helped into being by an agent. Know-how in this more conventional sense is associated with productive activity, poiésis, in contrast with science, *epistémé*.

However, Heidegger gives even this more conventional understanding of the term an unfamiliar twist. *Techné*, he claims, is not about the procedures of making but rather about knowing how the thing must come out in the process of its production. It consists essentially in bringing the process of making to completion in the conformity of the produced thing with its essence. This kind of know-how is directed toward the end or goal of production rather than the means. It is productive in the sense of bringing the thing forward, producing it like a witness in court; first as idea, then in reality. *Techné* promotes the specific movement in which a thing emerges. In so doing it goes beyond *physis* to bring forth another type of being which, Heidegger argues, is not the product of arbitrary will, but of a *logos*. "*Techné*," Heidegger writes, "is a mode of proceeding *against physis*, though not yet in order to overpower it or exploit it, and above all not in order to turn use and calculation into principles, but, on the contrary, to retain the holding sway of *physis* in unconcealedness" (Heidegger 1994, 155). It is in this specific sense that *techné* is engaged with presence as such and not merely the utilitarian concerns of everyday life. As Heidegger will write in a later work, for the Greeks, "Using commends the used thing to its own nature and essence" (Heidegger 1966, 196, compare Heidegger 1966, 187).

Logos

For Plato, as we have seen, the distinguishing feature of *techné* is the predominance of the *logos*. And now Heidegger places the *logos* at the center of the Aristotelian concept of *techné* as well. Thus, to understand *techné* we must first consider this important Greek word. It is usually translated as "reason" or "discourse." Heidegger rejects these translations. "*Logos*," he claims, is derived from the word "*legein*" which means to lay out, harvest, or gather. "*Logos*" is the gathering together of the relationships that make things intelligible and the making manifest of the results of this gathering. This definition suggests that the *logos* is related to the essence of things and to the articulation of that essence in speech. But note that Heidegger finds the *logos* at work not only in theoretical knowledge, but also in circumspection, the basic familiarity with things that accompanies action. At every level of cognition, *logos* signifies the functions of unifying and making explicit involved in the intelligent encounter with the world.

But what is involved in the work of the *logos*? What does it actually encompass? It is, says Heidegger, a kind of rule or law immanent to the elements it gathers. The gathering act is an interpretation of these elements as belonging together in a model of the thing. This model is not simply the empirical givenness of the thing but its finished and perfected form. In understanding this particular chair or table as what they are, I transcend their limited and imperfect realization in the here and now toward their "idea"; I relate them to what they are in their truth.

If, for the moment, we confine ourselves to understanding the *logos* in its role in *techné*, as interpreted by Plato, these abstract qualifications can be given a concrete meaning. Recall that for Plato each art is governed by a *logos*. The art of shipbuilding, for example, gathers materials and plans under the leading idea, the *logos*, the ideal model, of a ship that will be strong and reliable, and perhaps also suitable for carrying large quantities of goods, fast, or excellent in warfare, depending on its type. The *logos* selects and assigns each resource its place in the whole and measures the progress of the work against a pregiven result, formulated more or less explicitly by the maker either in an internal monologue or in conversation with others.

Eidos and Morphé

The *logos* refers to the act of gathering in which a model is identified and articulated. The Greeks call the model itself an "idea" or "*eidos.*" The *eidos* is the immediate result of the gathering in which *logos* consists. The *eidos* is the "look" that the finished thing must have to be a proper product of its *techné*. It is sighted in advance and only on the basis of this initial sighting can *techné* proceed. The *eidos* is roughly equivalent to the idea of "essence" we will explore in more depth below.

Heidegger reinterprets the concepts of *telos* (usually translated as "end") and *peras* (usually translated as "limit") in terms of this understanding of the *eidos*. We moderns conceive the end as a subjective goal and the limit as an external barrier to movement or extension. Accordingly, we think of technical activity as subordinate to a goal in the craftsman's head and the product as limited by the available resources, the environment, and so on. Heidegger reverses the terms of this modern understanding of the *eidos*. The end and limit are in fact the finished product itself insofar as it conforms to the *eidos* and embodies the specific limitation that makes it this particular thing rather than another. The *telos* is not in the mind of the maker nor is the *peras* external to the work. Heidegger claims, in a sense, that the *eidos* is discovered, "disclosed," rather than invented and thus the end or limit it places on the product and on the craftsman's activities is a truth rather than a subjective intention. The *eidos* is not so much an idea as the real being of the thing to be made, what it most intrinsically is prior to any and all "ideas" in the usual sense of the word. To effect this reversal, Heidegger emphasizes that the craftsman's conception of the *eidos* inhabits the work and the work process. "In other words, *eidos* is genuinely understood as *eidos* only when it appears within the horizon of one's immediate addressing of a being" (Heidegger 1998, 210).

The concept of *eidos* is closely related to that of *morphé*, or form. Form is the *eidos* realized in an appropriate matter of some sort. In this sense it is not what we normally understand as form. The *eidos* must appear, come into presence, through a process of formation of its material, the *hylé*. Form is a state of being of that material, not something extrinsic that happens to it accidentally. Form is the movement toward completion that overtakes and transforms the material, stripping it of its imperfection as it proceeds. We must not therefore conceive of the material as essentially what it is prior to production. Rather, the material exists primarily in the work process as what has not yet been "forged into its boundaries," granted the form it awaits in its primitive state (Heidegger 1995a, 118).

We can of course reconceptualize all this in common sense terms and think of *eidos* and form as subjective ideas in the head of the maker, matter as objective things in the world, and their encounter as a contingent happening caused by human will. This is precisely the modern conception of technology Heidegger claims is alien to the Greeks. We have, he says, fallen away from the original Greek conception through our inability to cling to the original meaning of *techné*. In that meaning, the emergence of the thing is thought through the process of formation. Work is not an accident that befalls indifferent raw materials but the entry of the crafted object into a world. With this conception the Greeks seem to have anticipated Heidegger's own phenomenology. The thing must not be conceived ontologically outside its relation to the process in which it emerges from the work of the craftsman. Rather, it is "revealed" in that process.

Dynamis and Energeia

These two categories explain the concept of *techné* at the deepest level. They encompass the activity of production and its result. As such they are dialectical categories, for each aspect of production is tied to a contrary aspect in many different ways. Just as raw materials correspond to form, so to clumsy action there corresponds skill, to every potentiality an actuality, and so on. On the one side there is a specific mode of "privation," *steresis*; on the other side, its corresponding fulfillment. This dialectical pattern is repeated over and over. Heidegger writes, "*Dynamis is in a preeminent sense exposed and bound to steresis*" (Heidegger 1995a, 95). This dialectical character of production is the result of its ontologically original function of revealing.

Dynamis is usually translated as either potentiality or force. In Heidegger's account of *techné* it has both these meanings. The material, *hylé*, has the *dynamis*, the potential, to become the finished work. In this sense, *dynamis* means "appropriateness." Each technical activity calls forth the appropriate material on which it must work to achieve its ends. The finished work itself is *energeia*, the actualized potential of its production process and materials. The *energeia* instantiates the *eidos*, brings it to presence.

The second meaning of *dynamis* refers us to the craftsman, the producer, who possesses the force or capacity to make the work. Aristotle subjects *dynamis* in this sense to a very complex analysis, which Heidegger explains at length.

In Aristotle's *Metaphysics*, these two senses of *dynamis* are distinguished as *poiésis*, the creative moment, and *pathein*, the moment of tolerating, undergoing. They are mutually implicated in a dialectic of action and passion, creation and receptivity. The creative power of the craftsman implies a material that can "bear" the transformations imposed on it. This "bearing" Heidegger attributes to the material as a quality he calls "bearance." Bearance is not merely the absence of resistance, but signifies the essential availability of the material for form. The clay is not simply there to be formed into a jug; insofar as it is part of the process of production, it *demands* the achievement of form. "With the transformation of the clay into the bowl, the lump also loses its form, but fundamentally it loses its formlessness; it gives up a lack, and hence the tolerating here is at once a positive contribution to the development of something higher" (Heidegger 1995a, 74; compare Heidegger 1966, 14).

There is yet a further dialectic of force identified by Aristotle. This is the relation of force to "unforce," that is, to the specific absence that threatens every force. As blindness is to sight, so every unforce is to its corresponding force. This relationship is clear from the fact that performances based on a capacity are not merely done but are always done either well or poorly. The criterion of performance is implicit in the very fact of performance and is derived from the good performance rather than the bad. The bad is condemned by its failure to conform to this criterion. A normative dimension thus inheres in the nature of *dynamis*.

Dynamis as force or capacity of production is characterized as a "how to," an effective way of doing. The craftsman's *dynamis* places him or her in a state of readiness to perform the work. This readiness is not so much an orientation toward a goal, a wish or striving, as a discrimination and selection of precisely those actions that enable the movement of the produced thing from potentiality to actuality. *Dynamis* thus has a third dialectical character. The force for producing is always an exclusion of acts that would be unproductive, a leaving undone of those many mistaken moves that would prevent rather than further the realization of the work. What is not done belongs just as much to the essence of force as what is done.

Finally, there is one last dialectical relation in the structure of *dynamis* which has to do with the role of the *logos* in *techné* as Plato explains it. This is the relation of each specific force to the contraries it mediates. The healing art aims at health by addressing sickness as its problem task. In this, the *dynamis* of healing, a form of human practice, differs from the *dynamis* of a natural object such as fire which does indeed turn cold to warm but does not "address" the coldness as such. Fire acts, to be sure, not through a *logos* but causally. In medicine's addressing of sickness can be seen the play of the *logos*, which animates the various aspects or phases of the movement in which the work consists. The physician acts in this gap between the contraries he addresses to favor one against the other. Nothing of the sort is involved in natural movement.

Energeia refers not just to the empirically real, but to the specific type of reality that embodies the *eidos,* the finished work. In this sense, Heidegger claims,

Aristotle places the actual before the potential, as more ontologically fundamental. The work as embodying the archetype or *eidos* is ontologically prior to the various materials, tools, plans, and activities from out of which the work finally takes shape under its guidance and in view of its end.

The priority of the actual establishes a strange circularity in the *Metaphysics* that shows up even more clearly in the *Ethics*. The theory of virtue is based on observation of the behavior of the actual good man. This made perfect sense to Aristotle and his world, but we immediately ask how the good man is distinguished from the bad without a prior theory of virtue. The ontological version of this thesis leads to the freezing of the potentialities of the thing in the given form of an "actual" model, very much the opposite of our modern sense of potential as unbounded possibility (Polt 2001, 32, 36).

Enantia

We have seen the dialectical character of Greek productionism. The word that Heidegger introduces to discuss this is "*enantia*," contrary. Contraries appear in relation to every aspect of *techné*, from the relation of *morphé* to *hylé* and *dynamis* to *energeia*, to the various forms of *steresis* (privation) associated with *dynamis*. But these Greek contraries are not modern antinomies. Each contrary implies its other and comes to rest in its other. *Hylé* and *morphé* cannot be thought separately, any more than can *dynamis* and *energeia*, force and unforce, movement and rest, doing and not doing. Not only are the contraries mutually implicated, they are engaged in a development, a *kinesis* with a preestablished *telos*.

It is interesting to note that Heidegger identifies the *steresis* character of the contraries as a central theme in both Aristotle and Hegel (Heidegger 2002, 135, 142). Reconciliation of the contraries is of course also central in both, albeit in different ways. For the Greeks reconciliation is a fact of nature. Their world is always already reconciled. But this is a world that no longer exists. Modernity consists in the diremption of the contraries into opposing principles. For moderns like Hegel, reconciliation is an arduous achievement, if it is possible at all.

Poiésis as Production

Heidegger argues that *poiésis*, production, was the model of all being for the Greeks. The Greeks did not imagine that *physis*, nature itself, was manufactured. Rather, the structure of production as described above is also the structure of being itself. The essence of production is "*being-finished-and-ready*, i.e., a kind of being in which motion has arrived at its end" (Heidegger 2002, 136). To be finished means to instantiate an essence, the "*eidos*," the look. The thing places itself into appearance in the *eidos* that encompasses its completion and so enters the world. Presence, *ousia*, is thus "producedness" and can be analyzed as *kinesis* in terms of such concepts as *morphé* and *hylé*, *eidos*, *telos*, and *peras*.

Of course the analysis must be modified to take into account the difference between *physis* and artifacts, what has its *arché* in itself and in another. This difference determines the place of the *eidos, which* can either guide the craftsman in placing an artifact in the world, or, in the case of *physis*, actually place itself into the world directly and immediately, without the intervention of another. This self-placing of the *eidos* into existence is, however, structurally similar to production.

Until the mid-1930s, Heidegger has a primarily positive view of this approach and *Being and Time* is influenced by it. The production model translates between ancient and existential ontology. At first Heidegger even describes Aristotle's position as more or less identical with the coming analytic of *Dasein*. For example, in his 1923 lecture on Aristotle, he writes:

> Thus the toward-which this primordial experience of being aimed at [in Aristotle] was not the domain of being consisting of *things* in the sense of objects understood in a *theoretical* manner as facts but rather the world encountered in going about dealings that produce, direct themselves to routine tasks, and use. What *is* amounts to what has been finished and made ready in the movement of going about the dealings of production (*poiésis*), i.e., what has come into a being-on-hand and is now available for certain tendencies to use it. Being means *being-produced* and, as having been produced, being of significance relative to certain tendencies to have dealings with it, i.e., being-available for them. (Heidegger 2002, 127–28)

This passage anticipates the later theory of worldhood as the readiness-to-hand of "equipment" rather than the presence-at-hand of things.

That theory advanced beyond Aristotle in tracing the source of the meanings governing production back to *Dasein*'s care rather than to objective essences. The essences of things are no longer reified as things themselves but understood from out of their place in everyday practical activity, phenomenologically interpreted. Paradoxically, this new understanding of essence is made possible by modern technology.

Modernity

The Greek Revealing

We are now in a position to understand Heidegger's account of the difference between the Greek and the modern encounter with being. In his 1937–1938 lecture course on truth, Heidegger notes that the Greeks discovered being but then failed to ask the question of being. They were blinded by their own discovery which led them no further than an investigation into the nature of beings. They turned too quickly from the fact of the revealing to what was revealed. Here is how Heidegger explains their failure.

Wonder is the "basic disposition, the one that was compelling at the beginning of Western thinking. It let the question of beings as such become a necessity, though in such a way that it precluded a direct inquiry into *alétheia*" (Heidegger 1994, 149).[2] Wonder directed the Greeks toward the astonishing presence of beings, the unusualness of the most usual, and they responded by seeking to "preserve" being through allowing the essences of beings to appear: " . . . as moved by wonder, man must gain a foothold in the acknowledgment of what has erupted, and he must see it in a productive seeing of its inscrutable disclosure . . . " (Heidegger 1994, 146). This disclosure is the revelation of essence through which beings are perceived as what they are. Heidegger continues

> [I]t is clear that this perceiving of beings in their unconcealedness is not a mere gaping, that wonder is carried out rather in a procedure against beings, but in such a way that these themselves precisely show themselves. For that is what *techné* means: to grasp beings as emerging out of themselves in the way they show themselves, in their outward look, *eidos*, idea, and, in accord with this, to care for beings themselves and to let them grow, i.e., to order oneself within beings as a whole through productions and institutions." (Heidegger 1994, 155)

With this the Greeks made the fundamental discovery that the very possibility of knowing things depends on knowing them *as* . . . ., that is to say, knowing them through their essence. The Greeks explained this with the concept of presence as producedness. Our everyday commerce with the world is based on informed anticipation. We do not first know individual facts or sense data but rather the "look" we bring to things in engaging with them. We anticipate the "what" of the thing as the condition for encountering it in all our relations to the real, not just in production proper.

This is the background to Plato's theory of ideas. Heidegger appears to accept a variant of the Platonic position. We must be acquainted, he argues, with the "essence" of things to know them. We must have already encountered "house-ness" to recognize a house, "birdness" to recognize a bird. All acquaintance with particular facts presupposes an ability to perceive them *as* something. It is through this "as" that they enter a world (Heidegger 1995b, 335). Thus, our experience is constantly guided by concepts, although in Heidegger these are understood to be tacit, prereflexive, rather than explicit in a knowledge of some sort. The particulars of sense experience are not what is most real and concrete. What is primary are the ideas that enable those particulars to emerge as what they are.

Of course this only pushes back the problem of understanding our encounter with the world because now we must explain how we "see" the *eidos,* which in turn allows us to see the particulars. Heidegger admits that the realm of essence is "uncertain, shifting, controversial, and groundless," at least for us moderns (Heidegger 1994, 73). The encounter with the essences of things, he argues, is a unique kind of intuition, a "seeing which draws forth, a seeing which in the very act of seeing compels what is to be seen before itself" (Heidegger 1994, 76). In this "productive seeing, a conformity to something pregiven is not possible, because the productive seeing itself first brings about the pregivenness" (Heidegger 1994, 77).

The concept of a seeing which produces its object has emerged more than once in the history of philosophy. It appears in the scholastic notion of divine creation and is later translated into idealistic terms as "intellectual intuition," the power of thought to posit its objects. The concept was introduced into aesthetics by Kant to explain artistic production. The artist produces the concrete work in all its sensuous details in the very process of conceptualizing it. Heidegger seems to be gesturing in this direction, although, faithful to his phenomenological method, he complicates things by asserting that for the Greeks this productive seeing is actually an uncovering of pregiven meanings and not an imposition. "This letting hold sway [of being] is accomplished by exhibiting beings in their forms and modes of presence and by preserving beings therein—occurrences in which poetry as well as painting and sculpture, the act that founds a state, and the worshipping of the gods first obtain their essence" (Heidegger 1994, 128).

The Greek revealing was both a noble and a restricted encounter with being. Its nobility lay in the recognition that the forms of beings, the *eidos*, are not arbitrary products of human will, but arise from being itself. The Greeks knew that being grants itself to man in a revealing which requires man as a witness. Heidegger comments, "The first task was then to apprehend beings as beings, to install the pure recognition of beings as such, and nothing more. This was quite enough if we consider what was simultaneously grounded with it: the primordial determination of man as that being which, in the midst of beings as a whole, lets beings hold sway in their unconcealedness" (Heidegger 1994, 128). In sum, the Greeks discovered the basic premises of Heidegger's philosophy, or rather, Heidegger has rediscovered his own premises in the Greek beginning.

But the Greeks were unable to get beyond the *eidos* to its source in a process of revealing they could not conceptualize. They knew the belonging together of being and human being but did not "think" it. Why not? For the Greeks, the discovery of the *eidos* exhausted the content of human witnessing. It is this turn from being as revealing to the revealed *eidos* of beings that eventually leads through the many stages of Western thought to the final culmination in technology.

The Modern Revealing

Like the Greeks, Heidegger affirms both the independent reality of being and the ontological significance of human witnessing, but the precise role of witnessing differs for each of them. Heidegger emphasizes the fact that the Greeks passed from wonder at being to the invention of the sciences without pausing to reflect on the nature of their encounter with being. It was the very strength of the

Greek—their harmonious relation to the world—that blocked their progress toward a deeper understanding. The Greeks did not question the essences they attributed to things and so did not ask how things came to appear in the light of their essence. That question, the question of being, can only occur where the very concept of essence is in question. We ask that question in the modern world because we incessantly take apart and reconstruct the beings around us in the works of technology. This assault on beings does not bring them to completion in pregiven forms but proceeds according to subjectively elaborated plans.

The modern technological revealing sweeps away all concepts of essence and leaves only a collection of fungible stuff available for human ordering in arbitrary patterns. Heidegger's point is clearly illustrated by Descartes' famous example of the piece of wax in his second "Meditation." The object before him appears to be a substance in the Aristotelian sense until he begins to deconstruct it analytically. The wax changes its qualities as it is heated up, and soon is reduced to a certain extension perceivable, Descartes proves, only by the understanding. This extension, he notes, is precisely the quality by which the apparent substance can be infinitely transformed into objects of different shapes (Descartes 1955, 154–55). Descartes does not discuss the technical implications of this analysis, but it is obviously relevant to his famous claim that science would soon render us "masters and possessors of nature" (Descartes 1955, 119).

We recognize, as the Greeks did not, the ungrounded nature of the *eidos*. While they knew its source to be outside themselves in being, they had no way of justifying this insight to the ages to come. "For in the essence of *techné*, as required by *physis* itself, as the occurrence and establishment of the unconcealedness of beings, there lies the possibility of *arbitrariness*, of an unbridled positing of goals and thereby the possibility of escape out of the necessity of the primordial need" (Heidegger 1994, 155). Modernity is the unleashing of this arbitrariness in the technological expression of human will.

Modernity is generally the object of Heidegger's critique, but he admits at least implicitly that it enables us to go beyond the Greeks in one respect. We have discovered the active involvement of human beings in the meaning of beings even if we express this insight in a distorted form as subjectivism and nihilism. With this we are free to move in either of two different directions.

We can dismiss essence as merely arbitrary and subjective, overlooking the whole question of being. This is the modern technological outlook. Modernity aims at a condition "where the absolutely meaningless is valued as the one and only 'meaning' and where preserving this value appears as the human 'domination' of the globe" (Heidegger 1998, 197). The danger of this outlook is not so much its threat to human survival as the incorporation of human beings themselves into the "enframing" as mere raw materials alongside things. Lost in this leveling is not just human dignity, but also awareness of the unique role of the human being as the site of experience, the locus of world-shaping encounters with being.

But there is a second path opened up by the deconstruction of essences. The concept of essence, Heidegger argues, refers to what is permanent and enduring. But just insofar as essences are dissolved in the acid of modernity, the role of the human being in revealing comes to the fore. It is not nature alone that reveals being; human being too is actively involved. The belongingness of human being and being in the making of worlds is the only constant that remains, and recognition of this fact is finally possible in modern times. Indeed, while shrouding being in the technological enframing, modernity also contains the "other possibility ... that [man] might experience as his essence his needed belonging to revealing" (Heidegger 1977, 26; see also, 28–29, 40–41). Heidegger's own philosophy is this recognition. Despite Heidegger's apparent nostalgia for the premodern past, he never suggests a return to ancient *techné*. Instead, he looks forward to a new era in which new gods will enable human beings to reclaim their place in a world no longer shrouded in a technological order. The new era will use technology but it will not be technological. It will have a "free relation" to the realm of production rather than understanding being on the production model.

Heidegger's Dilemma

From the Greeks to Dasein *Analysis*

In the struggle to avoid modern subjectivism Heidegger's vocabulary introduces a puzzling ambiguity. Such *physis*-derived terms as presence, revealing, bringing into the manifest, bringing forth, signify at one and the same time existence and appearance, the one hinting at materialism, the other idealism. Yet it is well known that Heidegger rejected both these doctrines. In this he believed himself to be following the Greeks who did not rely on the modern distinction of subject and object from which these ontological alternatives derive. The concept of revealing is supposed to transcend such antinomies. What looks like a confusion is in fact a deep insight: our conviction that existence and world are totally independent of appearing is a mistake, as is the contrary view according to which the real is our product.

Heidegger argues that human witnessing is implicated in principle in any concept of a world. It is meaningless to talk about a world "in itself" and humans certainly cannot exist without a world. Neither humans nor world can be considered the ground or origin of the other. Neither can be dissolved in the other. Rather their coexistence is absolutely fundamental. But this position leads to a dilemma. How can being *require* a "besouled" being without losing its independence? Heidegger insists that the presence of a witness "precisely makes it possible for such being to secure this self-reliance in the truth ... The independence of things at hand from humans is not altered through the fact that this very independence as such is possible only if humans exist" (Heidegger 1995a, 173).

With the Greeks, the *eidos* has the independence Heidegger demands but in a misleading objective form. He calls Greek ontology "naïve" for this reason. The harmony of the contraries is only obtained by artificially assigning them to each other. We see immediately "behind" the illusion and notice how easily they can be split apart. For example, Plato's idea of the *logos* of *techné* assumes an intrinsic connection between an end and a means where we see the two as externally related. This is why Callicles seems right to us despite Socrates' best arguments. But, Heidegger argues, there is something more complicated going on here that we tend to overlook. Plato and Aristotle's idea of *techné* binds the contraries together in a way that can be validated in a phenomenology of our practical engagement with the world, but they lack the means to express their insight properly. As a result they attempt to present it in the everyday language of thinghood. The essential connections they have identified appear accidental in that language, at least they do to us who are remote from the source of their insight in the revelation given to the Greeks at the origin of Western philosophy.

This limitation is overcome in *Being and Time.* There the meaning of beings is rooted in *Dasein's* care and not in objective forms as for the Greeks. The production model continues to operate but in a phenomenological context. Heidegger presents everyday *Dasein* as primarily handling objects, i.e., involved in *techné.* But the equipmental realm, now defined as the "world," is no longer approached through the structure of the product as it is by Aristotle. Instead, Heidegger develops a phenomenology of *Dasein's* use of objects. This approach grounds the *eidos* in *Dasein's* temporality. *Dasein* projects meaning on the basis of its need to be, that is, to be this or that person engaged with this or that thing or activity in the future. Meaning must be understood in relation to *Dasein* rather than taken for granted as merely given. But, as for the Greeks, meaning still has the same function of letting beings emerge as something definite.

Sartre would later interpret this approach as a reduction of meaning to human intentions. This was not Heidegger's idea at all. Rather, care "discloses" the world and with it the meanings of the things in the world. It is not subjective but relates *Dasein* to a tradition and a language. However, Sartre was not entirely wrong in one important respect. The grounding of meaning in care renders it contingent and indeterminate.

Dasein's relation to the model of production is ambiguous. The human being is not governed by a fixed *eidos*. Its *poiésis* is subordinate to a *praxis* of self-making. Authenticity requires that *Dasein* think itself as a totality, a finished work so to speak. This it can do only in relation to death. Authentic practice is informed by this sense of completeness. The production model haunts this formulation strangely because *Dasein's* completeness is its death, not the realization of a prior essence. The order of *steresis* and completion in *techné* is reversed, the ultimate privation following rather than leading the process.

The lack of a fixed essence of man spills over onto the world as Heidegger demonstrates the dependence of meaning on *Dasein's* indeterminate future. As a result, the concept of authenticity undermines any fixed definition of things, the meaning of which must be revealed in relation to authentic practice. But do meanings then retain enough independence to avoid being reducible to the subject? In other words, does Heidegger's theory actually fulfill his intention to remain faithful to the initial Greek discovery of revealing?

The Role of Art in the History of Being

In Heidegger's later work, he rejects what he sees as the implicit subjectivism that haunts this early approach. He remains convinced that meaning is not present-at-hand, but now he interprets it through an original concept of history as the advent of truth. The meaning of beings is granted in various contingent forms in the course of history. Each of these forms is an encounter with a partial truth about beings, an encounter that is lived as the structure of the world.

The history of being is a long decline from the original Greek discovery of revealing. Heidegger introduces an argument concerning time to explain this decline. He claims that the Greeks reduced *ousia*, presence, to what appears in the present moment. This leads to the objectification of the *eidos* as present-at-hand in the world, even as it reveals the world. A tension develops between the dynamic principle of revealing and a static understanding of what is revealed. Latin translations of Greek terms eventually cut them loose from their source in the idea of revealing. The present-at-hand *eidos* becomes the "whatness" of the thing, entirely separate from its existence. Still later in modern times it finally becomes a merely subjective idea in the mind. In the technological age subjectivity expresses itself in calculations and plans. This is the ultimate dissolution of the *eidos*. The human "conquest" of nature now prevails where revealing was once recognized as the dynamic principle of being.

In "The Origin of the Work of Art" (Heidegger 1971), Heidegger returns to the theme of revealing in an attempt to overcome the limitations of both the original Greek formulations and his own efforts in *Being and Time*. He presents revealing not in relation to *Dasein*'s care but rather as a dispensation emerging in the work of art. The emphasis shifts back from the using of tools to their product. The artist's *techné* now participates in disclosing a world through the work. These reflections on art succeed in de-subjectivizing the notion of revealing. Meaning emerges from a creative process rooted in being and includes human activity in an essential capacity. The fact that this activity is no longer purely individual, but relates to, indeed founds, a community makes possible a concept of essence with the required independence. Although now the essences of things are time bound, historical, unlike for the Greeks, they belong to a destiny and regain the dynamic character of a *logos* that rules over and gathers the things themselves.

With these reflections on art Heidegger provides a promising new model for understanding the revealing of beings. But it turns out to be an empty promise. The solution developed in *Being and Time* was not historical but applied to *Dasein* as such. It thus explained modern as well as ancient revealing. The creative process of art occupies the theoretical place of *Dasein*'s care as the fundamental disclosive activity of man, but it cannot do the work of that concept. The new model applies only to premodern times when art had the power of revealing and not to the age of technology in which art is reduced to a marginal "experience" and confined to the aesthetic realm instead of shaping the practice of life. The technological enframing that takes its place does not so much create meanings as destroy them, de-worlding things and reducing them to a "objectless" heap. To the extent that it reveals a meaning, what appears is an endless repetition of the same "standing reserve," *Bestand*, not the rich variety the Greeks found in their world. This explains the extraordinary vagueness of Heidegger's discussion of the saving power. The best he has to offer is the remote eschatological hope that art can recover the power of revealing or that the very extremity of enframing will lead to its collapse.[3] But he does not predict as much. In his later work he leaves the question open, and as we will see, this invites other initiatives.

A Hegelian Heidegger?

When Marcuse was his student, Heidegger was not yet resigned to this dilemma. He still sought a new revealing in "the act that founds a state." His references to a "revolution" and a "new beginning" were all euphemisms for Nazism. When he discovered that Hitler's plans were different from his own, he retreated from history into more and more obscure formulations of his goals. Heidegger neither describes the salvation he awaits nor prescribes a path to reach it. This abstention has impressed some readers with his profundity, while others have dismissed his blurry vision as a dangerous mystification. I would like to try a different approach, a kind of immanent critique and synthesis of Heidegger's reflections on technique. He would no doubt have rejected my interpretation, but it bridges the gap between his thought and that of his student, Marcuse, who also entertained a vision of a new era but went beyond his teacher in sketching it hopefully. The point of this exercise is to show that Heidegger's own theory implies a more concrete critique of technology and projection of its promise than he himself developed.

Let me begin this reconstruction of Heidegger's position by noting the moment of reconciliation in his thought. Heidegger argues that the Greek world still slumbers in the hidden recesses of everyday life, but that it can only be recovered by a radically modern gesture. Thus, his analytic of *Dasein* posits a quasi-Greek totality at the basis of human existence in the intimate familiarity and practical engagement with the things of immediate experience. At this basic level, the contraries are complementary, as they are for the Aristotle. In *Being and Time* there are no antinomies of subject and object, value and fact for *Dasein* in its everyday commerce with its world.

This "Greek" note in Heidegger's thought comes up against a dissonant modern note from the very start. The dissonance takes various forms throughout his career but always returns to disturb the idyllic unity of human being and world. Contraries continually degenerate into contradictions both existentially and historically. This is the significance of "fallenness," inauthenticity, nihilism. But Heidegger holds out a hope of recovery, a "*Verwindung*," at first at the personal level through the resolute grasping of the time of life, and later through a possible "new beginning" of the history of the West through which the antinomies of modernity would be left behind. These different versions of recovery cannot bring about a return to the happy age of the Greeks but remain within the general framework of modernity. But they do promise a reconnection with meaning and limit, a recognition of finitude, and a homecoming of sorts in the midst of modern homelessness.[4]

This notion of reconciliation suggests that beneath the explicit historical narrative of decline in which Heidegger situates technique there lies an implicit narrative of a very different sort. His story could also be told to say that the ancients understood the importance of being as the source of meaning, and the moderns the role of human being in its essential activity. But each age misunderstood its own deepest principle. The ancients confounded being with the essences of particular beings. The moderns confused the essential role of humanity in the process of revealing with technical command of nature. Stripped of these misunderstandings and adequately comprehended, this previous history opens us to what Heidegger claims is "a more original revealing, and hence . . . the call of a more primal truth" (Heidegger 1977, 28).

This "turn" amounts to the revealing of the revealing itself. Obscured throughout history by the exclusive focus on the things revealed, revealing itself will finally become visible. The transcendental account Heidegger proposes will enter existence as a disposition toward being. In sum, we await a new dispensation in which revealing as such is encountered in its essence.[5] On this unorthodox reading, "The Question Concerning Technology" would culminate in a kind of posthistorical synthesis of ancient and modern through self-consciousness.

But this is a familiar figure of thought that goes back to Hegel: the "end of history" as history aware of itself. The young Marx repeats this figure in the notion of communism as a "dream" from which the world need only awaken to possess its reality. The implicit structuring of Heidegger's essay on technology around the figure of self-consciousness suggests a way of reading him against the grain of his own self-understanding. This quasi–Hegelian reading is certainly untrue to other themes in Heidegger's thought, the very themes that led him into complicity with Nazism and later to a completely apolitical conception of a new beginning. Nevertheless, the Hegelian reading is not arbitrary. A student following Heidegger's courses in the late 1920s and early 1930s might easily have understood him in this way, or at least been inspired to revise fundamental ontology along these lines.

Indeed, Hegel's dialectic suggests a solution to the central problem of Heidegger's later work, the construction of a relation of human being to being that can replace both Greek bringing forth and the modern *Gestell*. This is the task Heidegger must address as he becomes dissatisfied with the solution offered in *Being and Time*. But despite his long struggle, his later philosophy disappoints precisely on this point.

Although Heidegger hopes for a new dispensation, his reflections on how meaning would arise in that context are theoretically opaque, evocative, and poetic, but resistant to philosophical elucidation. We go from "thinking" to "thanking" but never discover a new way, after the defeat of *techné* and art, in which human being and being can join creatively in the making of a modern world rich in meaning again. The late descriptions of the fourfold appear to offer an ontological utopia which is difficult to reconcile with the early phenomenological notion of revealing. Simply waiting around for art to regain its power in a new dispensation seems a sad default on the promise of the Western philosophical tradition. A never quite acknowledged religious impulse hovers in the background.[6]

The Hegelian alternative focuses on life as a conflictual process of self-making leading to a harmonious outcome. In its Marxist variant, this solution promises a new era through historical action. Meaning arises out of conflicts in the structure of the world. These conflicts are specific and empirically verifiable and so the theory does not end up invoking an abstraction such as the enframing in the place of essence. What will now occupy that place? At first Marcuse attempted to fill the Hegelian dialectical form with Marx's early ideas on the ontological role of labor. In his later work aesthetic categories take over that role.

Where would Heidegger have ended up had he based his one intervention in history not on the existential notion of resoluteness but on the *techné* of historical self-production, the internal tensions and conflicts driving history toward the realization of its potential? Certainly, his trajectory would have been quite different. But had he moved in this direction rather than toward Nazism, it would be difficult to distinguish his position from the existential version of Marxism Marcuse proposed. There is enough similarity, in any case, that it could occur to Marcuse to write a doctoral dissertation in which Hegel's thought is reconstructed in a Heideggerian framework as the implicit "solution" to the problem of modernity.

Chapter 3

The Dialectic of Life

Marcuse's Hegel

From Aristotle to Hegel

Marcuse's Hegel

Marcuse wrote two books on Hegel. The first one, *Hegel's Ontology and the Theory of Historicity,* was submitted as a thesis to Heidegger in 1930 and published in 1932. Heidegger's opinion of this work is unknown as he does not appear to have said much about it before Marcuse was forced into exile. In it Aristotle is presented as the key to Hegel, but as we will see it is a strange Heideggerian Aristotle. Of course we are not concerned here with either the real historical Aristotle, nor even with the fidelity of Marcuse to Hegel's or Heidegger's Aristotle interpretations. What is significant here is the way concepts from Heidegger's Aristotle influence Marcuse's interpretation of Hegel. The similarities that emerge from this comparison are striking. The difference, of course, is also significant: Hegel is already a modern thinker and unlike Aristotle can speak to us directly. We can engage with Hegel as a contemporary in the (unmentioned) version of his dialectic found in Marxism.

The second Hegel book, *Reason and Revolution,* was published in 1941 while Marcuse was in the United States. In *Reason and Revolution* Marcuse makes the bold claim that "Hegel simply reinterpreted the basic categories of Aristotle's *Metaphysics* and did not invent new ones" (Marcuse 1963, 122). This claim conforms with the earlier book. There Marcuse follows Heidegger in asserting that the central Aristotelian category at the basis of Hegel's *Logic* is *kinesis,* "motility," *Bewegtheit.* "The presentation of the Idea of Being as motility lies at the core of Hegelian ontology" (Marcuse 1987, 173). This focus "allows Hegel to revive the great discoveries of Aristotelian philosophy by removing the cover which tradition had spread over them. Aristotelian philosophy is set once more on its true path:

proceeding from the negativity and dividedness of being (the *dichas* of the categories, *morphé* and *steresis—on dynamei* and *on energeia*) . . . as the basis of its motility . . . progressing until that most actual form of motility and the most actual being—*noésis* and *noésos*" (Marcuse 1987, 43). Marcuse identifies the duality at the heart of Aristotelian being with the bifurcation of being in Hegel, the internal contradictions that drive the dialectic.

Despite the common reference to Aristotle, these two books on Hegel are quite different. The later one is clearly the work of a Marxist albeit a Marxist intent on recruiting Hegel to the cause. The earlier one is ambiguous. It does not quite interpret Hegel from the standpoint of *Being and Time,* but the Heideggerian influence is obvious. This ambiguity was noted in Adorno's review of the book and has become its defining feature. So convinced are most commentators that Marcuse's early Hegel book is simply an intermediary between Heidegger and Marxism that its difficult content is generally ignored. Once the transition is made and Marcuse is safely classifiable as a Marxist, his writing is more accessible and his politics more clearly articulated. In sum, he is more interesting to the sort of people who tend to write about Marcuse.[1]

There is, however, much to be learned from Marcuse's thesis, both about Hegel and Marcuse himself. But decoding Marcuse's message is not simple. Not only is the writing difficult, the constraints of a thesis dictate the omission of references to one of Marcuse's most important sources. He cannot cite the disreputable Marxist Georg Lukács, whose *History and Class Consciousness* was known to him and cited in other essays of this period.[2] The significance of Lukács for Marcuse's Hegel interpretation must be guessed in the absence of references. However, once one starts guessing, interesting connections appear. Still, making the connections is not always easy. The language of the thesis is to a great extent Hegelian, as is Lukács's language, but the links between them are not worked out explicitly.

Heidegger and Lukács have enough in common to explain how Marcuse could draw on both. Both are opposed to the naturalistic, positivist, and neo–Kantian methodologies so influential in their day in professional philosophy and Marxist theory. Both explore the philosophical implications of the crisis of European civilization and attempt to develop a concrete historical ontology based on human finitude in response. Marcuse finds in both elements toward a rational foundation for revolutionary opposition to capitalism and its culture. At the core of their contribution is a radical concept of history which Marcuse reads back into Hegel as the heart and soul of the dialectic. The historical ontology underlying the dialectic can link philosophical reflection to concrete social struggles. But this requires a restorative operation in relation to Hegel comparable to Heidegger's restoration of Aristotle and directly related insofar as Hegel was profoundly influenced by Aristotle.

The unifying theme of this interpretation is production, a central category for Aristotle and hence for early Heidegger and Lukács as well. Production is one of the central categories of Lukács' early Marxism, not just economic production but the production of history. This is the category under which Lukács explains the dereification of society through revolutionary action. Historical production is a unique practice of self-making which Lukács describes as the unity of theory and practice. We will find this category at work in Marcuse's interpretation of Hegel. Once again we are confronted with the ontic-ontological status of the human practice of making, although it is of course not Lukács but Marcuse who could have formulated the matter in this Heideggerian language. In sum his thesis is a heideggerianized reading of Hegel's Aristotelianism and, as such, aims to provide the basis for a reconstruction of Marxism as a fundamental ontology.

But reading *Hegel's Ontology* through Heidegger is difficult. Heidegger is mentioned only briefly in this preliminary acknowledgement: "Any contribution this work may make to the development and clarification of problems is indebted to the philosophical work of Martin Heidegger. This is emphasized at the beginning instead of being indicated throughout with special references" (Marcuse 1987, 5). This note invites us to approach Marcuse as a Heideggerian but does not explain how we are to do so. Properly, Hegelian terms must be translated into Heidegger's language in order to support such a reading. That procedure violates the text in important respects. I think we must imagine how Marcuse's book would have been read by himself and his colleagues, students of Heidegger. Every allusion that could be connected to Heidegger's thought would certainly have been so connected. In other words, the book was not written for naïve readers or Hegelians but for Heidegger and those around him. We get a hint of what this might mean from a postcard Marcuse sent to his fellow student Karl Löwith in July 1931:

> It is true that a longer work of mine on Hegel will appear this fall: it is an interpretation of the *Logic* and the *Phenomenology of Spirit* as foundations for a theory of historicity. The *Hegel-Marx* question is not explicitly addressed, although I hope that this interpretation will throw some new light on this connection. Neither does this work contain a critical discussion of Heidegger nor is it intended to do so. Rather, the whole is a necessary preparation for articulating the fundamental nature of historical happening. (quoted in Marcuse 1987, xii)

The reasons for Marcuse's reticence about Heidegger's influence are unclear. There is certainly enough Heidegger in the thesis that it is incorrect to argue that Marcuse was no longer under Heidegger's influence when he wrote it. It is true that he could hardly present Heidegger with a thesis in which Hegel was turned into a Heideggerian. Heidegger has unkind things to say about attempts to identify his thought with that of his illustrious predecessor (Heidegger 1994, 144–45). Nor would it have been seemly for Marcuse to present himself as Heidegger's champion in opposition to Hegel. Still, one wonders about the lack of references. In any case, there are three plausible links to Heidegger.

First, there is the form of the work. Marcuse's Hegel analysis is *methodologically* similar to Heidegger's contemporary readings of Aristotle and Kant and builds on Heidegger's conclusions. Just as Heidegger developed his ontology out of his interpretation of Aristotle, so, Marcuse claims, "Hegel acquires the ontological framework of his analysis through an examination of Aristotle's work" (Marcuse 1987, 18). Thus, insofar as Marcuse applies Heidegger's historico-ontological approach to the study of Hegel, he continues the research into Aristotle and attempts to attain the level of questioning at which his teacher aims. Marcuse's thesis sets out to free Hegel from the overlay of commentary based in this case not just on a scholastic tradition, but on Hegel's own late self-interpretation which distorted and diminished his original contribution. And just as Heidegger's 1929 book, *Kant and Problem of Metaphysics*, emphasized Kant's turn from an early emphasis on the imagination to a later focus on the understanding, so Marcuse identifies a similar turn in Hegel, from an early emphasis on life to a later emphasis on the absolute. In each case the thinker passed over a dynamic principle that could be developed in terms of a phenomenological ontology for a cognitive principle that recapitulated the errors of Cartesianism.

Second, Marcuse goes back to Dilthey to reevaluate his concept of life, which significantly influenced the development of Heidegger's concept of *Dasein*. In this Diltheyan interpretation, Hegel will then be shown to have anticipated Heidegger. "In unprecedented fashion from the beginning, Hegel replaces the transcendental I of cognition with the full concrete I of life, with the 'whole of human nature,' with the 'totality of our being' (Dilthey)" (Marcuse 1987, 245). This enlarged concept of the subject, like Heideggerian *Dasein*, can enter into the movement of being rather than simply observing it as a *cogito*.

Third, Marcuse interprets Hegel in terms of the Heideggerian concept of revealing. It is well known that for Hegel, being is contradictory, divided in itself and therefore in perpetual process. Marcuse reads the Heideggerian revealing into this notion of self-division and the associated notion of self-development. For Hegel as for Heidegger, being *appears* in producing itself.

There are now several historically distinct layers of theory and language involved in our account. It is important not to be confused by the hermeneutic complexity that results but to keep the focus clearly on the uppermost, i.e., the modern, layer. In this and the following sections I explain Hegel's relation to Aristotle as Marcuse interprets it. As with my account of Heidegger's interpretation of Aristotle, the point is not whether these modern thinkers got Aristotle right, but their appropriation of his insights. Marcuse's Hegel thesis introduces a further complication since he assumes a background in Heidegger and Lukács. Again, the point is not Marcuse's success in understanding these thinkers but his appropriation of their thought for his own purposes.

In sum, this chapter will test a hypothesis about Marcuse's Hegel thesis based on conjectures about the presence of these influences in his text. The hypothesis concerns Marcuse's implicit account of the relation of Hegel's historical dialectic to the production model of being in Aristotle, its Heideggerian repetition, and related concepts in Marxism.

Techné as Labor

Heidegger has already demonstrated the promise and limits of the Aristotelian *Metaphysics*, both of which it owes to its historical situation at the beginning of Western thought. He shows that in orienting metaphysics toward production, Aristotle opened the way to the understanding of being and he identifies anticipations of his own doctrine in Aristotle. Heidegger reinterprets Aristotle's objectivistically developed idea of production as the source of his own phenomenological analysis of worldhood. Many of the details of Aristotle's analysis are lost in the phenomenological repetition, but Aristotle's "discovery" of revealing is preserved and sharpened, taking into account the dissolution of fixed essences in modernity. The later Heidegger will relate the breakdown of ancient essentialism to technology, but in the early Heidegger this connection is not yet clear. In any case, the new theory of revealing was worked out in detail in *Being and Time* and in lectures, private discussions, and courses that Marcuse no doubt attended.

In Marcuse's thesis, Hegel's dialectic is shown to bear fruit precisely as a modern repetition of Aristotle in which the modern idea of labor does the work of *techné*. Labor manifests being in the form of actuality which involves not only entry into existence but more significantly, entry into a world which has about it the "needed belonging" of life, a living, knowing being, a *Dasein* in Heidegger's sense. Marcuse comments, "It is no accident that with the expressions 'deed' and 'activity' one hears the Greek *poiésis*, as an ontological category which defines Being as a product, as fabricated, and as 'prepared.' This certainly does not imply something produced by an other, being as prepared by humans; it means rather that Being is produced by and through itself" (Marcuse 1987, 79). As we saw with Heidegger, so with Marcuse the structure of *physis* is explained through *poiésis*.

As for Heidegger, so for Marcuse, there is a dereifying intent behind this conception. The goal is to break through the objectivistic veil to the "things themselves" as they are phenomenologically revealed. At that ontologically fundamental level, things do not stand alone, fixed and frozen in their nature awaiting a purely accidental encounter with a cognitive subject. Instead they exist in a dynamic relation to *Dasein*, which discloses them in its practical activities. Marcuse does not employ Heidegger's term "*Dasein*" here but instead returns to its source in Dilthey's concept of "life" which now takes on similar functions. Thus, Marcuse writes, "Life is consciousness and self-consciousness first and only because it is the 'universal medium' and 'fluid substance' of beings. . . . Life is a mode of being with whose existence all entities become de-objectified, are 'related' to life, and come alive" (Marcuse 1987, 232).

The appearance of the word "ontology" in the title of Marcuse's early Hegel book is significant. Heidegger claims that Hegel's *Phenomenology of Spirit* is "*the fundamental ontology of absolute ontology*. . . . To put the same thing in historical terms, we can say that since antiquity—in Aristotle no less than in Plato . . . .— the being of beings is determined as *eidos, idéa*, idea, and thus related to seeing, knowing, and *logos*" (Heidegger 1994, 141–42). Just as Heidegger claimed that

Aristotle addressed the "question of being," so Marcuse claims that Hegel's philosophy "is governed by the question of *Being*, and in the final analysis, by the question of the most authentic form of beings" (Marcuse 1987, 248).

Roughly defined in terms of one of its chief attributes, this ontological approach is a transcendental account of prior conditions. These are the general background conditions that make empirical facts possible. In Kant, particulars such as this or that thing, moment, or spatial location must be explained through the conditions making possible thinghood, temporality, or spatiality. This results in a peculiar doubling of terms; for example, transcendental space is a "form of intuition" that makes possible particular empirical perceptions of space. We have seen something similar in Heidegger in the case of technology, which appears twice in his theory, once as mode of revealing and the second time in the form of particular devices that enact that mode of revealing. In Marcuse's Hegel interpretation the concept of history is doubled. What Marcuse calls "historicity" is the mode of being of the happening of events in time. Historicity grants the meaning of historical happening and is therefore, in Heideggerian terms, its ontological condition.

The Greeks answer the ontological question with the original doubling of essence and existence. To be is to be revealed in the sense of being in a world *as* such and such. Being is what is brought forth, made manifest, and this implies having a meaning, which in turn implies the existence of *Dasein* as that being needed by being for beings to belong to a world. *Dasein* thus appears for Heidegger to be a very special kind of being in a necessary relationship to being itself. Marcuse identifies equivalents for these various Heideggerian concepts in Hegel. Hegel, in Marcuse's account, also attempts to understand how a world can form and reveal itself. And like Heidegger's concept of subjectivity, Hegel's covers the whole range of human possibilities, life itself, and not merely thought. Again, like Heidegger, Hegel does not rely on pregiven essences as did the Greeks. His idea of essence takes into account the modern discovery of cultural relativity. Marcuse follows up on these Hegelian innovations in search of a strong normative conception that, paradoxically, does not depend on some sort of final goal established in nature, tradition, or religion.

Despite the similarity of all this to the Heideggerian view, there is an essential difference. In Heidegger, the contingency of the relation of *Dasein* to world is never overcome. At most *Dasein*'s resoluteness enables it to be itself in the face of its "thrownness." Just as *Dasein* in Heidegger falls into a world, so in Hegel Spirit "'falls into otherness,'" but unlike in Heidegger it "overcomes this through 'labor,' and thus returns to itself. This whole process, which constitutes the Being of spirit, does not happen to spirit or take place with it; rather it is grasped and comprehended by spirit and is carried out and sustained via this cognition" (Marcuse 1987, 222). The process of revealing in Hegel is concrete, as labor and self-recognition in the object of labor. It is also social insofar as spirit is the life of a people and not just of an individual. Historicity then is alienation and return from alienation to a mediated unity with the other.

Revealing

There is a striking similarity between Hegel's concept of life as Marcuse interprets it and Heidegger's concept of *Dasein* as being-in-the-world. This is due in large part to the influence of Dilthey, but Aristotle too stands in the background. Like Heidegger's Aristotle, Marcuse argues that being "reveals" itself in the relation of *dynamis* to *energeia*. The movement of actualization is also an appearing. Marcuse attributes to Hegel the same insight and argues that it is this which enables him to recover the inner truth of Aristotle's philosophy. Hegel interprets Aristotle's concept of *energeia* as "a showing of itself as exposing, revealing, and displaying itself" (Marcuse 1987, 253). "Essence is a showing, revealing, and manifesting of itself. 'Essence must appear' (L, II, 101)" (Marcuse 1987, 81).

In Heidegger revealing involves the necessary relation of *Dasein* to being. Synthesizing Hegel and Heidegger, one might say that not only must Being appear, in appearing it requires *Dasein* before which to appear.

> The true absolute unity, which no longer stands over and against another and which has no other outside it, is the unity of subjectivity and objectivity or of thought and being. It is the unity of the necessary *difference.* Hegel insists on this original phenomenon: whenever being is encountered, it appears through the difference between subjectivity and objectivity. That is to say, it appears through difference in general and in a condition of bifurcation. Whenever the absolute 'posits itself in the form of existence, it must posit itself in a duality of form. For appearing and self-bifurcation are one' (ED, 85). (Marcuse 1987, 18)

Following Heidegger, Marcuse describes this appearing as an event. The unifying activity of life allows the world "to happen as the world" (Marcuse 1987, 13). The happening of the world—Heidegger calls it the "worlding" of the world—is the ultimate motility.

This partial identification of Hegel and Heidegger rests on the role of production in their thought. Marcuse shares with the early Heidegger the crucial conviction that the notion of being is modeled on productive activity in Greek thought and the thought of Aristotle in particular. As in Heidegger the *kinesis* or *Bewegtheit* explored in the dialectic is the revealing of being through a process of making. Although Hegel's repetition of Aristotle differs from Heidegger's, it too responds to the breakdown of ancient essentialism while preserving the Aristotelian discovery of revealing. It therefore offers a complementary perspective on the issues that concern Heidegger and promises to solve the same basic problems. The idea of explaining Hegel's bifurcated being on these terms seems original with Marcuse. Heidegger's own lectures on the *Phenomenology* do not hint at a similar connection. On the contrary, Heidegger accepts the conventional interpretation of Hegel's absolute and so asserts that his own position "is the exact opposite of what Hegel tried to demonstrate in his entire philosophy" (Heidegger 1994, 145).[3]

But despite this disclaimer the similarities also show up in the understanding of knowledge in Heidegger and Hegel as Marcuse interprets them. Recall that for Heidegger, knowledge is only possible on the basis of a prior disclosure of being to *Dasein*. Being-in-the-world is the fundamental unity guaranteeing the knowing subject access to the known object beyond all Cartesian dualisms. For Hegel the world is available for knowledge insofar as it exists as life. Life constitutes an initial unity of subject and object which makes knowledge possible, that is, it establishes a homogeneity of subject and object such that they can enter into a cognitive relation.

> Life is the presupposition of cognition but not as the specific mode of being of a particular existent in the world, but rather as a mode of being of the world itself. From the start cognition operates within the unity created by life and world, subjectivity and objectivity. . . . The "object" of cognition stands now in the prior relation of adequacy to cognition. "Intrinsically" it possesses the same mode of being as the subject of cognition, namely, the mode of being characteristic of life. (Marcuse 1987, 163)

Thus, prior to knowing as an epistemological relation, subject and object stand in an ontological relation as beings. "The unity of I and world, or the prior bonding between the subject who cognizes and beings, does not merely result from knowledge; nor is it grounded in the accidental constitution of human knowledge and experience. This is rather an ontological relation, one that holds among beings themselves, one that is true of the 'thing in-itself' (*Ding an sich*). This bond precedes all knowledge and in fact makes factual knowledge possible" (Marcuse 1987, 161–62).

The relationship involved in knowing is a self-realization of beings in which they are fulfilled. It is not a contingent relation of separate beings but internal to being itself. "The meaning and goal of cognition are understood thereby as a coming-into-truth of Being itself, as a communication of beings with their proper selves" (Marcuse 1987, 163).

Key Concepts

Levels of Being

Marcuse's thesis begins with a consideration of Hegel's notion of being as bifurcated or split at its very basis. This notion is often explained in terms of the idea that being harbors contradictions in itself. Contradictions between what and what? Every interpretation of Hegel addresses this question in one way or another. The Aristotelian basis of Marcuse's answer involves the appropriation of such metaphysical concepts as *kinesis, peras, dynamis,* and *energeia* in the context of Hegel's distinction between the levels of being. These levels go from being-there, roughly equivalent to simple thinghood, to "essence" which is a more sophisticated concept of reality founding the highest level, life, the human world.

At the level of essence, beings exist in a self-relation such that they can encompass and master their own transformations and the environment in which they exist. This level of being, which Hegel analyzes in his "objective logic," corresponds to the Aristotelian analysis of substance. From there Hegel moves on to the "subjective logic" of life and knowledge: substance as subject. At these levels, being not only preserves itself in the midst of change, it stands in essential relations with its environment, both as doer and knower. These categories are developed in terms of notions of activity and totality influenced by current Marxist theory, especially the writings of Lukács. In the following exegesis I will discuss the "Key Concepts" of Marcuse's interpretation of these levels of being in Hegel.

Kinesis

Common sense holds that empirically existing things are all that is. This view, which Aristotle attributed to the Megarians in the *Metaphysics,* leaves out of account the internal dynamics of becoming through which things are "brought forth," the "how" of the thing.[4] Hegel's explanation of these dynamics begins where Aristotle left off. He calls the empirically existing thing "existence" or "being-there" (*Dasein*). It realizes in actuality the *dynamis* implicit in its being. This *dynamis* contains the potentialities or "truth" of the thing. Hegel calls it "in-itselfness." What the thing is in itself always transcends its existence.

The bifurcation of being consists in the split between in-itselfness and being-there. Beings are not only divided in themselves, they are in motion due to the tension their inner division creates. Thus, the bifurcation means that being is never simply itself, but always "in another," possessed of unrealized possibilities and involved in the process of transformation that moves it forward. "Being has the fundamental character of being 'split' into two: it *is* in being *other*, as equality-with-self and transformation. It carries its negativity within itself, and is negativity in its innermost essence. This fundamentally split and dual character of being is the ground of its motility, of its happening" (Marcuse 1987, 42). Thus, "The first phenomenon encountered in the course of the ontological interpretation is that of being as motility (*Bewegtheit*) and its basis, namely, the absolute difference between in-itselfness and existence (*Dasein*)" (Marcuse 1987,181). This motility is the Aristotelian *kinesis* once again.

But if being is divided, fraught with negativity and condemned to constant movement, then the question arises how the fragments are held together. Hegel's concept of motility addresses the problem of achieving or maintaining unity in the midst of change. This unity is actuality, *energeia*, but as in Heidegger's Aristotle, so in Marcuse's Hegel, actuality is not simply "there" but is itself a type of movement. "Actuality constitutes itself through a distinctive mode of motility; actuality *can be* only as motility" (Marcuse 1987, 103). Hegel calls this unity of motile, bifurcated being, "being-by-oneself-in-otherness." This is the encompassing term for *energeia* and *dynamis* in their necessary relation, "the being for oneself (*energeia*) of in-itselfness (*dynamis*) " (Marcuse 1987, 148).

> Existing in the condition of negativity, being "must posit the unity that is contained within it", must absorb each negativity into itself as its very own, sublate it, and must relate itself to itself through it. Thereby it must win the unity of its existence, and preserving this, it must unfold itself out of it. Hegel calls this grasping of negativity through its comprehension, the "negative relation to self". (Marcuse 1987, 176)

The split in being is thus not a simple fact; it is an active self-relation, a for-itselfness. Marcuse calls the category of for-itselfness "the most comprehensive in the entire logic" (Marcuse 1987, 179). Note the presence of the term "self" in this account. Marcuse describes the stages of motility in terms of the concept of self-hood as an inner division that unifies itself. Things too can have a "self" in this sense, at least formally, since they unify a manifold of determinations. Although the concept of selfhood is not confined exclusively to human beings, human self-hood most clearly exemplifies the unifying process. The negative relation to self which is at the basis of our being is also at the basis of the unity of things (Marcuse 1987, 179).

Being-There and Limit

At the lowest level of "determinate" or "immediate" being, things appear to be self-subsistent and independent of other things. At this level they do not have a necessary relationship to other beings, their own process of change, or the accidents of their own being. They simply are without an "interior" or a relation to their own "self." This level of being corresponds to the notion of objective thing-hood comprehended superficially by the "understanding" or common sense. However, even at this level a first division appears between their possibilities and their given form.

It is easy to verify this in everyday experience. No matter how cursory and uninformed our perception of things, no matter how simple the things, they lie under a horizon of possibilities. The simplest object could be other than it is and this "otherness," although it may be vague and undefined, belongs to its nature as much as its positive qualities.

> Immediate being appears in its determinacy as the mediation of its intrinsic being, but this latter transcends its determinacy and reaches over to its own potency and possibility. It determines itself "as the other of itself". In this "difference" between its in-itselfness and its immediacy lies the "drive" of its movement which leads beyond immediacy. Being sets itself in movement. (Marcuse 1987, 175)

The second level is the elementary process of change of the determinate being of level one. Once being is set in movement things lose their integrity and solidity. They are not yet capable of self-production as is an essentially grounded substance that can maintain itself through change. Instead, in changing beings go beyond their "limit," the Aristotelian *peras* or *telos*, and lose their identity. Their in-itself-ness places them into relation with that which succeeds them in the process of change.

> The Being of immediate beings constitutes itself first and foremost through movement which is the complete *perishing* of the individual something, the going beyond its own limit that is its in-itselfness, thus the movement of going beyond its own self. The "end" of individual beings is incorporated within their being in such a manner that the latter is first fulfilled when they reach their end. The individual being is *finite*. (Marcuse 1987, 54)

Again, common sense tells us that ordinary beings are constantly changing from one thing into another. This process of change appears external to the things themselves, something that befalls them from without. Yet it must be explained in terms of the possibilities contained in the things. The log burning in the fireplace transforms into smoke and heat according to its own nature. Its existence is annulled in the process but not arbitrarily. Viewed in this light the world consists in a vast system of possible exchanges and transformations. Beings are not independent of each other but are bound together in essential relations.

At this level change reveals that the implicit or true being of a being is another being rather than a further development of itself. At a higher stage of development being will preserve itself in the midst of change but here things perish in revealing their truth, that is, in going beyond their limit to be what they "truly" are, namely, something else. "What immediately happens to the something in its being-for-another is not an alien, external occurrence. On the contrary, this constitutes the being-there of the something. Through it, its in-itselfness fulfills itself as determination. Its own being 'sends it beyond' its respective determinateness as its limit" (Marcuse 1987, 59).

Change at this level is interpreted through the Aristotelian category of *steresis*, or privation. The inability of beings to maintain themselves beyond a specific "limit" is defining for this lower level of being. Marcuse writes that for immediate being, "The in-itselfness of the something is a specific form of *im*potence (powerlessness.). . . . Precisely because of its powerlessness immediate being is *at the mercy* of the motility of its being: it can neither sustain itself in the course of this movement nor can it keep it within its bounds. Its in-itselfness changes with every determinateness that impinges upon it" (Marcuse 1987, 50–51). Being's powerlessness is the fact that its movement is its death. The being-in-itself of immediate being is that into which its "powerless" being is transformed. The living thing, understood not in terms of its inner dynamic but as a mere succession of states, offers a clear illustration of this concept of powerlessness. Perishing is a necessary aspect of life. The seed perishes in becoming the plant; the leaf withers with the seasons and new leaves grow.

The concept of powerlessness resembles Heidegger's analysis of Aristotelian bearance, the particular type of *steresis* in which beings go over into something else. But as with Aristotelian *steresis*, the passage to another is not arbitrary but reveals the truth of the original being that dies in changing. The concept is also similar to Aristotle's notion of matter. Just as matter goes beyond itself "appropriately" in taking on form, so beings realize their potential in the process of change even as they lose their identity in becoming another. Hegel extends the notion to encompass all change from one thing into another, understood at this level.

Finitude

Like Heidegger, Marcuse identifies *peras* and *telos*, the categories of finitude. "The limit is the 'principal' (L, I, 115, *archê*) of beings themselves (the Aristotelian category of *telos*)" (Marcuse 1987, 54). But this finitude is a new kind of infinity, the infinite movement that belongs to the essence of being. It is not an endless progress—Hegel's "bad infinity"—but an internal movement of self-realization. "Infinity is only the most consistent expression for the absolute and universal immanence of motility; it is the 'unrest of self-movement' within the being of beings" (Marcuse 1987, 60). Marcuse explains this Hegelian finitude as a radical philosophical atheism.

> For the first time the concept of finitude is removed from the theological tradition and placed on the ground of pure philosophical ontology. It is no longer the finitude of being as *ens creatum* in contrast to a creator God that is meant here. The finite is not contrasted to anything else, not even to the infinity of beings themselves, which Hegel dismisses precisely as the "bad" infinity. From this point on, Hegel opens the wholly new dimension of the universal *historicity* of beings and clears the way for understanding the essence of the *historical.* The process of happening of finite beings is not a development toward some previously determined or undetermined goal. It is not at all a happening to and from. It is a pure happening in-itself, immanent to beings themselves. The finite being does not *have* a history; it *is* history. The history of humans is only a specific *mode* of this universal process and is to be understood only in unity with it. (Marcuse 1987, 55)

This conception of finitude implies no reference to an infinite God and so appears incompatible with Hegel's own frequent references to the divinity. Surely the concept of the absolute represents a final end of some sort. Marcuse argues that the deeper import of Hegel's dialectic contradicts these usual interpretations and self-interpretations. If history is really ontologically fundamental, the happening of being cannot have a predetermined goal but must be "a pure happening in itself" (Marcuse 1987, 55). Human history is a specific realization of this historical character of being. But this means that there can be no end of history, no final reconciliation, no ideal the realization of which would interrupt the ceaseless movement, the restlessness of being. Essence then can no longer be taken for granted as an atemporal meaning and purpose but is also thrust into history.[5]

In what does the universality of this process consist? Does it embrace nature as well as human history? Or does nature transcend history under the sway of eternal laws? These are tricky questions Marcuse addresses rather obscurely in his thesis. He notes that for Hegel, nature is both absorbed into life as a moment in its self-development and remains independent of life as its presupposition and basis. The dialectic of determinate being described above would presumably correspond to this relatively independent status of nature. But just how independent is it? Hegel does not want to grant its independence full ontological status. Nature is only a moment in the process of self-development of spirit. Its mere externality is overcome as it enters history. Spirit "is nature as well as self-consciousness, and . . . through its own history transforms an intrinsically ahistorical nature into unity with history. This is accomplished in that Spirit recognizes and comprehends nature as a form of its existence and lets it become its 'world'" (Marcuse 1987, 313). This still leaves in suspense the question of what nature was before it was so generously incorporated into spirit as world. Marcuse attempts to clarify this ambiguous statement of the case in his contemporary Marxist writings.

The Dialectic of Essence: Dynamis and Energeia

Marcuse is famous for having written a book entitled *One-Dimensional Man*. What is less well known is that the notion of dimensions plays a role in this early Hegel thesis where it signifies the relation of essence to immediate or determinate being. With this concept of dimensions Marcuse addresses the problem of the *eidos* which lies at the center of Heidegger's Aristotle interpretation. In Marcuse's account Hegel, like Aristotle, offers a solution to the Platonic split between the *eidos* and actual being. Marcuse writes that the "two dimensions . . . are not isolated and self-subsistent worlds that need to be brought subsequently in relation; they are dimensions of being which are from the beginning ontologically dependent on one another, and which only continue to exist through each other and which only move themselves within their conflictual unity" (Marcuse 1987, 75). The two dimensions, essence and existence, coexist necessarily in the self-manifesting of essence in existence. They cannot be thought independently of each other and their unity is the motility of being.

At the level of essence, the possibilities of things are their own, rather than another's. The self-relation of the thing is active, unifying it around what it can become instead of passing over into another as its possibilities are realized. The thing "posits" itself as a unity in its multiple determinations and encounters with other things. It can do this only through realizing its in-itselfness in its existence, achieving actuality. Hegel's concept of actuality is "equality-with-self-in-other-ness" or "being-by-oneself-in-otherness." This refers to the fact that beings sustain themselves through change as always themselves and yet other in the many different ways in which they evolve, interact with their causes and effects, and relate to themselves in various processes of self-definition and self-awareness. Actuality, Marcuse argues, derives directly from "the Aristotelian categories of *dynamis* and *energeia*" (Marcuse 1987, 42).

Actuality involves a specific temporality, a connection to that which it has always already been, its essence. Marcuse uses a Heideggerian neologism to explain his interpretation of the temporality of essence. The essence is not behind appearances, nor is it a pure ideal, but rather it "prevails" in the order of appearance. In Heidegger's terms, "it 'essences' in them—*west in ihnen*'" (Marcuse 1987, 77). Beings "essence" in passing from one realization to the next. The essence is the unity of these various manifestations. Substance and accident are related essentially because the substance is the totality of accidents, not something behind them. It is not a mere sum but a whole governed by a *dynamis* Hegel calls "actuosity." Being is thus self-generating and self-unifying. Marcuse concludes, "Essence has no independent being 'alongside' existent things; it always only exists as what 'has proceeded from negativity and inwardness,' and the 'being thrown into the externality of being' (L, II, 97)" (Marcuse 1987, 81).

For Hegel, the concept of essence is fulfilled in life, which masters itself and its environment and so reproduces itself as what it is through a process of development. "Hegel names this grasping of negativity through its comprehension, the 'negative relation to self.' First, through this relation does being become an entity which exists 'for itself,' that is, a 'subject, person, a free being'" (Marcuse 1987, 176). But even beings which are not conscious can participate in this third stage of development implicitly, without knowing that they do so, as does, for example, the Aristotelian substance.

Hegel understands substance in terms of two related ideas: potentiality and movement. Being "is never simply and immediately what it can and ought to be, but finds itself and moves itself within the difference of in-itselfness (potence) and existence" (Marcuse 1987, 91–92). Nothing simply is; whatever is is in movement between its given form and its potentiality. The concept of potentiality or possibility refers to what any actual being truly is in itself. "The possible is the in-itselfness of the actual" (Marcuse 1987, 95). Actuality lays out the "horizon of possible determinations" and realizes one among them in every particular case (Marcuse 1987, 93). The notion of potentiality Hegel invokes here is derived directly from Aristotle. It refers to the force of the thing that holds it together as it realizes itself, becomes what it can best be. Essence as potentiality is thus striving and struggle and not simply an ideal form.

Substance now stands in normative subordination to its own potentialities.

What a being is at any given moment is in question in terms of what it should become in conformity with its essence. The normative aspect of the notions of *dynamis* and *energeia* comes to the fore. When Hegel says that the actual is the rational and the rational the actual, he is not merely describing the existing state of affairs. He is making a demand. Untrue being must give way to true being. The revealing of the true being is a process of development.

However, this interpretation opens up new problems. The modernized idea of *energeia* is no longer bound to a pregiven *eidos* but creates itself. This is freedom in the modern sense without the arbitrariness and externality associated with the materialist account. As for the Greeks, so for Hegel, a harmonistic necessity binds beings to what they can become, but this necessity is no longer pregiven. A totality continues to exist, but now its logic must be discovered in its development rather than positing that development in terms of the *eidos*. This self-creation is teleological without a prior *telos*, aims at an end it itself creates. This is the work of history.

Hegel avoids regression to ancient dogmatism by deriving essence from the tensions in appearance and between things. Essence is both the internal relation of the thing in itself to its determinations, and the external relation of the thing to the other things with which it necessarily coexists. Essence is relatedness and the development that proceeds out of relatedness. "Existence, as designating the Being of things which are, has proved to be a structure of relationality in a double sense: first, as the behavior of individual existents toward every factual determinacy of their thereness (*sich-verhalten*; self-related activity); second, as the ontologically appropriate universal interrelationship among individual existents, through which alone they are what they are. The *essence* of existents is contained within the process of development of this relationality" (Marcuse 1987, 90). This is eminently true of the living human being. Hence, "All of what I can become as this determinate individual is already there, *not* in the sense of a mystical predetermination, but in the sense that my concrete person depends on the 'existing multiplicity of circumstances' out of which and within which alone it *becomes* what is possible for it" (Marcuse 1987, 94–95).

Life and Labor

The originality of Marcuse's thesis lies in the attempt to pursue the productionist argument to its logical conclusion, that is, to develop an ontology based on the model of production that does not flinch at the last moment and turn to a contemplative foundation. This links his position to Aristotle, Heidegger, and Hegel, but it also carries him in a very different direction explored by Marx. Marx first interpreted Hegel's notions of labor and history in terms of a theory of class struggle and revolution. In addition to the master–slave dialectic, on which he comments as early as the 1844 *Manuscripts*, Marx built explicitly on Hegel's doctrine of essence in *Capital*.

This doctrine is a historicized transformation of the Aristotelian interpretation of being in terms of the structure of *techné*. Marcuse worked out the shift from Aristotelian *techné* to Hegelian "historicity" through the analysis of Hegel's concept of life. Hegel understands productive activity as a diremption within life. Life requires a world in which to deploy itself. The living subject "makes" this world and in confronting it confronts itself. This world is not nature in the sense of the natural sciences. Rather, it is what correlates with the tendencies of life, its needs, movements, perceptions. In modern terms, we could call it life's "niche," that segment of reality to which it necessarily relates.

The living thing exists in relation to an objectivity it creates or appropriates. The reference to objectivity suggests a cognitive relation, but life is less knowledge than activity. "The ontological relation of life to the totality of beings must not be distorted into the epistemological relation of consciousness to objectivity" (Marcuse 1987, 232). Activity involves phases of "objectification and deobjectification, falling into otherness and reabsorption back into being for self, a process of externalization and unification. This process was concretely defined as activity, namely, as the exhibiting and producing of itself through conscious activity which is necessarily a 'transaction with and transformation of beings'" (Marcuse 1987, 296). The world is incorporated into the self in the essential movement of life.

> Driven by this need, individual Life now turns against its objectivity in order to "overpower" it and to "appropriate" it. This is a process of infusing with life the external world that opposes life. Worldly objects are made to "correspond" thereby to life (habitability, ability, enjoyability, usefulness, applicability are not simply present as aspects of life but are posited with life itself and find completion in its movement). The object is overwhelmed to the point where the living individual "deprives it of its particular nature, converts it into a means for itself, gives its own subjectivity as its substance". (Marcuse 1987, 158)

Here the activity of making a world takes a literal form in the concept of labor as objectification developed in the *Phenomenology*. Desire and labor are forms of activity in which life brings forth itself and its world. The intrinsic contents of the self are objectified in the world through labor. Life is thus a concrete process of revealing, the highest and fullest revealing. It is through labor that thinghood achieves its fullest actualization. The object as indifferent barrier, as the "negative" other of life, is overcome. "Labor is at the same time the fundamental relation of self-consciousness to thinghood, whereby the pure negative objectivity of the latter is sublated and animated. Thinghood first attains its subsistence through this affirmation" (Marcuse 1987, 257). Life is the true meaning of being insofar as it masters its own possibilities and exists through knowing and freely disposing of itself. "Self-consciousness had recognized that the world constituted only the cycle of its activity and that essentially it had to manifest and prove itself in the world. It recognized that actuality is in essence an object of 'work'" (Marcuse 1987, 276).

Work takes on an extended sense in Hegel and refers eventually not merely to the making of artifacts but to all forms of objectification, including the creation of institutions and culture. The structure of productive activity in the narrow sense becomes the model for historical creation in general. This concept of work as the objectification of the life of community was "perhaps Hegel's greatest discovery" (Marcuse 1987, 246). This is the essential concept of historicity which does not simply explain change, but which is the basis for an account of the world-hood of the world in terms of human activity. "The world subsists and is real only through the knowing and acting self-consciousness whose 'work' it is" (Marcuse 1987, 300).

Hegel's historical production is similar to Aristotle's *techné* in that it involves a constructive engagement with things by which they enter a world, and similar to Heidegger's revealing in that this engagement is understood as constituting the world from the standpoint of "factical life." "The Being of life shows most explicitly that the self-actualization proper to life presents the true meaning of being. The actuality of life is full effectivity, a process of displaying and exposing one's possibilities outside oneself" (Marcuse 1987, 253). But still more important are the connections between this interpretation of Hegel's concept of life and Marxism, particularly the Marxism of Lukács. These connections become obvious in Marcuse's contemporary essays. He writes, for example, that in the master–slave dialectic Hegel "is concerned here with the process of reification and its transcendence as the basic happening of human life, which *Marx* then represented as the basic law of historical happening" (Marcuse 1978b, 440). I will return to this theme in the next chapter.

The Absolute

Hegel's dialectic culminates in the absolute, which has a complicated relation to his concept of life. The absolute is doubly ambiguous. In the first place, it may be interpreted as a special form of knowledge or as a highest being. This ambiguity gives rise to two different ways of interpreting the division of the system into levels of being. These levels may form a hierarchy of distinct types of being, with the living and knowing subject at the top, or they may merely describe different ways of understanding being, different categorial schemes. In fact, the system seems to include both: the levels of determinate being and substance can describe anything at all, but life and knowledge are specific types of being.

One way of resolving the ambiguity is to consider each level a broader context embracing the lower levels. For example, the process of change described at level two is explained more profoundly in terms of the concept of essence introduced at level three. In the usual understanding of Hegel, the knowing subject provides the ultimate context, the absolute that embraces all being-there and substance in its truth. But can a contingent human knowledge form a necessary context of being itself? This was precisely the weak spot Kierkegaard identified in Hegel. It is an idealistic move that Heidegger too rejects.

The second type of ambiguity has a biographical basis. In the earlier works Hegel's absolute is life as practical engagement, while in the later works the absolute is a theoretical abstraction distinct from life. Heidegger is critical of Hegel's notion of a cognitive absolute, which he sees as a typical Cartesian evasion, substituting epistemology for more fundamental ontological issues. Marcuse shares this critique, but he draws very different conclusions from it.

Marcuse complains that life described on the terms of cognition is dissolved in the absolute and history eliminated. Hegel's phenomenology attempted to combine two incompatible perspectives and to reconcile life as historicity and the absolute as a form of cognition beyond history.

> As soon as *cognition* is defined as life, history follows; as soon as life is defined as *cognition*, however, historicity is pushed away from the history of life. The truth of life is then defined in relation to an absolute and thereby unhistorical mode of knowledge. The *Phenomenology of Spirit* is Hegel's first and last attempt to unite as equally fundamental both motives and to construct the historicity of absolute spirit on the basis of history. We can describe this attempt with a brief formula: to show how life, as historical, carries within itself the possibility of its own ahistoricity and how it actualizes this possibility in the course of history. (Marcuse 1987, 227)

In Hegel's later work, even this concept of life is displaced more and more by an ahistorical cognitive absolute.

Heidegger interpreted Hegel's thought in its entirety through this problematic move, but Marcuse argues that the earlier concept of life can support a true "fundamental ontology" oriented toward history. This is because life implies world, world in Heidegger's sense. The unity of the living thing and its world can be conceived phenomenologically as an ultimate context embracing all levels of being. Even the nature of the natural sciences can be founded in the world, if not reduced to it. All forms of knowledge can take their place within life. Cognition understood as a life function necessarily involves a people and a history. Thus, historicity lies at the center of the theory so understood.

Marcuse's analysis of the absolute preserves the priority of life against Hegel's tendency to reduce it to a stage in the development of knowledge. This puts him at odds with the mainstream of Hegel interpretation which accepts Hegel's distinction of philosophical wisdom and practice. Philosophy comprehends the necessity underlying the dichotomies of practical life after the fact and thereby transcends them. Like the "owl of Minerva," it flies at dusk. But wisdom in this sense does not normally play a role in practical life. The naïve individual who attends church or sees a great work of art is in the presence of the meaning of practical life in a pretheoretical form. The philosopher alone raises these representations of meaning to their concept in self-consciousness.

The absolute so conceived unifies all being in itself through knowledge. The philosopher (Hegel) knows himself and his world as his own and so is not dispersed in the multiplicity of beings, nor compelled by them to "work" for his own survival, but subsists among them in unity while freely affirming their difference from himself. He is at home in them as the realization of the conditions of his own selfhood. Yet he does not deny their plurality but rather preserves it even in unifying being with himself. "Hegel's intention is to attain an 'absolute' meaning of being in relation to which all that is can be understood in its mode of being without presupposing, however, a generalized unitary ontological meaning from the outset" (Marcuse 1987, 22). Such a generalized unity would be Friedrich Schelling's identity of subject and object Hegel dismisses as the "night in which all cows are black." "On the contrary, the plurality of all oppositions among beings should be preserved in and be a part of this meaning. This meaning of being should at the same time provide the possibility of overcoming the fixed oppositions of subjectivity and objectivity, consciousness and 'being' through an originally unified principal which would allow us to understand this duality in its proper unity as proceeding from itself" (Marcuse 1987, 22).

This extremely abstract formulation can be concretized. At the risk of banalizing Hegel's insight, consider the notion of challenge. A challenge is not simply an obstacle although it may at first appear such. Unlike the object of work, the challenge is not overpowered and transformed, it is "met." Nor is meeting a challenge the annihilation of the challenge as such. To meet a challenge is to encounter the apparent obstacle as an opportunity for growth, self-development. The challenge must therefore be respected in its right to challenge and not evaded simply to achieve a goal. Indeed, the true goal can only be reached by maintaining the challenge in its challenging nature. The challenge is ours and yet to be a challenge it must be other. In meeting the challenge appropriately the individuals meet themselves as they would hope to be. They thereby transcend "the fixed oppositions of subjectivity and objectivity" while preserving "the plurality of all oppositions among beings." The mainstream cognitive interpretation of the absolute would say that the self-conscious understanding of the growth process is not necessary to growth but can be known by the philosopher in a wisdom that recollects growth in its truth in the eternal "afterwards" of knowledge.

Hegel places the self-consciousness of life beyond life. But this seems to imply an accidental relation between knowledge and its objects that the absolute was precisely supposed to transcend. The moment of realization, like the emergence of the philosopher from Plato's cave, is incommensurable with life and its flow. Absolute knowledge here is external to life, a metaphysical afterthought so to speak. History, as the flow of life, "ends" in a knowledge that transcends it. This timeless knowledge can then also encompass timeless nature as well and so achieves completion. Yet history must continue, as perpetual temporal movement if not as destiny. Hegel interpreters have never agreed on how to make sense of the combination of an atemporal knowledge that seems to inaugurate a stage of history beyond history, and an essentially temporal concept of being.

This version of the absolute does not carry the existential significance of the Heideggerian conception of authentic *Dasein*. Here wisdom is possible only in escape from the cave and not in the cave itself. But there is another interpretation of Hegel's concept in which wisdom is more than pure theory. In this alternative, the absolute is a specific way of life that understands itself as such. In the former case life is a mere stage in the growth of knowledge, subordinate to the disincarnate wisdom of the thinker. Only in the latter case can Heidegger's essential advance toward a concrete philosophy be preserved in a Hegelian context.

If we are not satisfied with a cognitive absolute, but insist with Marcuse on a living absolute actively engaged with being in a world, then we are on a difficult path. The absolute as an ultimate self-consciousness can encompass all being, nature and history, object and subject, fact and value, but life appears to be limited to one side of the dichotomies. Marcuse's solution to this dilemma is to assume that the encounter of life with being is no contingent relationship of subject with object but has an essential character. Life is neither a *cogito* nor an object of knowledge. It is rather a universal mediator, incorporating everything into its process. Life is not a subject standing over against objects. In its transcendental function, life creates a world on the one side and a living being in that world on the other side. Subject and object emerge from this common source. Hegel's term for this underlying unity is "totality." "The totality is that being which lies at the ground of all beings, which is present in them, and which gives unity to the multiplicity of all that is" (Marcuse 1987, 22).

How is this conception of totality related to knowledge, which is surely an aspect of the absolute in any interpretation? Marcuse shifts the emphasis from what is known to the "being of knowledge in the totality." He gets from a concept of the absolute as knowledge to this alternative view by emphasizing the structure of knowing rather than its content. Knowing now appears as a specific way of being in the world, a form of motility. Knowledge is not considered in an epistemological light, but rather ontologically. Knowing is a mode of being of subject and object rather than an accidental relation of subject to object. As "possessing the structural unity of self sameness in otherness, knowledge is the . . . highest form of being" (Marcuse 1987, 264).

Knowledge is not just an accumulation of things known but is a model for being as a whole. It has the structure of a totality that does not annul the difference between its moments. It exemplifies the principle of being-oneself-in-otherness. Knowledge unifies, allowing plurality to exist while holding all its objects together in consciousness. This is an ontologized version of Kant's transcendental unity of apperception. Hegel's absolute is not a detached knowing, the object reduced to the subject, but rather knowledge as a model of the kind of unity that can be attributed to being in its multiplicity and internal opposition. "The 'principal' of absolute synthesis which is not 'merely a form of knowing but also a form of being' is the 'one true reality' (ED, 236). Its occurrence is that of the *totality*" (Marcuse 1987, 36).

Let us return again to the example of challenging to clarify this abstract formulation. In analyzing this example Marcuse would emphasize the fact that life, as essentially a process of growth, encompasses the challenge and the challenged in a single system. The system is not truly complete so long as it is unself-conscious. Of course challenges are constantly met in unself-conscious practical life. However, the stage of the absolute is reached only when the individuals recognize self-consciousness as a necessity both of their being and of the challenge itself. In self-consciousness, we not only meet the challenge and grow but affirm growth as the meaning of challenging as such. The challenge no longer appears as an accident from which growth proceeds accidentally, but as essential to the human condition. The knowledge of this is itself a dimension of growth, true maturity. If I do not understand how meeting challenges has made me what I am, I have not fully grasped the challenge that now stands before me. Indeed, it may appear to me as a mere obstacle rather than as an opportunity to transcend myself and I may attempt to evade it. Hence self-consciousness is essential to challenging considered in its systemic unity. This is "unity through difference" transcending the opposition of subject and object, theory and practice.

Such self-consciousness displaces the center of my being toward the system. I am no longer a worker attacking a thing to be worked on, a life confronting an environment, an ego facing an other, or rather, I *am* that ego but *also* the other insofar as I accept and affirm myself in my role in the system. In this sense life is the unity in difference of subject and object, not the subject opposed to the object or independent of it in pure knowledge. Life is not a specific type of thing in the world, but a way in which the world exists and shows itself, being-at-home-in-the-other-as-such is, in Heideggerian terms, "being-in-the-world" itself, authentically lived.[6]

From Hegel to Marxism

For Hegel, production is an emerging out of implicit being, that is, the in-itself in the sense of *eidos* or essence. It manifests being in the form of actuality, the for-itself, which involves not only entry into existence but more significantly, entry into a world that has about it the "needed belonging" of life, a living, knowing being, a *Dasein* in Heidegger's sense. In Hegel, this producing is the activity of the product itself. Being, in its initial positing, produces itself as an existing being-there and drives itself onward toward higher forms of existence. Because this productive activity is historical and happens in the events that shape the human world, it involves human action.

Having reached his own version of this conclusion, Heidegger posits being-in-the-world and analyzes its structure. As we have seen, this structure includes falling into inauthenticity as an intrinsic possibility of *Dasein*. Thus, being-in-the-world is tied to its opposite, the objectivistic view it both undermines and founds. Heidegger's various attempts to escape this pessimistic conclusion are unsuccessful, wavering between individualistic authenticity, Nazi activism, and passive waiting for "new gods." This latter, his final stance, is a hangover from the sort of apocalyptic expectations that were common among early 20th century Central European intellectuals, but it seems decidedly odd today.

Marcuse's Hegelian alternative promises a different way out. The movement of dereification in Hegel is a development out of a contradictory unity, driven by an internal motility from level to level and fulfilling itself at the highest level in the absolute. Since the absolute is interpreted here as a movement of human life rather than as pure cognition, it has a historical content. Dereification is more than a theoretical transcendence of objectivism, more even than individual authenticity, and certainly other than Nazism and mystical messianism. Its content is identified implicitly with socialist revolution. This historical conception of dereification converges with Lukács's Hegelian version of Marxism in which the class conscious proletariat stands in for the absolute.

It is clear from Marcuse's other writings in this period that this analysis of Hegel contains a coded reference to Marxism. In Lukács, knowledge, i.e., Marxism, enters into (proletarian) consciousness and so life understands itself and expresses itself as transforming practice. This is the Lukácsian version of the absolute that, in more abstract terms, Robert Pippin attributes to Marcuse's Hegel: the "subjects can and do understand the 'totality' of [their historical] ... period as their own historical doing, and thereby actively *assume* the role of subject" (Pippin 1988, 78). Marcuse's thesis sets out from just such an interpretation of Hegel to open a path from Heidegger's early work toward a radical reevaluation of modernity and its prospects. This path, which of course Heidegger did *not* follow, represents a significant alternative to Heidegger's later works.

Marcuse's Marxism is explicit in "On the Problem of the Dialectic." He explains that

> This "ego" of human life, to which the dialectic thus "returns," is not primarily knowing thought but the full being of life happening in the real world. The necessity of the dialectic lies in the necessity of this life to be able to control reliably the essence of being in all life situations. The "dialectic of the self-consciousness" is not a free floating dialectic of knowing; it is tied to the concrete being and action of human life. (Marcuse 1978b, 436)

This concept of self-consciousness joins theory and practice in a unity. Life "can only fulfill its essence if it mediates its entire immediate existence (which measured against its actual possibilities is essentially an 'otherness,' a 'loss of its self') with its self-being; it makes this existence its own by changing it, 'appropriating it' ('assimilating it'). Only in this change through the process of sublation does the living ego remain equal to itself in otherness" (Marcuse 1978b, 438). The key to Marcuse's extremely abstract presentation of the Hegelian absolute as a dimension of life lies in the transcendence of reification. Lukács introduced this problematic into Marxist circles in this period. His theory of practice is essential background to Marcuse's Hegel interpretation. I will therefore turn to Lukács's influence on Marcuse in the next chapter.

Chapter 4

Interlude with Lukács

Totality and Revolution

The Concept of Totality

It is time to broaden the contemporary context of Heidegger's and Marcuse's forays into the history of philosophy. In this chapter I will focus on one particularly significant figure whose influence on Marcuse is unquestioned and who may also have had some impact on Heidegger. Georg Lukács was a prominent literary critique and essayist in the German language from shortly before World War I until the end of the war when he joined the Hungarian Communist Party. After that extraordinary conversion, Lukács wrote a book entitled *History and Class Consciousness*, which revolutionized Marxist theory if not the capitalist world.

Marcuse's first doctoral thesis on the artist novel borrowed the theoretical framework of Lukács's early *Theory of the Novel*. In his 1930 essay on "The Problem of the Dialectic," Marcuse writes, "Lukács's book, *History and Class Consciousness*, is recognized and appreciated as a contribution to the development of Marxism which is essential and whose importance cannot be overestimated" (Marcuse 1978b, 421).

Lucien Goldmann argued that Heidegger's *Being and Time* was a response to *History and Class Consciousness* (Goldmann 1973). Goldmann tried to show that the Heideggerian concept of being was a de-Marxified version of Lukács's concept of totality. Although Goldmann's argument has not been generally accepted, it is true that on the last page of *Being and Time* Heidegger makes a clear reference to Lukács's notion of the "reification of consciousness" (Heidegger 1962, 487). And Heidegger's emphasis on practice and his critique of the contemplative stance of traditional philosophy certainly resembles Lukács's *praxis* philosophy.

Perhaps more significant than these questions of influence is the easily verifiable fact that Lukács's concept of totality has parallels in Heidegger and Marcuse.

The main function of this concept in Lukács is to mark the place of the lost unity of self and world for which modern consciousness longs. That unity was represented by ancient Greece in Lukács's pre–Marxist works and by a future communist society in his later works. At both stages in Lukács's development the totality is also the source of the intelligibility of the historical world. The comparison with Lukács's early works proves fruitful for gaining a deeper understanding of Heidegger and Marcuse regardless of the ties that may or may not have linked them in their time. I will turn to that comparison now.

The Greek Ideal

In Heidegger's account, Greek productionism is structured around "*enantia*," contraries. Contraries appear in relation to every aspect of *techné*, from the relation of essence to existence, matter to form, movement to rest, potentiality to actuality. But these Greek contraries are not modern antinomies. Each contrary implies its other and comes to rest in its other. Essence and existence cannot be thought separately, any more than can matter and form. Not only are the contraries mutually implicated, they are engaged in a development—a *kinesis* with a preestablished *telos*. Reconciliation of the contraries, ideal and real, is central to the Greek view of life.

The Greeks live in a world in which everything has its place and achieves the ideal in striving for self-completion according to its own inner tendencies. But this world no longer exists. Modernity consists in the diremption of the contraries into opposing principles. Facts now stand opposed to values, and *techné* becomes technology, the arbitrary imposition of a measure, a plan, and a goal on raw materials that have no *telos* and no inner tendencies of their own. Heidegger attempts to restore the original harmony through what he calls the "saving power" that accompanies the growth of technology. We have examined this saving power in an earlier chapter. Here I would like to consider the significance of the Greek ideal in shaping Heidegger's thought and especially his conception of an authentic relation between human being and being.

The underlying harmony Heidegger identifies in Greek *techné* is ontologically fundamental for modern times, too, although now it is profoundly masked by everyday reality; Heidegger evokes this harmony first with the notion of being-in-the-world and in his last period with the idea of the "fourfold." These concepts refer to a unity of subject and object, value and fact prior to their separation in modern culture. But this unity is obscured by inauthenticity and technology and can no longer be fully lived. In Heidegger's early work what philosophy knows might break through occasionally in the form of authentic resolution. In his later work philosophy itself, or at least the philosophical life dedicated to "thought," can give an existential weight to insight into the ontological depths. But this is not a revealing, that is, the form of life of the age. Salvation would consist in the practical realization in existence of what philosophy recognizes in theory. The implicit harmony would become explicit, active in everyday life and thought. This new era would "bring about a change in human nature, accompanied by a transformation of metaphysics" (Heidegger 1968, 209).

What is the meaning of this appeal to a renewed harmony of human being and being from out of their technological strife? It is a return to the Greeks, a "new beginning." Hence Heidegger's interest in the problem of *techné* with which the Greeks thought the revealing for the first time. But there is something overwrought about this intense preoccupation with the Greeks. The Greeks, he assures us, are the founding fathers of Western thought. We must return to them for inspiration to grasp the basic insight that has unfolded even as it degenerated throughout the last 2,500 years of Western history. Only modern German is a "philosophical language" on a par with ancient Greek. Such idealizations of Greece have been standard clichés in German culture for centuries and once inspired a book entitled "The Tyranny of Greece Over Germany" (Butler 1935). But in addition to these general clichés, Heidegger's appropriation of Greece depends on a specific theme found in Schiller, Hegel, and his own contemporary, Lukács.

Schiller and Hegel proposed a remarkable theory of Greek culture according to which Greek art, and in particular the epic poetry of Homer, revealed a world in which meaning was not in question as it is for us moderns. The forms of things, social roles, and the meaning of life were given to the Greeks as *true*, as there to be discovered, and not as arbitrary inventions of human will. We have won the creativity of the subject but lost the truth of the object. The Greeks were at home in the world and we are homeless. They possessed a wholeness of life that embraced subject and object, "is" and "ought" in a fruitful and resolvable tension, but we are condemned to live them as antinomies, as an unhealed wound in the heart of being. Hegel's dialectic, which claims to reveal the secret of "being at home with itself in its other," is an ambitious squaring of this particular philosophical circle (Hegel 1968, 175).

Such ideas were certainly familiar to any German reader of the classics in Heidegger's day. But it is a curious fact that they resurfaced in 1916 as contemporary philosophy in a book that excited much comment at the time and was likely known to Heidegger. This book is Lukács's *Theory of the Novel.* The central category of Lukács's analysis of epic literature is "totality," by which he means not all and everything but rather the unity of the antinomial opposites of modern life, the proximity of the ideal and the real. The Greeks lived the totality we can only represent aesthetically or philosophically. In the Homeric epic there is no *fundamental* opposition between duty and interest, art and reality, individual and community, between, ultimately, the soul and the world in which it finds itself. Every act and every object in this world is, just as it is, artistic and ethical in its natural form. The gods are companions, not judges of men. The tools and speech of everyday life are beautiful and find literary expression without lyrical or illusionary aesthetic transformation.

This notion of totality may or may not have influenced Heidegger directly. That would be difficult to show since Lukács's conception of Greece was familiar. It is nevertheless interesting that the following passage from *The Theory of the Novel* sounds remarkably like Heidegger's interpretation of *techné*.

> Totality as the formative prime reality of every individual phenomenon implies that something closed within itself can be completed; completed because everything occurs within it, nothing is excluded from it and nothing points at a higher reality outside it, completed because everything within it ripens to its own perfection and, by attaining itself, submits to limitation. Totality of being is possible only where everything is already homogeneous before it has been contained by forms; where forms are not a constraint but only the becoming conscious, the coming to the surface of everything that had been lying dormant as a vague longing in the innermost depths of that which had to be given form; where knowledge is virtue and virtue is happiness, where beauty is the meaning of the world made visible. (Lukács 1968, 34)

Lukács emphasizes the function of self-development and completion. He introduces the idea that limitation comes not merely from without but is assumed by the thing limited. Form realizes the tendency of content here as in Heidegger's analysis of bearance. The last phrase announces the agenda of Heidegger's later aesthetics.

In classical German philosophy, the idealization of ancient Greece inspired a modern ideal of wholeness achieved anew through the complex mediations of dialectics and citizenship. These mediations would preserve the advance of modernity, the discovery of the autonomous subject, while resolving the theoretical and practical antinomies of modern life resulting from that discovery. For Heidegger such a reconciliation of ancient and modern appears as the inauguration of a new epoch beyond human powers of prediction or creation.

Lukács's trajectory was quite different. In the course of his reprieve of this tradition, he quickly passed from the nostalgic position outlined in *The Theory of the Novel* to a Hegelian–Marxist reconciliation within a transformed modernity. Like the epic community, the proletariat in his *History and Class Consciousness* lives and acts in solidarity, transcending the alienated individuality of bourgeois society. The proletariat too belongs to a world of which it need only achieve consciousness to bring its works to completion. Its actions are not arbitrary impositions of will but realize a necessity inscribed in things themselves. But if the proletariat resembles an epic community living in the "presence of the totality," this presence is not simply given but won through the creative practice in which the class makes its own history. The resolution of the antinomies requires a historic "labor" of revolutionary world making.

Historicizing the Absolute

According to the early Marxist Lukács, being is essentially historical. History cannot be reduced to nature nor is it a merely regional form of being. History is ontologically fundamental insofar as our world, everything we can know and touch, is historical. Furthermore, the thesis that being is historical blocks any transcendental move to a suprahistorical ego or atemporal categories. Being cannot be grasped without active involvement in history as there is no external place to stand. The most fundamental such involvement is economic production in which the working classes have always been engaged. However, only under capitalism are workers able to comprehend the social world they create through their labor. In so doing they discover that they have objectified themselves in the world in an alienated fashion Lukács describes as reification.

Reification is the appearance of social processes in the form of thinghood. The concept derives from the Marxist notion of the fetishism of commodities interpreted in Hegelian terms as a "form of appearance," or "form of objectivity," a modality of essence. Reified thought is the sociological equivalent of the objectivistic and mechanistic empiricism criticized equally by Hegel and Heidegger. And as in their theories, so in Lukács reified appearances mask a more fundamental totality in which subject and object are unified rather than split apart in an eternal antinomy. It is only on the ground of this prior unity that the bifurcation between them can open up. Labor, disalienated through revolution, will restore that unity through the self-conscious appropriation of social reality by the proletariat.

Heidegger's phenomenological ontology also abstracts from nature in placing historicity at the center of its interpretation of being and so can be reconciled with Lukács's version of Marxism in this respect. However, unlike in Heidegger, Lukács's critique of reification has revolutionary political implications. It does not lead beyond history but to the next stage of history. Since the working class is the basis of history, its consciousness that it is such is itself historical and can have historical consequences. The revolution disalienates history through dereifying capitalist society and exposing all the hidden social processes that underlie its thing-like form. Then human action returns to itself not as an alien power but as self-expression. The form of this unity of actor and object, the totality, is not merely a theoretical postulate but also a real historical force.[1]

This Lukácsian dialectic lies in the background of Marcuse's explanation of Hegel's concepts of life, work, and the absolute. However, Lukács is the great structuring absence of the book which is, after all, an academic thesis presented to a very conservative faculty. The fact that Marcuse cannot mention Lukács or suggest a Marxist alternative to Hegel creates problems for the reader. The discussion of the higher levels of Hegel's dialectic is exceedingly abstract. It is hard to imagine how it would have been interpreted by a Marxist schooled in Lukács at that time. But this is what we must do if it is to make sense as an expression not only of Marcuse's scholarly interests but also of his intense political convictions. The most important such connection links Marcuse's obscure elucidation of Hegel's absolute and Lukács's theory of practice.

Recall that Marcuse explains the absolute as self-conscious life. The life process is a kind of quasi-transcendental totality positing organism and environment, consciousness and being. Where the living consciousness knows itself as a moment of life in this sense, its world is dereified and freely enacted. The world achieves full intelligibility in the subject's self-consciousness. This interpretation appears to be a euphemized expression of the notion of proletarian revolution as conceived by Lukács, also in terms of Hegel's absolute.

Lukács distinguishes between two fundamentally different types of practice, a "contemplative" practice characteristic of bourgeois society, and a transforming practice that "penetrates" its objects. The model of contemplative practice is the relation of the worker to the machine (Lukács 1968, 89). The machine is self-contained; it has its own logic, the law of its operation; the worker is external to the machine and tends it without actually controlling its autonomous functioning. For Lukács, this type of subject-object relation exemplifies the reified practice of a capitalist society, whether it be entrepreneurial activity, buying and selling on markets, or scientific research (Lukács 1968, 98). Contemplative practice is thus not simply passive as the term suggests, but technical, manipulative in character. It modifies the world, to be sure, but it leaves its objects *essentially* unchanged. Indeed, it presupposes the law of its objects which it comprehends and applies according to the Baconian principle that "Nature to be commanded must be obeyed."

Despite the frenetic activity of a technical civilization, its practice does not affect the essence of its objects, their law, only their manifest form, their appearance. Activity at the level of appearance depends on a passive relation to law, which practice merely "contemplates" and does not attempt to change. The activism of the bourgeois subject is based on fatalistic acceptance, "realism," at a deeper level. This realism shows up in the notion of values as ideals irretrievably cut off from the facts of the world. Philosophy's reified subject-object conception raises this structure to the highest level of abstraction. According to Lukács, when Kant demonstrates that the world of experience is rigorously determined by scientific laws, he opens that world to unlimited technical progress while excluding in principle any role for values (Lukács 1968, 160–61).

Contemplative practice separates theory, in which law is comprehended, from practice in which it is applied. This separation distinguishes it from both *techné*, in which knowledge of the *eidos* guides the realization of intrinsic potentialities, and from the "sight" that guides the activity of *Dasein* in immediate relation to the equipment of its world (Heidegger 1962, 98). In these latter cases knowledge is a phase of the practical activity, a *logos* in Plato's sense, rather than an external value neutral complement to it.

In contrast to contemplative practice, transforming practice attacks the laws themselves. This nontechnical practice grasps the essence of its objects and changes them at the deepest level. Self-consciousness is the implicit model of this type of practice. We change what we are immediately in becoming aware of ourselves. Self-consciousness is simultaneously awareness and action; it transcends the gap between theory and practice. Lukács's innovation is to conceive of social transformation on this model, as a highly complex and socially mediated expression of self-transformation. Disalienation in the social sphere thus involves collective self-awareness. This is a social interpretation of Hegel's absolute. A more precise explanation of what this means follows.

Lukács never claims that we can dispense with contemplative practice and substitute transforming practice for it everywhere. His point is rather that society is fundamentally modified when the proletariat achieves self-consciousness. This transformative power of self-consciousness is familiar from certain unusual everyday life situations. We are aware of the difference between self-contradictory beliefs or self-deceptions that are immediately cancelled by self-consciousness and other beliefs that are not modified when we become aware of holding them (Dumouchel 1991). The market is the social equivalent of the former. When buyers and sellers act on the market, they form a collective subject unconscious of itself. Their practice is determined by the "law" of the market they each use to get ahead, but that law itself is the combined effect of their very attempts to use it. The condition for the emergence of such a system is its fundamental misrecognition by social subjects. This misrecognition consists in the preconceptual structuring of the social as a realm of individual activity on alien objects. By becoming conscious of the consequences of their action and coordinating voluntarily, the individuals can overcome its contemplative limitation and the corresponding reified form of objectivity of their objects; they can change the "law" of their action and create a different social world together.

As a Marxist Lukács projects such radical results only in the case of labor. Workers "produce" society through their labor and their participation in capitalist institutions. When they come together, therefore, nothing can stop them from transforming the society they constitute unconsciously *qua* workers. But the condition of this transformation is self-consciousness, workers' recognition of their own real social role. That recognition itself constitutes a fundamental social change because it changes what it is to be a worker, from passive, reified social atom to collective agent: "the act of consciousness overthrows the form of objectivity of its object" (Lukács 1968, 178, trans. modified). Lukács writes

> In the commodity the worker recognizes himself and his own relation to capital. Inasmuch as he is incapable in practice of raising himself above the role of object his consciousness is the *self-consciousness of the commodity*, or in other words it is the self-knowledge, the self-revelation of the capitalist society founded upon the production and exchange of

commodities. . . . [W]hen the worker knows himself as a commodity his knowledge is practice. *That is to say, this knowledge brings about an objective structural change in the object of knowledge.* (Lukács 1968, 168–69)

Lukács's distinction between nature and history must be understood in relation to this distinction between types of practice. There is a domain in which transforming practice is possible, in which we can reconstitute our objects by becoming socially self-conscious, and alongside it, there is another domain in which our action will always be contemplative, technical. The first domain is society, the second is nature. Self-consciousness immediately alters the logic of collective action in the social domain. Lukács does not articulate the boundaries of history and nature very well, but he is at least clear that the dialectic applied to physics and chemistry, as Engels suggested, is reduced to a crude allegory of knowledge. Thus, there can be no dialectic of the "nature in itself" studied by natural science.

In Lukács, the dialectic is not a metaphysical or methodological principle but the actual moving force of history, within which human beings are situated as potential agents of radical change, historical "producers." For Lukács true transforming practice involves not just an understanding of the epistemological dependency of reified objectivities on society, but an ontological dialectic of the subject and object underlying those objectivities (Lukács 1968, 24n).

Lukács's theory of practice can be summed up in three equivalences: in the social domain, we *are* in the strongest sense the object, that is, society, and thus our knowledge of society is self-knowledge and our self-knowledge action. Historically concretized in the idea of proletarian revolution, these cannot be immediate equivalences but imply various mediations such as political parties, theoretical knowledge, and so on. Nevertheless, the three equivalences lie in the background of these mundane activities and guarantee in principle the possibility of their success.

This account of Lukács' theory of transforming practice appears congruent with Marcuse's Hegel interpretation. Marcuse agrees with Lukács that only human history is fully dialectical and that Hegel erred in taking the dialectic for an all encompassing system culminating in absolute knowledge. Hegel's self-interpretation contradicts his own most original discoveries in his early work. Marcuse traces his vulnerability to this unfortunate self-interpretation back to his attempt to apply the dialectic to nature, to "absolutize historicity," which leads to a "smoothed over" version of the dialectic (Marcuse 1978b, 417–18, my translation). Blurring the boundaries between nature and history risks tilting the whole enterprise away from practice toward theory. This, Marcuse argues, is what eventually happens in Hegel's later work and in the tradition of interpretation derived from it. Marcuse's concerns here converge directly with Lukács's own restoration of the dialectic. Their principal contribution is to uncover the dynamic theory of historical agency implicit in the Hegelian dialectic. It is precisely this aspect of the dialectic which cannot survive its extension to nature. Applied to nature it becomes either a regressive emanationist metaphysics or a methodological prolegomena to the positive sciences.

In his thesis Marcuse must stop short of explicitly drawing the Marxist conclusions toward which his argument tends. He comes close in many passages of *Hegel's Ontology*, but he cannot supply the Marxist content. Nevertheless, consider how he might have concretized these remarks on labor as the underlying structure of Hegelian historicity.

> The fundamental element, common to these categories and which has a wide range of reference is the concept of "activity." Activity is the living unity of knowing and acting, whereby knowledge means consciousness of self and action, the actual letting happen of the self. Activity is essentially "transformation" and "bringing forth." Every activity "aims at" a transformation (PhG, 196); it changes something in the one who performs it; it turns it around in its present condition; it "turns it upside down". . . . The concept of bringing-oneself-forth further specifies that the life process is concretely a self-manifestation, self-risking and self-assertion. (Marcuse 1987, 262)

Lukács's three equivalences clearly haunt this abstract statement of the case while the repeated reference to "bringing forth," "*hervorbringen*" harks back to Heidegger. One imagines Marcuse, with his Berliner's irony, smiling to himself as he constructed sentences which would be read so very differently by Heidegger than by his politically sympathetic colleagues.

Can we go further toward integrating this interpretation of Hegel with Marcuse's Marxism? The figure of self-consciousness as simultaneously self and social transformation seems to be present in all his later thought and to have found the early formulations of Critical Theory. Here is an example from Max Horkheimer's classic essay on "Traditional and Critical Theory": "In genuinely critical thought explanation signifies not only a logical process but a concrete historical one as well. In the course of it both the social structure as a whole and the relation of the theoretician to society are altered, that is both the subject and the role of thought are changed" (Horkheimer 1972, 211). This change, which Lukács described as the unity of theory and practice, situates revolution in the place of the absolute. It echoes still in Horkheimer's text insofar as the transformation of thought transforms social being.[2]

Technology and Nature

Modernity is haunted by nostalgia for a simpler world. But it is impossible to return to an objectively given totality. Now meanings are recognized as human creations. But how then can we cross the gap between the creating subject and the indifferent world? We left Heidegger struggling to overcome the centripetal force of modernity in a unified conception of being-in-the-world. Heidegger's early analysis of production in Aristotle was formative for this conception of worldhood. However, worldhood has an ambiguous status in Heidegger's work. On the one hand, *Dasein* is being-in-the-world, inconceivable out of connection with its environment. On the other hand, the truth of *Dasein's* being is discovered in the breakdown of its world. Anxiety, dread, boredom, living-toward-death are all stances through which the individual gains access to the complete groundlessness of worldly existence. The totality lost in the remote Greek past could not be regained either in the depths of *Dasein's* being-in-the-world nor in the mythic politics of the Nazi state. In the latter Heidegger productionism is treated negatively, as the fundamental error of Western metaphysics. Although Heidegger begins his analysis with production, it ends in existential and eventually quasi-religious themes far removed from these beginnings.

Hegel offers a strangely similar spectacle. The master–slave dialectic places work at the center of the theory and promises a reconciliation of human being and world. Its generalization as an ontological model suggests that all meaning and truth arise in a productive relation to reality. According to Marcuse, this Hegelian historicity sets the agenda for later approaches to understanding history. "The self alienation of consciousness and its actuality, the disappearance of what it originates from, its imprisonment in the objectified world, the 'desire' to sublate and to take back this alienation—these are precisely the categories through which the specific historicity of human life is treated in post–Hegelian discussions on the subject of 'history'" (Marcuse 1987, 298). With these remarks, Marcuse's thesis comes as close as it can to alluding to the contemporary Marxist version of Hegelian dialectics. However, like Heidegger, Hegel abandons these productionist beginnings and his theory concludes in the ether of the absolute, a purely cognitive relation to reality which Hegel himself compares to the self-thinking thought of the Aristotelian God. Marcuse's interpretation of the absolute as life corrects the emphasis and steers the dialectic back to the realm of practice.

Here he rejoins Lukács, as we have seen. Lukács's interpretation of Marxism launched the Hegelianizing approach to revolution that Marcuse combined with Heidegger's fundamental ontology in his early works. The crucial link is the notion that there exists *a form of self-consciousness which is both the revelation of a world and the transformation of that world.*

Such a conception is incompatible with the conventional understanding of nature in itself as the ultimate reality. Nature can be "revealed" to consciousness and worked on by technique but certainly not transformed by self-consciousness. The nature in itself of the modern sciences is the correlate of a knowing subject abstracted from reality. A social epistemology may dereify it, but this dereification is not the self-consciousness of an identical subject-object. Only a dialectic such as that of Lukács, which excludes scientific nature and interprets being as history, can transcend the antinomies of the contemplative relation to reality.

Heidegger's phenomenological ontology also abstracts from nature in placing historicity at the center of its interpretation of being and so can be partially reconciled with Lukács's version of Marxism. But Heidegger's *Dasein* has no concrete social identity despite the attempt to fill it out with traditional and national content at the end of *Being and Time.* In this respect it is as abstract as the *cogito* it replaces. Marcuse's synthesis of Heidegger and Lukács overcomes this limitation by interpreting *Dasein* socially, in terms of its position in a collectively created social world. Hegel's master–slave dialectic introduces social division into the motility of history. This then prepares the way to an assimilation of Lukács's historical dialectics.

Marcuse's early theory is an extraordinary synthesis of Heidegger and Lukács but it also suffers from their limitations. On the one hand, the abstractness of the Heideggerian conception of *Dasein* and its care is only partially overcome by reference to the Marxist concept of class. Already in the early 1930s it is becoming clear that class struggle is not the only force driving history. Marcuse attempts to deepen Marxism by going beyond the conventional emphasis on class interest to a more radical theory of the alienation of labor, but he does not address the latest stage of capitalist development in which the proletariat is no longer a revolutionary force. If revolution is going to unify theory and practice, another type of agent will be required. The sources of resistance must be deeper than alienation or interests which the system can mask and manipulate. Marcuse will search for that alternative in Freud and aesthetics in his later work.

Then, too, Lukács's version of the dialectic succeeds all too well in distinguishing nature from history. The social world is a network of people and things in intricate patterns that are not easily unraveled. Lukács distinguishes nature and society in theory, but although he knows they cannot be truly separated in practice, he has no account of their connection. This inconsistency makes it impossible for Lukács to develop the critique of technology implicit in his theory of reification. He criticizes the structure of capitalist technology; he sees technology as part of history rather than nature, and yet he has nothing to say about its transformation. The resulting antinomy of history and nature threatens the whole theory. Does the coming to self-awareness of a social group engaged in complex technically mediated relations really resemble the immediate unity of subject and object in self-consciousness? Demonstrating this would certainly take some elaborate qualifications if it is possible at all, and yet we do not want to fall uncritically into acceptance of reification in every domain of complex relations between people and things as does Jürgen Habermas, for example. His "media theory" freezes the "system" of such relations in its given form while allowing democratic initiatives only in a lifeworld purified of things (Habermas 1984).[3]

Marcuse's alternative in his later work is to extend the dialectic to technology itself. For Marcuse history excludes the abstract nature of the natural sciences but it explicitly includes the whole range of natural relationships and objects touched by human activity such as landscape, environment, and raw materials. As he explains in an early essay, the historical dialectic applies to all human "works and creations, but also of nature as an occupied life-space and a power to be used" (Marcuse 1978b, 418).[4] These have a dialectical form explored in the "objective dialectic" of thinghood, the lower levels of the dialectic that correspond more or less to the Aristotelian concept of production.

Marcuse's originality in the Marxist tradition appears in his insistence that the power of the imagination can fill in these two gaps in the classical theory, updating the approach to agency and technology. The organized work of the imagination is aesthetic activity, based on aesthetic experience, and it is therefore to aesthetics that Marcuse turns in his later work for this constructive dimension of his theory. I explain this remarkable revision of Marxism in the next chapter.

Chapter 5
Aesthetic Redemption

Marcuse's Theory: A Preliminary Sketch

Introduction: Back to Weimar?

Although there are several competent expositions of Marcuse's later thought, I intend to offer an account of his ideas here and in the next chapter. This may seem redundant, however, I will take the occasion to propose a hypothesis about Marcuse's thought as a whole, and indicate a direction I think it can be usefully continued. While I do think there are ideas worthy of further development, let me be clear at the outset: I agree with most commentators that there are insuperable problems in the dizzying multiplication of categories in which Marcuse attempted to cloth his position after *One-Dimensional Man*. At times Marcuse seems to regress to an impossibly old fashioned metaphysics. He invokes Plato's ideal forms and talks of "objective values" (Marcuse 1972, 69); his startling late theory of sensation looks like an attempt to re-enchant the disenchanted nature of modernity. A different and more interesting interpretation of these ideas is possible. What I will offer here is a diagnosis and a suggested cure for Marcuse's restless search for an adequate discourse. Once the restlessness itself is noticed, it becomes obvious that he was trying to express an intuition which he lacked the means to fully explain.

Marcuse shared the ambivalence toward modernity of many intellectuals in the Weimar Republic of his youth. Of course most intellectuals held traditional positions. The reactionaries were resolutely hostile to "civilization" and idealized an imaginary German "*Kultur.*" Liberals struggled in the face of growing chaos to maintain their old faith in progress. But a far more interesting position emerged in the writings of certain thinkers on both the Right and the Left. Ernst Jünger, Oswald Spengler, Heidegger, Walter Benjamin, and Marcuse, along with many in the arts attempted to combine cultural critique and modernism in a revolutionary perspective. The advent of an alternative modernity was supposed to grant technology a different function in ways corresponding to their different political convictions. Working all this out was not easy and led to some fairly confused thinking, especially on the Right (Herf 1984).

What was the difficulty with which Marcuse contended? I believe it was his own past, his complicated relationship to the doctrine of his teacher, Heidegger. This is of course only a hypothesis and were he here today, he might very well reject it. But his failure to explore the philosophical implications of his later thought satisfactorily requires an explanation. After all, this is the same person who wrote *Hegel's Ontology, Reason and Revolution,* and a dozen careful and profound studies of the history of philosophy between the two wars. The major postwar books are on a different plane in terms of theoretical development and consistency from the later writings. What happened? It was not age per se that blocked Marcuse's philosophical path. All who knew him can testify that he was as sharp as ever to the end.

But perhaps something connected in a different way to age was involved. The concerns of Marcuse's last work hark back to his early writings under Heidegger's influence. Individuality and experience are central categories once again and these ultimate texts attempt to found critical consciousness in an ontology that has a suspiciously phenomenological aspect. Like the early Heidegger, the later Marcuse rejects naturalism and a purely cognitive concept of subjectivity in favor of an active and needy subject that encounters a world correlated with its powers. Implicit in both Heidegger's and Marcuse's critiques of technology is a reference to Aristotle, interpreted phenomenologically. Both were concerned with the implications of the breakdown of Greek essentialism for modern technology and for the "pre-ontological" understanding of the world that accompanies it. Heidegger's early thought is thus far more significant for Marcuse's later critique of technology than is usually supposed.

But by 1968 Marcuse had lost touch with this background in his wide-ranging search in Marx and Freud for a more concrete explanation for the catastrophic outcome of the Enlightenment. He would surely have felt a return to phenomenology impossible. Yet I will argue that there are resources in phenomenology which he might have applied to the explanation of his later project. Without those resources, he was condemned to try one discourse after another, like badly fitting clothes, in the pursuit of an adequate means of expression.

The best evidence for this hypothesis is the structuring absences and parallels in the texts themselves. But there is also a historical fact: Marcuse came to Heidegger in a period of social turmoil when Left and Right contended for power against each other and against a failing liberal state. In this period political choices were existential choices, choices of morality and identity, not mere matters of opinion. From 1933 to 1968, the non–Stalinist Left was too weak to offer much hope to someone of Marcuse's rather skeptical bent, and more importantly, too dogmatic to innovate new responses to a rapidly changing capitalist society. Opposition was largely reduced to the expression of radical opinion and membership in Stalinist parties. What seemed new about the New Left, at least to the generation of 1968, was in fact a renewal of the sort of existential revolt with which Marcuse was familiar from his own youth. Marcuse was well aware of this and it sent him back to the themes of his early work.

Curiously, the New Left horrified Adorno and Horkheimer and even Habermas for a time. They saw in it only a pale reflection of fascist anti-liberalism. This set them irremediably at odds with their students.[1] Marcuse made the opposite choice and studied the New Left as exemplary of new possibilities of resistance accompanying the organization of modern capitalism. He searched the movement for signs of a possible future as Marx had searched the Paris Commune. As a result he was the hero of his students and hundreds of thousands of others who knew only his writings. A whole generation of scholars remembers Marcuse in that specific context, and dismisses him along with its youthful illusions. This is a mistake. Marcuse's later theory is an echo of the deeper note of his Weimar period. Restoring that historical connection, even against Marcuse's explicit self-understanding, is the only way to do justice to his later work.

The Concept of Potentiality

Marcuse's career as a philosopher begins with a synthesis of Heidegger and a Marxism strongly influenced by Lukács's early writings. But Marcuse is already discontent with what he perceives as the abstractness and ahistoricism of *Being and Time*. For Marcuse, authenticity is not the return of the individual to himself from out of alienation in the crowd, but reflects the social character of existence, the fact that the world is a shared creation. Marcuse's early existential Marxism thus culminates in a call for a philosophy that unifies theory and practice in a critical encounter with its time and the issues of the day (Marcuse 1978a, 398ff).

This existential politics once adopted remains integral to Marcuse's thought for the remainder of his long career. The structure of the "world" in something close to Heidegger's sense is at stake in all serious political struggle. But Heidegger's terminology, such categories as existence, *Dasein*, authenticity, quickly drop by the wayside. Instead of developing an existential analytic of political engagement along Heideggerian lines as he first proposed, Marcuse turns to Marx and Freud. Under the influence of the Frankfurt School, which he joins in 1933, Marcuse develops the notions of technological rationality, one-dimensionality, and a historicized version of instinct theory. These offer sociological and psychological alternatives to Heidegger, who practically disappears as a reference. But as we will see, vestiges of Heidegger's ontology persist in his thought to the very end.

It is commonplace to find traces of Heidegger's critique of the *Gestell* in Marcuse's concept of technological domination. In his interview with Frederick

Olafson, Marcuse remarked that Heidegger may exceptionally have achieved genuine historical insight in his later writings on technology. "The *Frage nach dem Sein* recedes before the *Frage nach der Technik*" (Olafson 1988, 98). But the connection goes much deeper. The most important vestige of Heidegger's influence is Marcuse's theory of the two dimensions of society. Although his presentation of this theory in *One-Dimensional Man* does not reference Heidegger, on examination it reveals a remarkable resemblance to the argument of "The Question Concerning Technology." In fact Marcuse sketches a sort of "history of being" that parallels Heidegger's account in his famous essay.

Was Marcuse aware of the parallel? After all, his student days lay far in the past. His text could have sources other than Heidegger. But there is a defensive footnote that gives the game away. In the middle of his argument concerning being and potentiality, he digresses to say, "To avoid a misunderstanding: I do not believe that the *Frage nach dem Sein* and similar questions are or ought to be an existential concern" (Marcuse 1964, 136). This clear reference to Heidegger, negative though it is, leaves no doubt that Marcuse intended his own "history of being" as a politically charged alternative to Heidegger's.

Marcuse notes that reason in ancient Greece distinguishes between true and false not only in language but also in experience. Truth and falsehood are not merely propositional, but involve the disclosure of being and apply in the first instance to things before applying to statements. The Greek conception of the thing, substance, was not static, but included an inherent movement toward higher forms. In fact the Greek word *"dynamis,"* "potential," already implies a kind of energy and striving toward essential truth. All being aspires to its end, to a perfected form which realizes its potentialities. The struggle of being for form is negatively evident in experience itself, in the suffering and striving world, the internal tensions of which reason analyzes. But since the essence is never finally attained, it actually negates every contingent realization in the imperfect objects of experience. The "is" contains an implicit reference to an "ought" it has failed to some degree to achieve. This "ought" is its potential, which is intrinsic to it and not merely projected by human wishes or desires (Marcuse 1964, 124–25, 133–34).

The role of the arts is to bring existence to its essential form. Implicit in every art is a finality corresponding to the perfection of its objects. The art of government aims to make men just; the art of education strives to develop the rational faculty that is the human essence. No such finality is implicit in modern technology that emerged through the destruction of *technai,* inherited crafts based on traditional values.

There is an obvious similarity between this description of the Greek concept of truth and Heidegger's interpretation of ancient productionist ontology. However, in contrast to Heidegger, Marcuse emphasizes the normative structure of production which he generalizes to being as a whole.[2] Hegel's influence is at work in this difference in emphasis. Of course neither Heidegger nor Marcuse suggest a return to the objective essences of the Greeks. But they do regard Greece as an emblem of the lost totality they project into the future in one form or another. Heidegger praises the Greeks for recognizing being as a source of meaning beyond human will. Marcuse draws a related conclusion with very different political implications: the Greeks maintain the difference between the two dimensions of being, essence and existence, the ideal and the real. They thereby preserve the truth of critical reason, the notion that what is is fraught with tension between its empirical reality and its potentialities.

Modern technological rationality sacrifices that truth in liquidating all reference to essence and potentiality. It aims at classification, quantification, and control. It admits no tension between true and false being and makes no distinction between preferences and potentialities. The empirically observed thing is the only reality and truth and falsehood apply only to propositions about it. And just because it is wholly defined by its empirical appearance, the thing can be analytically dissected into various qualities and quantities and absorbed into a technical system that submits it to alien ends. What ancient ontology takes for an intrinsic finality—the perfected form of things, the *logos* of a *techné*—is now treated as a mere personal choice. Modern reason flattens out the difference between the essential potentialities of things and merely subjective desires. It declares its "neutrality" over against the essences which governed the earlier *technai*. Arbitrarily chosen values are placed on the same plane as essences and no ontological or normative privilege attaches to the latter. It is this abstention from essentializing that gives modern reason its peculiar positivist self-understanding as purified of social influences.

For example, an analysis of the state conducted on classical terms would relate it to ethical ends, such as justice. Today the social sciences focus exclusively on the machinery of coercion and propaganda without regard for the purpose of the whole. Politics is about who gets what and how they get it, not about the realization of a norm. But how can the end of government, justice, be placed on the same plane as the will to power of a Callicles? A bias reveals itself in this equivalence, a bias which is all to the benefit of Callicles whose ambition is now taken no less seriously than a true public purpose since both are regarded as mere preferences. It is this abstention from any judgment as to what is accidental and what essential that is the original violence of modern reason, which places it in the service of the status quo.

Things no longer have intrinsic potentialities transcending their given form, but are simply there, unresistingly available for human use (Marcuse 1964, 146–48). Means and ends, realities and norms belong to separate realms, the one objective, technical, the other subjective. Nineteenth century positivism glorified the one, while romanticism exalted the other. But in the 20th century the subjective world no longer escapes operationalization. It too is brought under control through mass communications, management techniques, and psychological manipulation. Human beings are incorporated into the system as just one more fungible component. A one-dimensional society emerges in which critical reason is easily dismissed as unmotivated neurotic discontent. Indeed, a few marginal critics may even be functional for the system, proving the full extent of its liberalism by their ineffective complaints.

The class system perpetuates itself now by suppressing the potential for a humane and egalitarian social order made possible by technological advance. This is the crux of Marcuse's social critique: advanced society is, in a certain sense, *technically* outmoded by its own achievements. It is capable of "pacifying" existence but artificially maintains competition as the basis for inequality and domination. As Marcuse put it in his later speech on ecology, radical political struggle today consists in "existential revolts against an obsolete reality principle." "The specter which haunts advanced industrial society today is the obsolescence of full-time alienation" (Marcuse 1992, 35, 37). Technological rationality contributes to maintaining and reproducing the domination that is built into the inherited structure of society.

The "continuity of domination" is secured above all in the world of work. If workers' self-actualization and self-government are treated as preferences rather than as a human and social potentialities, they lose the normative force to counter capital's drive for profit and efficiency. Self-actualization and self-government on an assembly line remain the merest fantasies while real products roll off the line and prove its worth. This is what Marcuse meant when he wrote, "Today, domination perpetuates and extends itself not only through technology but *as* technology, and the latter provides the great legitimation of expanding political power, which absorbs all spheres of culture" (Marcuse 1964, 158).

So far Marcuse's theory recapitulates Heidegger's contrast of ancient *techné*, based on the realization of essential potentialities, and modern technology which "enframes" nature and society in a rationality of calculation and control. He acknowledges Heidegger's influence in a short article written in 1958 that offers a kind of prospectus of *One-Dimensional Man* (Marcuse 1989, 123–24). And as with Heidegger, the implicit standard against which technology is judged is a notion of growth and development that first appears in Greek *techné*. But within this shared framework a difference appears. For Heidegger, philosophy can only reflect on the catastrophe of technology, but Marcuse goes beyond earnest contemplation of the present to project a concrete utopia that can redeem the technological society. Despite the enframing, critical reason is still capable of formulating transcending demands and realizing the dream of freedom.

The Pursuit of the Concrete

Theory and Practice

Marcuse is a utopian thinker. He conceives of a redeemed technological rationality in a liberated society, much as Plato, at the end of the *Gorgias*, imagines a reformed rhetoric that would serve good ends. Heidegger's utopian impulses were safely checked after the mid-1930s, and during World War II Adorno and Horkheimer seem to have lost not only hope but even the capacity to imagine a better future.[3] Marcuse followed a different trajectory. From the 1950s on, his writings attempt to articulate a vision. Eventually this utopianism enters into his conception of instrumental rationality itself where it is formulated as a positive technological alternative. Technology is to be reconstructed around a conception of the good, in Marcuse's terminology, around life. The new technical *logos* must include a grasp of essences, and technology must be oriented toward perfecting rather than dominating its objects. Marcuse thus demands the reversal of the process of neutralization in which technological rationality was split off from substantive rationality and subserved to domination.

There is no easy way to argue this through an appeal to Marxist social theory, conceived as Marx conceived it, as a "counter-science." Although Marcuse makes such an appeal, he admits its weakness in advance. The problem has to do with the structure of the materialist dialectic that grounds all transcending concepts in the tensions of existing reality rather than in a realm of ideals. In Marx the gap between ideal and real is destined to disappear as theory becomes consciousness and philosophical speculation enters the real world as mass politics. The early Marxist Lukács called this "the unity of theory and practice." In a 1929 essay much influenced by Lukács, Marcuse describes it as "the noblest desideratum of all philosophizing" (Marcuse 1978a, 397).

The significance of this "desideratum" is explained in Lukács's critique of Kantian ethics. Once reason is purified of the teleology postulated by ancient ontology, "ought" and "is" stand in unmediated opposition. But this amounts to a confession of impotence. In failing to identify and further those mediations in the real by which the "is" can develop beyond its limitations, ethics concedes the inevitability of the given. "The 'ought' presupposes a being to which the category of 'ought' remains *inapplicable* in principle" (Lukács 1971, 160). By contrast, for Marxism, ideal demands become practical realities in the context of class struggle. The unity of theory and practice would transcend the antinomy of "ought" and "is" could it be achieved.

But as social struggles weaken in advanced industrial society, the gap between concrete reality with its internal tensions and the vision of a better society grows ever wider. In the early 1960s, when Marcuse wrote *One-Dimensional Man*, the unity of theory and practice appeared permanently lost. Hence the pessimistic tone of much of that book. Marcuse was forced to concede that potentialities could only be derived philosophically, by identifying technically possible remedies for the massive private distress and public squalor produced by a repressive society, without much hope of finding a corresponding will to change in a population blinded by ideology and "false needs."

But how then are the amorphous resistances or symptoms of distress related to these remedies? What can verify the diagnosis if not the voice of the victims? Without their assent, what distinguishes the philosophical analysis from the mere discontent of a beautiful soul? Worse still, if that discontent motivates action at some point, what will stand in the way of educational dictatorship (the "philosopher king"!) imposing a rational solution to the riddle of history on the unthinking masses?

"Aha!" exclaims the impatient critic of Marcuse who has held back through these all too lengthy explanations. "Now everything is clear. We are descending the slippery slope from utopianism to totalitarianism. Superior knowledge will prevail over the actual public will. A new 'rational' order will be imposed, not through the state as in earlier totalitarian experiments but through the technical system. Plato's *Republic* anticipated Marcuse's program, lacking only the up-to-date erotic and environmental references that are supposed to make the rationalistic pill easier to swallow."

The objection is implicit in Bruno Latour's brilliant reading of the *Gorgias* as a conspiracy between Callicles and Socrates to expel the *polis* from the halls of reason to the benefit of either pure power or pure knowledge (Latour 1999, chap. 7). Callicles' cynicism and Socrates' idealism complement each other. The one sees only manipulation in the assembly, while the other condemns it for not coming up to scientific standards of rational inquiry. What is overlooked, Latour complains, is the possibility of a practical rationality suited to the actual conditions of the assembly, in sum, democracy.[4]

But Marcuse was no Platonist. True, his critique of Plato is different from Latour's and concerns Plato's hostility to pleasure rather than his dissatisfaction with the *polis*. Indeed, Marcuse shares that dissatisfaction. He asks how it is possible to liberate a society that has made "unfreedom . . . part and parcel of the mental apparatus." And he replies

> From Plato to Rousseau, the only honest answer is the idea of educational dictatorship, exercised by those who are supposed to have acquired knowledge of the real Good. The answer has since become obsolete: knowledge of the available means of creating a humane existence for all is no longer confined to a privileged elite. The facts are all too open, and the individual consciousness would safely arrive at them if it were not methodically arrested and diverted. The distinction between rational and irrational authority, between repression and surplus-repression, can be made and verified by the individuals themselves. That they cannot make this distinction now does not mean that they cannot learn to make it once they are given the opportunity to do so. Then the course of trial and error becomes a rational course in freedom. Utopias are susceptible to unrealistic blueprints; the conditions for a free society are not. They are a matter of reason. (Marcuse 1966b, 225)

Reason is not identified with the Platonic *epistémé* here, but with public debate in a society where dissent is no longer suppressed and concentrated media power no longer distorts communication.

I do not believe later ambiguous statements cancel Marcuse's basic democratic commitment as expressed in this passage. What concerns him in essays such as "Repressive Tolerance" is the successful manipulation of the masses by the media and by the structuring of daily life around an artificially maintained struggle for existence. The freedom of the community requires the unfreedom of those who impose these manipulations and structures, that is, the end of private ownership of the media and the corporations. This is a socialist argument, not a totalitarian one as Marcuse's critics sometimes claim.[5]

Nevertheless, it is true that throughout much of his post–World War II career, Marcuse believed that progress toward freedom was blocked by the attachment of the masses to the very system that oppressed them. Such unwelcome realism is called "elitist" by the defenders of the elite power of the Rupert Murdochs. The question of which needs are "true" and which "false" arises from their exercise of power, not from the arrogance of the intellectuals. As Marcuse puts it, "As long as the individuals are indoctrinated and manipulated by a superimposed society (manipulated down to their very instincts), their answer to this question cannot be taken as their own. But by the same token, no 'tribunal' can justly arrogate to itself the right to decide which needs should be developed and satisfied" (Marcuse 2001, 52). An impasse? To be sure. But this is real impasse, not one of Marcuse's devising.

Two oppositional attitudes are possible in this situation. On the one hand, critics can retreat into what Lukács once called "the Grand Hotel Abyss" and negate the world abstractly in the name of an impossible ethical exigency: the world *ought* to be otherwise, nothing that is is right (Lukács 1968, 22). On the other hand, critics can follow a Hegelian line in seeking out the smallest signs of a historical transcendence and *project* a possible future. This is the difference between Adorno's negative dialectic and Marcuse's utopianism.

But where are these signs to be found in the one-dimensional society Marcuse describes? Marcuse's early interpretation of Marxism prepares a surprising response to which he returns in his later work: lived experience. In his early work class struggle is understood on existential terms as a mode of being-in-the-world. With the eclipse of revolutionary consciousness, opposition must emerge from another experiential source. In the next section I will explore Marcuse's various attempts to identify a new basis for resistance.

Experience as Foundation

The reference to experience is crucial for Marcuse's project insofar as he seeks to construct a rational critique of modernity. Modern thought defines itself by its rejection of authority and dogma, by its basis in the self-certainty of the autonomous individual. Science is founded in the carefully observed evidence of empirical experience. If there is anything that science does not explain, i.e., if philosophical critique still has an object, it must be verifiable in a different type of experience. The existential interpretation of experience appeared in the 1920s, not just to Marcuse but to many other philosophers as well, as a specifically modern response to naturalistic scientism and neo–Kantianism. Experiential thinking offered a way of recovering essential insight without lapsing into premodern dogmatism. As Douglas Kellner writes, "Marcuse's lust for the concrete was thus rooted in a fundamental drive of twentieth-century philosophy" (Kellner 1984, 396). It is true that this drive led some philosophers, including Heidegger, to interpret the experiential truth in national, racial, or religious terms in opposition to Enlightenment universalism. But it also took a progressive form in Marcuse's demand for social and political freedom.

Unfortunately, Marcuse's argument from experience has not stood the test of time very well. He started out by announcing the idea of a "concrete philosophy" founded in individual existence, *Dasein*, and never entirely abandoned this approach although the Heideggerian reference was quickly dropped (Marcuse 1978a, 385ff). The concrete appears here as the activity of the existential subject, itself constituted within a world in Heidegger's sense. But Heidegger's analysis of *Dasein* fails to achieve the level of concreteness implied by his own notion of historicity. The historical world cannot be understood without reference to the divisions within the community whose history it is. Marcuse asks

> [I]s the world "the same" even for all forms of *Dasein* present within a concrete historical situation? Obviously not. It is not only that the world of significance varies among particular contemporary cultural regions and groups, but also that, within any one of these, abysses of meaning may open up between different worlds. Precisely in the most existentially essential behavior, no understanding exists between the world of the high-capitalist bourgeois and that of the small farmer or proletarian. Here the examination is forced to confront the question of the material constitution of historicity, a breakthrough that Heidegger neither achieves nor even gestures toward. (Marcuse 1978c, 364–65)

Marcuse believes he can achieve this breakthrough with a Hegelian–Marxist interpretation of the dialectic. As we have seen, his Hegel thesis worked out the alternative to Heidegger in terms of a historical dialectic of life. Life resembles Heidegger's *Dasein* in seeking its unity and wholeness through a future-oriented construction of its own potentialities. It does not have a prior essence but must create itself under the given conditions. In this sense it is "historical," a being that relates its past and future. Yet Marcuse's concept of life differs from Heidegger's *Dasein* in that the master–slave dialectic introduces social division and labor into its motility. The expression of its "care" in work and world leads to objectification and mutual recognition, themes entirely absent from Heidegger's existential analytic. Marcuse conceives the notion of the human "essence" in Hegelian–Marxist terms, as self-conscious unity of self, community, and world, and on this basis he argues that it can only be realized through overcoming the alienation of the worker under capitalism.

The phenomenological concept of world is now divided by class struggle. The worldhood of this world includes politics as an essential moment. The problem is to find an authentic, that is, philosophical, politics capable of articulating the situation of contemporary *Dasein*. Following Lukács, Marcuse interprets that politics in terms of the struggle against reification, with reification cast in the role of inauthentic objectivism in Heidegger. The equivalent of authenticity now appears as solidarity in that struggle. All Marcuse's later attempts to reach the concrete, through such concepts as the "new sensibility," sensuousness, the aesthetic, the instincts, resonate with this original existential Marxist approach.

The motility of life promises revolutionary social change, but it is closely tied to a rather traditional Marxist politics that is no longer plausible after the triumph of fascism and the rise of post–war consumer society. Marcuse addresses these conditions after he joins the Frankfurt School with a radically historicized version of the Freudian instinct theory. Freud enables him to elaborate a richer concept of erotic and aesthetic experience as the basis for an entirely new kind of politics.

Marcuse's early Hegel interpretation haunts his later Freud interpretation. In *Eros and Civilization*, he recasts the Hegelian idea of life in terms of Freud's metapsychology (Marcuse 1966b, chap. 5). With Freud Marcuse describes the affirmation of life in peace and reconciliation as a libidinal attachment to the world, a sort of generalized erotics. The death instinct is mobilized in the struggle for survival and takes exaggerated forms in competition, violence, and aggression. The balance between the instincts is historically relative. The great wealth of modern societies could tip that balance in favor of life if obsolete institutions, technologies, and character structures were transformed. The possibility of such a transformation is now rooted in the aesthetic sphere which, following Freud, Marcuse grounds in *eros*.

Like Adorno, Marcuse turns to aesthetics for some trace of negativity in the face of the breakdown of the link between theory and practice. This turn belongs to a long tradition, particularly strong in Germany, of aesthetic opposition to the status quo.[6] Marcuse was prepared for this move long before he encountered the Frankfurt School: his first thesis explained the "artist novel" as a social critique of bourgeois society. Aesthetic radicalism reappears in *Eros and Civilization* where Marcuse reminds us that Schiller introduced art into social theory as a mediation between the abstract forms of civilization and the brutality of raw sensuous content (Marcuse 1966b, 186ff). Aesthetic education would prepare the people for freedom by refining their experience of the world. This was the original concept of "cultural revolution." Aesthetic mediation between "ought" and "is" represents an alternative to the Marxist unification of theory and practice through class struggle. Although aesthetics lacks the power directly to transform reality, at least it is a realm of actual experience. As such it moves beyond the idealism of pure ethical exigency.

In *Eros and Civilization* Marcuse identifies beauty with that which is "life-enhancing." "For the aesthetic needs have their own social content: they are the claims of the human organism, mind and body, for a dimension of fulfillment" denied by the established society (Marcuse 1969a, 27). The "ugliness" of modern societies is not merely unsatisfying to the senses of sight and hearing but offends against the "life instincts," i.e., against a wide range of needs that cannot be channeled into profit making and war. Erotic liberation in an advanced society is not about having fun, as supercilious critics have charged, but far more seriously concerns reconstructing modernity to serve the enhancement of life rather than the struggle for existence.

Marcuse's aesthetics raises as many problems as it solves. On the one hand, it grounds the argument in experience, a potentially universal domain in which all can participate and which can support a rational discourse. On the other hand, it valorizes one of the dimensions of experience that is most difficult to universalize rationally, art. Is Marcuse's aestheticism compatible with democracy? Democratic public reason is an intersubjective process, but insofar as the aesthetic is disclosed to an attuned sensibility, it appears to be private. The idea of beauty individualizes the encounter with the aesthetic as a higher truth available only to the happy few.

An Essay on Liberation addresses these objections in a surprising way. Marcuse's argument there is rooted not in the study of anti-capitalist struggle but in the history of the artistic avant gardes. His aesthetic theory attempts to recapitulate the turning point in the development of modernism when radical experiments in overcoming the split between art and life proliferated in the first years of the century. That movement, which preceded the conquest of the masses by the media, projected a concrete utopia that reappeared in the 1960s in the New Left counter-culture. On Marcuse's view, technological civilization can only be released from the bind it is caught in by a return to the promise of those early avant-gardes. But he insists that this time, even as art spreads it influence over the whole surface of society, it must retain its autonomy to play its transcending role. The end of the affirmative culture of the bourgeoisie is not the end of art (Marcuse 1969a, 47–48, Marcuse 1972, 108, 121).[7]

This aesthetic transformation is now possible, Marcuse argues. The weakening grip of one-dimensional society explained the emergence of "new needs" and a "new sensibility" among youth. It was not just that young people held radical political opinions. Mere opinions would have inspired readily cooptable demands for particular reforms within the system, not a bad thing, but not revolutionary either. The new sensibility operated at a more basic level than politics, at the level of the form of experience itself. Marcuse's notion of an "aesthetic *Lebenswelt*" (life-world) refers to an order of experience in which the aesthetic qualities of objects are revealed immediately to sensation. The aesthetic *Lebenswelt* entered everyday life on a mass scale through the New Left with revolutionary implications.

Aestheticizing Technology

The incredible inflation of aesthetics in Marcuse's thought has two rather different motives. In the first place, with speculative metaphysics discredited, he needs an experiential basis for identifying potentialities transcending the given. Second, he needs a more concrete and imaginatively rich value criterion than morality by which to measure the social world. Even if the advanced industrial society criticized in *One-Dimensional Man* could meet basic moral standards, it would still constitute a social universe hostile to human beings and nature. This is related to problems in its technical structure that must be met with aesthetically informed solutions.

The new sensibility of the New Left was supposed to accomplish these goals. It brought broadly conceived aesthetic criteria to bear on social life, inspiring demands for radical change (Marcuse 1969a, 28). Marcuse interprets this phenomenon repeatedly in different conceptual frameworks, once in Freudian terms as a recovery and release of erotic energies, a second time in terms of the early Marx's concept of sensuousness, and a third time in terms of the concept of beauty, which he relates to the history of art, to Plato's theory of recollection and to Kant's theory of the imagination. I will discuss these alternative accounts in the next chapter. The constellation formed by these analyses raises the exciting but rather marginal cultural innovations of the 1960s to the level of a world-historical experiment in the political realization of artistic ideals. There are obvious problems with this view, but focusing on them may cause us to overlook what is most interesting in Marcuse's theory, namely, his innovative approach to the politics of technology.[8]

Benjamin introduced the theme of the "aestheticization of politics" in a critique of Jünger's writings on modern war (Benjamin 1979). It was been widely assumed ever since that there is some essential connection between aestheticization and fascism, to which Jünger was attracted. But Martin Jay points out that there are also progressive interpretations of the aestheticization of politics, for example, Hannah Arendt's writings on Kant's aesthetic theory (Jay 1993). Arendt attempted to show that what Kant called "reflective judgment" can be generalized from art to politics (Arendt 1982, 106). Politics on this account is properly doxic rather than epistemic, a matter of opinion rather than knowledge, based on the imagination rather than on understanding, and precisely in this apparent deficiency lies its link to our freedom. Political judgment is not scientific but it does contain an appeal to the other for agreement. It is thus neither universally valid nor merely personal, but constructs an intersubjective bond through a special type of rational discourse.

To this example of a progressive aestheticization of politics cited by Jay, we can add Marcuse's radical politics of technology. In *An Essay on Liberation* Marcuse turns to Kant for a social theory of the imagination. In Kant the gap between the abstract universal categories of the understanding and sense experience is filled by the imagination. The imagination mediates between the senses and reason, raising sense experience to universality while bringing concepts down to earth as the organizing principles of its projections. It is the faculty of synthesis that enables a multiplicity of elements to be united both in judgment and perception.[9] So too the

imagination in Marcuse mediates between lived experience and technical principles, defining things through their realizable potentialities in a free society. Marcuse
holds out the possibility of a redeemed technology that would respect the potentialities of things and recognize the responsibility of human beings in the shaping
of worlds. Marcuse's new technology would enhance life rather than invent new
means of destruction. It would be environmentally aware and treat nature with
respect (Marcuse 1992). Recognition of humanity's place in the order of revealing
requires valorizing the sensibility and imagination through which the potentialities of things are manifested. A receptive—Marcuse calls it a "feminist"—
subjectivity would animate this technology, replacing the aggressive subject of the
existing technological rationality (Marcuse 1974).

There is a certain similarity between Marcuse's project and that of Arendt. Is it
a coincidence that both these Heidegger students affirm the disclosive power of art
and attempt to transpose it to the political domain by drawing on Kant's third
Critique? Where Arendt found a model of political judgment in Kant's theory of
the imagination, Marcuse took the more radical route of applying that theory to
technology. Just as Arendt found resources in Kant for validating the debates of the
polis, so Marcuse found resources for bringing technology into the *polis* as one
among many controversial issues to be decided there.

Marcuse's theory of the new technology depends not only on Kant but also on
the Frankfurt School's speculative critique of the positivistic limitations of Enlightenment reason. The questionable historical validity of this theory is less important
than the perspective it opens on the future. According to Adorno and Horkheimer,
the original mode of experience was more primitive but in some respects richer
than the restricted experience that emerges with class society. Capable in principle of responding to the objective world in its many dimensions, in practice
reason and sensibility are channeled into the struggle for survival. Experiential
contents that go beyond what is required for victory in that struggle are derealized
and treated as mere fantasy. The realm of art differentiated out as the imagination
and reason split apart in this context. Reason became technical while the imagination conserved counterfactual images of a harmonious world, a persistent
negativity that was safely confined to a marginal artistic realm (Adorno and
Horkheimer 1972, 32ff). Marcuse argues that the recovery of a richer concept of
reason incorporating the imagination is possible once again now that technological advance has in principle ended the struggle for survival.

A transformed sensibility "free for the liberating exigencies of the imagination," arrives at very different ways of understanding and mastering the world
(Marcuse 1969a, 31). It perceives potentialities in the objects themselves, as potentialities *of* those objects, and not as arbitrary desires or wishes of the subject. These
potentialities are known through imaginatively informed aesthetic judgments of
social reality.

What kind of knowledge is this knowledge of potentialities? This is the question of what Heidegger called "productive seeing," which Marcuse will treat as the

mode of abstraction appropriate to a modern reconstruction of the concept of essence. Once metaphysics and tradition are ruled out of order, it is only through the imaginative grasp of reality that reason can go beyond mere cataloguing and quantifying of objects toward an appreciation of their essential truth. Reflection on aesthetic experience supports a type of judgment that can identify the significant "Form" of reality, distinguishing essence from accident, higher potentiality from limited empirical existence. Following Hegel, Marcuse calls this abstractive act associated with aesthetic perception an "aesthetic reduction" (Marcuse 1964, 239–40). It strips away the contingent aspects of objects that restrict and stunt them in order to get at what they could be if released to their free development. The aesthetic reduction verifies at the theoretical level the claims of aesthetic experience and translates that experience into knowledge. Here beauty is the symbol of the good, the disclosure of being in its fullness.

This theory of the imagination is obviously derived from the model of art but it paints not just the canvas but all of nature. With the abolition of scarcity in advanced societies, the artistic imagination can overflow the boundaries of art to occupy the place of the Kantian transcendental imagination. This is one way of interpreting the project of the avant-gardes, which attempted at an early date to abolish the institution of art in order to realize its principles in everyday life. That project returns in the New Left. Responding to the revolt of the repressed sensibility, the New Left "invokes the sensuous power of the imagination" and projects a fundamental reorganization of the faculties (Marcuse 1969a, 30). From its marginal position the imagination moves to the center of the stage as the integrative faculty reconciling the demands of art and technology and incorporating nature into history. In a liberated society it would become "productive" in reality, like the imagination of the artistic creator, and would guide technical practice in the work of "pacifying existence."

> The rationality of art, its ability to 'project' existence, to define yet unrealized possibilities could then be envisaged as *validated by and functioning in the scientific-technological transformation of the world.* (Marcuse 1964, 239)

> The liberated consciousness would promote the development of a science and technology free to discover and realize the possibilities of things and men in the protection and gratification of life, playing with the potentialities of form and matter for the attainment of this goal. Technique would then tend to become art, and art would tend to form reality: the opposition between imagination and reason, higher and lower faculties, poetic and scientific thought, would be invalidated. Emergence of a new Reality Principle: under which a new sensibility and a desublimated scientific intelligence would combine in the creation of an *aesthetic ethos.* (Marcuse 1969a, 24)

Technology and Rationality

Technological Rationality

Marx claimed that at the end of the capitalist era social advance would be a condition for technical advance. But traditional Marxism reduced this Marxian idea to a complaint that capitalist society makes a bad use of technology and puts obstacles in the path of economic growth. This was not Marcuse's idea at all. On his account, growth of the existing technical base would be a disaster. This technology cannot simply be "used" to realize radical ends. What sense would it make to try to turn the assembly line into a scene of self-expression, or to broadcast propaganda for free thought? The systemic character of modern technology blocks recourse to it for these purposes. Technology has a logic of its own independent of the goals it serves. To the extent that this is true, merely changing goals would not change that logic, which is the source of the ultimate threat.

To make a difference at that level, not just the *ends* of production, but the *means* must be transformed insofar as they incorporate domination in their structure. A true alternative would change the base as well as the institutional superstructures. A postrevolutionary society could create a new science and technology that would place us in harmony rather than in conflict with nature. The new science and technology would treat nature as another subject instead of as mere raw materials. Human beings would learn to achieve their aims through realizing nature's inherent potentialities instead of laying it waste for the sake of power and profit (Marcuse 1972, 65). Marcuse writes

> Freedom indeed depends largely on technical progress, on the advancement of science. But this fact easily obscures the essential precondition: in order to become vehicles of freedom, science and technology would have to change their present direction and goals; they would have to be reconstructed in accord with a new sensibility—the demands of the life instincts. Then one could speak of a technology of liberation, product of a scientific imagination free to project and design the forms of a human universe without exploitation and toil. (Marcuse 1969a, 19)

This emphasis on technical transformation distinguishes Marcuse from both Heidegger and the rest of the Frankfurt School. True, technology has the power and consequences Heidegger, Adorno, and Horkheimer deplore, but it also holds a promise. In Heidegger the most one can hope for is a "free relation to technology," a salutary change in attitude; and Adorno and Horkheimer offer little more with their concept of Enlightenment tempered by "mindfulness [*Eingedenken*] of nature" (Heidegger 1977, 54; Adorno and Horkheimer 1972, 40). Far more radical, Marcuse calls for change in the very nature of technological rationality, which would be fundamentally modified by the abolition of class society and its associated "performance principle." The question of technology then is not only an ontological question of what technology is making of us; that question needs to be posed, to be sure, but we must also ask the political question of what we can make of technology.

Marcuse's argument culminates in the demand for a radical change in technological rationality. But the very concept of technological rationality is obscure. The difficulty is at least partly his fault. He sometimes equates "technological rationality" with the ratio of technology in general, or the existing technology only, and he sometimes employs it in modified forms such as "post-technological rationality" or the "technological rationality of art" to refer to a future liberated *techné* (Marcuse 1964, 235, xlviii, 238, 239). A common reading stemming from Habermas identifies Marcuse's notion with the generic interest in technical control, abstract efficiency (Habermas 1970).[10] On that reading, fundamental technological reform of the sort Marcuse advocates would be impossible, violating a basic condition of human existence.

In Habermas, technical reason, stripped down to its essential constituents, is sharply distinguished from other forms of thought and feeling. It is a quasi-transcendental or anthropologically general faculty, "blended" with other faculties in concrete situations but tending toward its pure form in highly differentiated modern societies. Judged from the standpoint of this generic theory of technical action, Marcuse's historical theory is incomprehensible or insignificant. On these terms, either his critique of technological rationality implies the need for an entirely new kind of technology that would not involve control and efficiency, a nonsensical idea, or he merely wrote in a confusing way about the need to apply technology to new purposes, a trivial idea.

(1) If the new aestheticized technology is based on completely new technical principles, then the whole theory is unbelievable. Who is going to invent those principles, and what will they be like? Although it sometimes sounds as though Marcuse intends a total break with the past, the revolution that interests him is not supposed to refute elementary arithmetic, change a decimal place in *pi*, or find aesthetically pleasing substitutes for the lever and the wheel. Nor would it, as Habermas suggests, require personal communication with nature rather than technical control of it. Marcuse does not believe it possible to replace technology as we know it with some sort of mystical union. That view he attributes to his old friend Norman Brown and distinguishes sharply from his own position (Marcuse 1968, 238ff).

(2) Perhaps Marcuse has more modest ambitions and merely hopes that current technology will be used to enhance rather than to destroy life. But if he intended nothing more innovative than this, it is difficult to figure out how *practically* his position differs from a simple change of goals. Of course we could make toys and medicine instead of weapons, but would that require *fundamental* technological change? If the new technology is simply a new application of the old, it is difficult to see what all the hoopla is about. Indeed, on this interpretation Marcuse's position is indistinguishable from ordinary technological

optimism, with its all too familiar technocratic implications (Alford 1985, 175–76). But Marcuse himself consistently talks in terms of the need for a change in *rationality* and not merely in applications.

This is the Marcusian enigma that has bedeviled his critics. I want to suggest a different interpretation that, while it deflates Marcuse's speculative ambitions somewhat, at least does not take him for a dreamer. This interpretation accords with his own emphasis on the importance of situating abstract concepts like "rationality" in a concrete social context (Marcuse 1968, 223–24). From that standpoint, his concept of technological rationality cannot be identical with the formal concepts of efficiency and control, but must have a content as a socially specific pattern of goal orientation; nor can it be a mere ideological "reflection," for then it would have neither technical efficacy nor truth value.

The Forms of Reason

Marcuse was acutely aware of several likely misunderstandings of his work. He worried that he would be taken for a reactionary who condemns the whole project of Enlightenment in criticizing modern technology. He acknowledged the risk that his new theory of sensation would be confounded with spiritualistic re-enchantment, a mere projection of "secret hopes" onto a sublimely indifferent nature. Anticipating these criticisms, he writes therefore that

> The critique of technology aims neither at a romantic regression nor at a spiritual restoration of "values." The oppressive features of technological society are *not* due to excessive materialism and technicism. On the contrary, it seems that the causes of the trouble are rather in the *arrest* of materialism and technological rationality, that is to say, in the restraints imposed on the *materialization* of values. (Marcuse 2001, 57)

The notion of "materialization of values" is the counterpart to Marcuse's critique of the neutrality of technology. Technology is not essentially value neutral but rather, under capitalism, the neutralization of the traditional values that governed it in earlier times adapts it to the pursuit of profit and power. These narrow capitalist values no longer respect the object, human beings, limits of any kind. Value free technology is "free" to treat everything and everyone as raw materials. The Heideggerian enframing reappears here seamlessly integrated to Marcuse's Marxism.

In Heidegger this type of technology is contrasted with Greek *techné* and a similar contrast is implied in Marcuse's critique. As we saw with Plato, *techné* combines objectively conceived values with technical principles. Marcuse proposes that the neutrality of technology can be overcome through restoring values to their place in the structure of technical reason. But in what would the new technical values be grounded? Ideology critique and cultural relativism have demystified the objective values the Greeks believed in. There is no way "back to virtue," as some philosophers have recently proposed. Instead, Marcuse argues that modern technology must be redesigned by the "productive imagination" selecting from a range of possibilities on the basis of a preference for human freedom and fulfillment, the affirmation of life (Marcuse 1964, 220). No doubt Marcuse's theory would be more sympathetically received today had he avoided such "unscientific" assumptions and either invoked a transcendental ground for values à la Habermas, or the freedom of the postmodern subject willfully to construct identities and realities.

Marcuse paid no attention to the latter view which was only beginning its ascent during his last years, but he does have an implicit answer to the Habermasian objection. His position is based on the older Frankfurt School conception of a holistic form of reason that is in some sense truer than the truncated instrumentalism of modernity. Habermas completely reversed his position. Indeed, he sees an ultimately salutary differentiation of reason from myth in precisely the phenomena condemned by his predecessors.

Marcuse remained faithful to their fundamental insight, which Horkheimer expresses in the notion that in modern times "the content of reason is reduced arbitrarily" (Horkheimer 1947, 20). Horkheimer calls the value neutral rationality of the existing society "subjective reason." It strips away the value commitments of an earlier "objective reason" that was based on essential insight. This earlier form of reason prevailed in the *logos* of the ancient arts. According to Horkheimer, "subjective" and "objective" reason are not opposites or alternatives but fractured moments of a totality that can only be anticipated today. He concludes that "The task of philosophy is not stubbornly to play the one against the other, but to foster a mutual critique and thus, if possible, to prepare in the intellectual realm the reconciliation of the two in reality" (Horkheimer 1947, 174). The early Frankfurt School thus held out the hope of reconstituting a richer concept of reason that would incorporate both values and science.

This conception, with its faith that we can find traces of the ideal in the real, could not be further from the over-burdened subjectivity of both transcendentalism and constructivism. It is true that Horkheimer, like Adorno, remained stubbornly bound to a negative dialectic, a pure critique. As Patrick Murray notes, their "reconciliation-without-identification between spirit and nature remains a promissory note" (Murray 1982, 228).[11]

Habermas dropped the promise. He restored a version of objective reason in a domain, communication, which he held separate from scientific-technical rationality. Normativity was saved but at the expense of reconciliation. Marcuse transgressed Horkheimer's self-imposed limitation and went on to fulfill the promise. His redemption of technology reconciles the antinomial moments of rationality identified by Horkheimer.

Whereas for Habermas scientific-technical rationality responds to a pure interest in control, Marcuse argues that control is itself subordinated to the interest of life. He recognizes of course that technology can be used to destroy life, but, he writes, "Then we are this side of discourse and logic, for logic and discourse developed as instruments of the effort to 'save' and fulfill life" (Marcuse 2001, 40). Marcuse thus posits a "*final technological cause*" (Marcuse 1989, 124). "Discourse and logic," subordinated to an objective purpose, are of course the *logos*. On this account Plato's version of *techné* would be normal rather than modern "differentiated" "value free" technology. Indeed, Marcuse claims that "advanced industrial society is not defined by technological rationality, but rather by the opposite. Namely, by the blocking, by the arrest, and by the perversion of technological rationality" (Marcuse 2001, 84). In this passage "technological rationality" refers to the "inherent end and purpose of technology" throughout history, i.e., to serve human needs (Marcuse 2001, 84). With this in mind, "authentic" technical progress can be distinguished from its repressive simulacrum (Marcuse 2001, 85). We are back to the contrast of *techné* and *empeiria*.

This is the normative basis of the critique of technology in *One-Dimensional Man*. The book concludes with a theory of the rationality of civilizational "projects." Marcuse adopts the Sartrean term to indicate that his analysis operates at the existential level, the level of the *a priori* forms of social experience and practice. He argues that we can judge these projects by the extent to which they fulfill the available technical potential for supporting life. A "transcendent project" would compare favorably with the existing civilization if it not only preserved and furthered the latter's technical achievements but also promised "a greater chance for the pacification of existence, within the framework of institutions which offer a greater chance for the free development of human needs and faculties" (Marcuse 1964, 220).

Marcuse claims to be judging the "truth" of civilizational projects in terms of the value they accord life. He defends this normative conception of truth, arguing that "the very concept of reason originates in this value judgment, and . . . the concept of truth cannot be divorced from the value of Reason" (Marcuse 1964, 220). But this argument is not as telling as Marcuse supposes. The issue is not the origin of reason but its destiny. The problem is precisely that truth has been divorced from the value of reason in the course of modern history. It is this which gives rise to the "dialectic of Enlightenment." This unfortunate fact is related to a change in the conception of nature. Only an alternative conception of nature can undo the damage at the theoretical level. The question then is whether Marcuse has such an alternative and whether it is convincing.

I will return to the question of nature in more detail in the next chapter. In brief, Marcuse argues that the scientific concept of nature belongs ultimately to history and is conditioned by the same forces that condition the uses and meanings of nature in its social context. If this is true, then the nature studied by natural science is an abstraction from a richer whole that can only be understood in social and historical terms. On these terms, it makes sense to claim that reason is essentially practical, essentially committed to the fulfillment of human needs, and not a pure spectator (Marcuse 1964, 218–19). This is more or less the conception of reason as *logos* that prevails in Plato and Aristotle and which Heidegger recovers in a modern form through a phenomenological interpretation of *techné*. Surprisingly, this conception of reason is compatible with the most recent trends in technology studies.

Marcuse and Technology Studies

Science and technology pose different problems for Marcuse's theory which he did not clearly distinguish. We can make sense of his approach to technology in a relatively straightforward way. But to do so persuasively we need to show how Marcuse's philosophical categories play out in the new field of technology studies. Marcuse's own discourse has powerful philosophical and political resonances which cannot be duplicated at the sociological level, but neither can contemporary research into technology be pursued exclusively at Marcuse's level of abstraction.

The environmental movement and the computerization of society have brought us into contact with technology in new ways Marcuse did not anticipate. They have made us far more aware of the contingency of design on social and political choices than we were a generation ago. At the same time, sociologists and historians of technology have shown that applications are not designed in function of abstract technical principles alone but emerge from concrete technical disciplines applied in social contexts. Naturally, those disciplines incorporate technical principles, but they include much besides. As social institutions, they operate under the influence of "actors," social groups with the power to define problems and select solutions. Designs that flow from these sources accord with the interests, ideology, and way of life of those groups. Of all the various ways in which a device can be designed to accomplish a certain purpose, that one will be chosen that satisfies both technical and social criteria.[12]

Unfortunately, Marcuse never developed concepts at this concrete sociological level, but he did give a more abstract interpretation of technological rationality that can be applied in a social context. Social constructivism, actor network theory, and the study of large-scale technical systems have developed useful concepts that are anticipated by Marcuse or easily applied to the explanation of his thought. We can thus translate Marcuse's insights into the basis for a radical sociology of technology. Here are some examples of anticipations and convergences that give a hint of this potential.

- The notion that technological design is not governed by efficiency or scientific principles but is decided by socially situated actors resembles Marcuse's critique of the neutrality of technology and his notion of socially determined technological projects (Bijker, et al., 1987). Marcuse goes beyond current technology studies in facing the political implications of the nonneutrality of technology. If actors impose designs accommodated to their way of life, then surely we should judge the results in terms of some sort of normative criteria (Marcuse 1964, 220ff).

- This approach to the social bias of technical decisions presupposes two further constructivist principles, the technical underdetermination of design and the interpretative flexibility of artifacts. It makes sense to analyze technology in social terms only if the meaning of artifacts is socially determined and contested, and workable alternatives are available (Bijker, et al., 1987). Marcuse presupposed something similar as the basis for his own notion of reconstruction of the technical base. In my own work I have tried to show how this presupposition can be made explicit and defended.

- Actor network theory proposes a concept of "delegation" according to which a value may be embodied either in discourse as a moral imperative, or in design through technical choices that enforce appropriate behavior. For example, the value of safety may be supported by a sign reminding users of a device to handle it carefully, or by a design which makes it impossible to use the device without taking the necessary precautions (Latour 1992). Marcuse might be said to offer the "macro" version of this "micro" thesis according to which norms are embodied in devices and constrain ("script") behavior (Marcuse 1964, 9ff).

- Finally, the theory of large-scale technical systems explains how technologies such as electric power and the airline industry bind huge populations and things together in both causal and symbolic relations. This approach has parallels in the Heideggerian enframing and in Marcuse's version of it. Some historians and sociologists of technology have in fact made the connection between Heidegger and their empirical research (Hughes 1989; Gras 1993). Marcuse adds a much needed perspective on the political implications of the systematization of society.

As these examples show, Marcuse allows us to draw rather more radical conclusions from technology studies than is customary. I realize that many students of technology dismiss both Heidegger and Marcuse and insist that we are wasting our time on useless abstractions when we could be doing useful empirical research. I do not think philosophers need to take lessons in empiricism from social scientists. These are old debates too tedious to repeat once again. Marcuse operates at a high level of abstraction, to be sure, but our task is to relate levels of abstraction—all we have to work with in the end—not to claim a false concreteness for empirical facts that owe their meaning to such nonfacts as traditions, the imaginary, and the global social context.[13]

This is what I have attempted to do in my own writings, borrowing freely from Marcuse and technology studies. I have introduced the concept of the "technical code" to explain Marcuse's concept of technological rationality in a more concrete sociological context. The technical code consists in fundamental social imperatives *in the form in which they are internalized by a technical culture*. These imperatives—Marcuse would call them "*a prioris*"—appear in technical disciplines as standards and specifications that have an apparently neutral aspect. Husserl once said that "Tradition is forgetfulness of the origin."[14] This is certainly true of technical disciplines which live in blissful ignorance of their own past, proclaiming their autonomy for all to hear while historians uncover the many acts of power that shaped them. The history takes us back to the actors who struggled to impose their interests and vision through encoding emerging technologies (Marcuse 1968, 215–16; Feenberg 1999, 87–89). The process continues today and we need the concepts to understand it.

This theory of technical codes has implications for the relation of technology and values. We can no longer accept the Weberian conception of technology as a value-free enterprise. Sociology of technology routinely tracks the influence of values on design. But this also calls into question the usual understanding of values. Are values, as is commonly supposed, subjective feelings rather than solid facts? Marcuse relativizes this distinction. He argues that values appear as values rather than as (technical) facts to the extent that they have been excluded from reality in the interests of a repressive organization of society. Technology itself could accommodate them were it "liberated" from the constraints of the existing society (Marcuse 2001, 54).

We might reformulate this insight to say that design embodies only a subset of the values circulating in society at any given time. Those not so embodied appear discursively rather than technically, but the two forms of value are not irrevocably cut off from each other. The "ideological" values can enter the technical realm through different design choices ("delegations") imposed by a different relation of political and social forces. This is an argument of particular importance for environmentalism. Conservative opponents of environmental reform routinely contrast "rational" technology with supposedly "irrational," "emotional," or "ideological" values. This contrast is spurious as a general rule if not in all particular cases.

Such fundamental social imperatives as environmental protection are beginning to shape an alternative technological rationality in Marcuse's sense. These imperatives are the "technological *a priori*" embodied in the devices and systems that emerge from the culture and reinforce its basic values. As we have seen, Marcuse argues that life affirming values are actually internal to technology and are not an arbitrary imposition. While this claim is excessively general, it can be given a concrete content in terms of technical codes. Each such code affirms life within the limits of the technical knowledge and the repressive structure of the dominant regime. Ethical and aesthetic mediations play an essential role in this process, integrating technical principles to a design that coheres with social and natural values. What makes capitalism special is the progressive reduction and neutralization of such mediations, the inherited *logos*, wherever they conflict with a narrow pecuniary interest.[15]

This reductive process is the source of the apparent purification of technological rationality in modern times, and not, as Weber and Habermas claim, the emergence of an original essence of technology from out of the undifferentiated social magma of premodern society. If capitalism is unique, that is not because it has freed technology from "nontechnical" concerns. Rather, capitalism is the first social system to repress the underlying population primarily through technology rather than through religion, ritual, and violence, and the first to treat it as essentially neutral rather than governed by an inherent *logos*. In this sense "neutral" capitalist technology can be said to be "political" without mystification or risk of confusion.

The Affirmation of Life

A variety of different rationalities operate at the level of the concrete forms of technical culture and it is up to us to judge between them and choose the best according to the immanent criterion implied in the life affirming mission of technology. Environmentalism has allowed us to give a concrete content to this notion as Marcuse himself noted at the end of his life (Marcuse 1992). A technological rationality oriented toward the preservation and enhancement of human life and nonhuman nature contrasts sharply with one oriented toward competition for control of resources and short-term exploitation.

We are supposed to be able to discover what this means concretely in any given situation by essential insight, by a reason informed by aesthetic sensibility and imagination and capable of identifying "objective values." This claim is both speculative and normative. It lies beyond the scope of social science and requires a very different kind of rationale.

The difficulties of interpretation are manifold. Marcuse's own explanations are suggestive but fall short of our expectations. Perhaps this is inevitable with such an ambitious claim. But in a broad sense, the idea of affirmation of life is obvious and compelling. Who can deny that monstrous indifference to life prevailed throughout the 20th century in wars, genocides, tyrannies, and exploitation? Why *not* demand the affirmation of life in opposition to this disastrous evolution which threatens human survival? On the other hand, working out Marcuse's concept philosophically proves difficult.

What concretely does it mean to affirm life in the context of technical action? Whose lives and why some rather than others? How would agreement be reached on these and other specifics and how, once a consensus formed, would it be operationalized in technological design? Can the value of life be reconciled with technical action at all? All of these questions require answers before we can evaluate Marcuse's claim that technology can be reconstructed to respect the value of life. Here I can only sketch some points for reflection.

The recognition of the potentialities of nature is not about chemistry and physics but the uncovering of an "existential truth" (Marcuse 1972, 69). The existential connection between human beings and nature lies in their commonality as life. It is absurd to imagine humans outside nature. They are a part of it, they belong to it, and this is not merely an objective state of affairs but implies inbred harmonies that are unexplainable from a scientific standpoint but which are nevertheless real. These harmonies appear most obviously in the aesthetic relation to nature.[16] They penetrate science itself in the preference scientists show for simplicity and elegance of explanation. They can also guide practices that are respectful of nature. This is not to demand inaction. Obviously, as a part of nature, human beings intrude on the world around them, take up space, kill and eat, just like other animals. But it is still possible, within the limits of human self-assertion, to foster peace and order in the world rather than violence and destruction. It is possible to organize a life-affirming way of life.

Life-affirming technology would thus not necessarily be more primitive than modern technology. The point is not to avoid disturbing nature but to avoid "violating" it (Marcuse 1972, 69). This position need not imply some pristine nature as a standard but it does entail recognition of the difference between traditional techniques and current capabilities. No doubt the builders of earlier generations turned farmland into cities and cut down trees for lumber. Going further back, farmers modified and domesticated the landscape to make it suitable for growing food. We inherit all these achievements and should not shun them because of the changes nature suffered at human hands. But surely we can distinguish the pace and scope of such interventions from modern methods. Even where true violations of nature took place, as in the deforestation of much of the Mediterranean coast, the fact that the destruction took centuries is reassuring: at least humans and animals had time to adjust.

Nature is violated in a more urgent sense where hills and mountains are leveled for mining or real estate development, species annihilated as their habitats are destroyed, forests clear cut, genetic modifications of plants and animals introduced without regard for future consequences, and all this done at the accelerated pace of modern business and government. That our civilization is certainly based on earlier violations of nature is not a reason to continue the practice, especially not now that our technologies are so much more powerful than those employed in the past. It is true that low tech methods of destroying the rain forests are proving quite effective, but this is a practice that should be stopped, not enhanced by modern logging techniques!

What would a life-affirming technological design look like? In one sense this is not a difficult question to answer because so many technologies already enhance life in obvious ways. Life as a value is present in the technical codes under which technologies are designed, the standards and practices in fields such as engineering. Consider, for example, the attention to safety in so many manufactured objects. So, in one sense, the demand for life-affirming technical designs is trivial. But in another sense it is not trivial at all but deeply challenging.

Quite radical changes in technologies will have to occur over the coming decades for something resembling our modern world to survive. The technologies we use today cannot preserve our mobility in space, our access to information, food, shelter, and medicine, and our security of life in the face of global warming and the massive pollution produced by modern industry in its present form. The system will soon suffer further stress from the economic development of India and China, with, as a consequence, rapidly rising world demand for oil and other raw materials. In one sense this is no surprise. What would be surprising would be technological stagnation; of course technology will change. In another sense, this is a contentious issue: *how* will technology change, in response to what criteria of development, in service to what values? World business has one answer, the movement for global justice another. From the standpoint of Marcuse's theory, a criterion based on the affirmation of life distinguishes their responses.

Technology and Values

Marcuse and Political Philosophy

How plausible is Marcuse's project? It is easy to dismiss his aesthetic reference in the name of standard notions of discursive rationality. This seems to be the line taken by most critical theorists under the influence of Habermas. However, the result is a rather narrow version of political philosophy, more or less identified with argument over moral rights, which does not take us far toward comprehending the complexity of modern political life and the conflicts to which it gives rise. Must we conclude that contemporary Critical Theory considers creative responses to social and political problems irredeemably irrational? It is precisely a theory of the rationality of such responses which Marcuse offers in a strained but nevertheless suggestive attempt to understand the political and social creativity of the 1960s.

Marcuse's approach differs fundamentally not only from Habermas's but from liberal political philosophy which also focuses on procedural notions of democratic rights. That focus results from an exclusive concern with consensus as the basis of social life. Without some procedural agreement ordering the community, substantive disagreements degenerate into disruptive violence. Liberal political theory interprets the fact of consensus in modern societies, which do not have an established worldview, in terms of an ideal of rational agreement on democratic rights. Even if we disagree on everything else, at least we agree on the correct procedures for handling disagreements. While there is no doubt some truth in this approach, it is often justified by exaggerating the degree of dissensus in modern societies. The supposed normative chaos of modernity is largely a myth which justifies thinning out the claims of political theory to rights alone.

In recent years some philosophers have noted the poverty of this liberal view. But attempts to fill in the picture with a complementary idea of the "good" usually fall back on mere traditionalism clothed in the rhetoric of multiculturalism. The critique of proceduralism has merit, but since technology also supplies a background consensus that everywhere trumps tradition, communitarians must ignore it to make their point. They are at one with liberalism in overlooking the central role of technology in organizing modern social life. This is not merely a practical matter.

The extensive coordinating functions of modern technology would break down without deep agreement on meanings and norms. This fact has become self-evident in the era of mass mobilization for consumption by the media. We can easily identify some of the chief elements of the technological consensus by simply watching television attentively. It is because we belong to this technological culture, as Heidegger pointed out in his own way, that we form a technological society. And it is precisely this technological culture which is incompatible with community. Transforming it is now the task.[17]

I do not think Marcuse would have sympathized with communitarianism in any case. It would have made no sense to him to go back to the tight restrictions of traditional community at the current level of development. It is possible and necessary to go forward toward a greater measure of peace, freedom, and fulfillment. I suggest that Marcuse's notion of an aesthetic criterion for the new technical *logos* be interpreted as an attempt to articulate a substantive, future oriented conception of democracy.

Is such a future imaginable? Not if technology and humanity are reified as permanently opposed domains. Marcuse's projection of a pacified society assumes that the "existential truth" of nature can be as widely perceived as the lies propagated by the media today (Marcuse 1972, 69). The citizens of a free society would be informed not merely by conflicting opinions and tastes, but also by consensual notions of beauty, order, appropriateness. Aesthetic forms would enter daily life and shape a different experience and ultimately a different technology which would in turn reinforce that experience. Is it likely that a new type of aesthetic consensus would emerge in a benevolent social environment in which human beings were free, their basic needs satisfied, their creativity nurtured? Why assume that people in a liberated society would be any more likely to share an aesthetic consensus than they are in the unfree society of today?

While it would take us far afield to respond adequately, a word of protest is necessary. These objections presuppose that the aesthetic has exclusively to do with high art and that the disputatiousness of intellectuals and artists characterizes modern society as a whole. Nothing could be further from the truth. Walt Disney long ago established a universal aesthetic consensus. If the cultural elites feel left out and sadly unable to defend their preferences, that is their problem. The modern world establishes aesthetic values, as have earlier societies, and reinforces and generalizes them through incorporating them into artifacts of one sort and another. What is different today is the role of organizations. Relatively self-conscious and short-lived corporations and political parties rather than the eternal church do the job.

The evolution of sensibility is a vast underlying tide on which these modern organizations navigate. Marcuse suggests the possibility of an evolution that would be reinforced and generalized through changes in technological design. Once one grasps the force of the technological consensus underlying our way of life today, it is more plausible to imagine changes at that level winning widespread agreement. This is not a reason for such changes, of course, but it matters politically that they could be widely shared were they to occur, independent of the question of justification. To be sure, there are problems with Marcuse's approach, but at least it offers a properly modern solution to the conundrum of rights and goods while promising a path to the realization of more liberating projects than those of either tradition or business.

Techné *Again: Epilogue with Plato*

Marcuse is engaged in defining the "good" in something like the sense in which modern political philosophy uses the term, but also in Plato's original sense. Plato's *Gorgias* is thus once again relevant to our inquiry. In that dialogue, the Good as such is divided into four subsidiary goods: pleasure, usefulness, beauty, and justice. All human beings pursue the Good according to Plato, and his fourfold division encompasses the motives that drive most people most of the time, identifying undeniably transhistorical aspects of human life. Yet each society grants a different meaning to the four goods and organizes their relations differently. This historical aspect of the Good was not recognized in antiquity, but it is obvious to us and subverts the claims of a moral universalism such as Plato's.

Classical reason, with its substantive value content, is victorious in Plato's dialogue but was later defeated by the positivist and relativist heritage of the Enlightenment. But now Marcuse will revive it in a new form as an alternative to the technological rationality of the post–war liberal technocracy. Like Socrates, Marcuse must recover essential thinking to find a place to stand to judge a society obsessed with wealth and power, but the logic of his argument is quite different from Socrates. The link between rationality and teleology has been broken for centuries. Callicles' descendants rule modern societies and this state of affairs cannot be reversed at the purely conceptual level, for example, by refuting hedonism (Marcuse 1964, 148). Indeed there is a sense in which hedonism, with its refusal of erotic restraint, offers a glimpse of liberation from a repressive, survival-oriented society (Marcuse 1968, 188).

This interpretation differs from Plato's in many respects, not least in defining the Good as the affirmation of life, *eros*. Usefulness (*ophelia*) in the simple form Socrates introduced it is no ally of philosophy now, but founds an operational rationality that replaces philosophy. From the standpoint of this modern rationalism, obligations flow from system requirements and not from essences; they do not transcend a bad reality as they did for Socrates, but guarantee its smooth functioning. The "natural justice" of our time is efficiency. With the exception of efficiency, all norms, both ethical and aesthetic, enter the limbo of conventionality to which Callicles long ago consigned them. The old philosophy is now considered outdated and speculative. Beauty has been reduced to packaging, a sales pitch, measured by its commercial value.

Thus, Marcuse, again like Socrates, must confront the skeptical critique of philosophy, and he too must pursue the argument under the limitations imposed by the adversary. Socrates accepted Callicles' challenge to argue "according to nature" rather than convention and was eventually able to overcome their opposition. Marcuse must also appeal to a common, i.e., modern, ground of argument in order to recover the full range of values. This ground is experience.

Just as Plato overcame the opposition of nature and culture in the myth of Rhadamanthys, so does Marcuse through the aesthetic interpretation of experience. I will discuss his method in detail in the next chapter, but for now it is sufficient to mention his conclusions. Needs and technology freed from their form in a repressive society play the role of *hedoné* (pleasure) and *ophelia* (usefulness). Although these are "natural" principles, Marcuse interprets them culturally. They are relativized through a theory of the historical development of the instincts and the social critique of technological rationality. *Kalon* (beauty) and *diké* (justice) return as aesthetics and ethics, cultural principles which now take on some of the characteristics of nature through Marcuse's Freudian interpretation of their "biological" basis.

In addition to the distinctions with which Plato worked, Marcuse introduces another axis, the difference between practice and theory, the realm of experience and that of objective representation. This second axis is related to the experiential requirements of an emancipatory politics. A democratic transformation of society must respond to practical public concerns. This was not an issue for Socrates. On the side of practice, we must include the "new" needs and aesthetically informed perceptions of a liberated sensuousness. The theoretical side consists in basic technical principles and ethical ideals. These must be reconciled with each other and with practice in a new technological rationality.

To each of these four goods there corresponds a specific privation: the old false needs of a competitive consumer society, the ugliness of the environment it creates, the immorality of exploitation, violence, and war essential to the workings of the

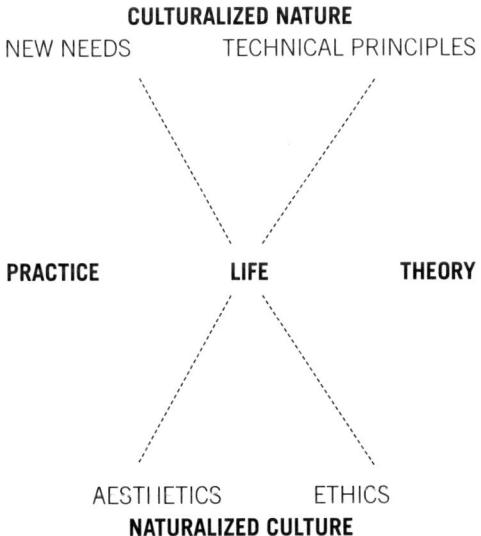

system, and finally the accidental failures of particular techniques and the more profound failure of the technological system as a whole to serve vital human needs and to protect the environment. All these privations are evoked and represented in one way or another by the small cultural elites that function as the critical consciousness of the society. From the Bohemian artistic subculture of the 19th century to the counter-culture of the 1960s, a critique unfolds that is progressively more concrete and realizable: the end of utopia.[18] The challenge of the late Marcuse is to theorize the generalization of that critique to the population as a whole through a transformation of sensibility.

Aesthetics here is not a matter of contemplation, but should be interpreted in classical terms as an ontological category. In its application to human affairs, it expresses the reflexive significance of the actors' actions for their own existence. In the myth of the Islands of the Blessed that concludes the *Gorgias*, the naked souls of the dead are judged in their reality. So the Marcusian aesthetic evaluates naked societies, stripped of their self-congratulatory media images. A society where homelessness, urban squalor, prisons, and war are commonplace defines itself by these "actions" on terms we can reasonably condemn on aesthetic grounds in this classical sense.

Nor is Marcuse's project so impractical as his very abstract language makes it appear. At one point, he mentions "gardens and parks and reservations" as a small example of the "liberating transformation" he awaits (Marcuse 1964, 240). More significantly, I think we already have weak versions of modern *technai* in such fields as medicine, architecture, and urban and environmental planning. Technical cultures based to a significant degree on life enhancing values derived from a long history and a wide range of experiences contend in these fields with narrow technocratic ambitions and commercialism. Each of these disciplines posits an idealized essence, such as health, the home, the city, the natural balance. Democracy requires the public discussion and refinement of these ideals in a context freed from propaganda, advertising, and technocratic and determinist ideology. This is not yet possible, but despite the obvious limitations of these disciplines, they offer at least an imperfect model for the new technological rationality Marcuse advocates. Generalizing this form of technological rationality and controlling it through democratic political debate is no mere fantasy but a concrete project of resistance to techno-corporate power.

We are familiar today with two main kinds of politics. They are instrumental politics aimed at power, laws, and institutions; and identity politics through which individuals attempt to redefine their social roles and their place in society. I would argue that Marcuse, like the New Left itself, represents a third kind of politics. I call this a "civilizational politics," a politics of collective self-definition that concerns not power, laws, and institutions, but the very meaning of our humanity. On these terms, the political question is: What kind of people are we, what kind of world do we want to live in, what can we expect as a basic minimum level of justice and equality in our affairs? The New Left replied that we cannot go on as before and in so doing it echoed Marcuse's "great refusal" of advanced industrial society. Not out of generosity or personal self-sacrifice, but out of a larger sense of who and what we are, we need to acknowledge the mediocrity of the society and the injustices at its base. Ideologies that stand in the way, even if they be identified with "rationality" itself, must be overthrown. One widely distributed leaflet during the French May Events of 1968 announced, "Progress will be what we want it to be" (Feenberg and Freedman 2001, 77) That in a nutshell is the hopeful political message Marcuse tried to send, and it is not exhausted.

Chapter 6

The Question Concerning Nature

The Two Natures

In the dominant technocratic and positivist conception, scientific-technical reason is understood as an indifferent spectator on a reality passively awaiting quantification and control. In practice, this modern form of reason escapes many of the social involvements and limitations that confined it to a subordinate role in earlier societies. But we have seen that in the case of technology, the escape is more apparent than real. Although it frees itself from tradition, it comes under the sway of competing contemporary social forces. These forces respond to different conceptions of nature. The dominant conception of technology is contested by social movements that emphasize respect for nature and its inherent potential for growth and development. What about science? Does it address the same conception of nature as technology? Is nature as an object of technology identical with the nature of natural scientific research? Is science too caught up in the politics of nature that emerge around technology?

In this chapter I will consider Marcuse's answer to these difficult questions. The path I will trace here is arduous because Marcuse's position is unclear. He follows Heidegger in arguing for the priority of technology over science. The project of technological domination thus defines the scientific concept of nature; presumably the overthrow of the former would lead to the transformation of the latter and to the invention of a new science. That science will change in the future is not in doubt, nor that the changes it will undergo will bear some relation to changes in the broader culture. But this vague general dependence of science on society is quite different from the rather more specific conception of technological change Marcuse envisages. I will argue here that the two natures of science and technology are not identical and that the attempt to tie technological transformation to a change in the scientific conception of nature is a false path, a dead end.

Why did Marcuse follow this path? That, I think, is a consequence of the way in which he mixed a Heideggerian critique of technology with the early Marx's notion of the alienation of nature. Scientific nature becomes the object of transformative practice when reinterpreted on these terms. The result is no more plausible today than were Marx's similar conclusions in 1844. Marcuse could have avoided this outcome had he pursued the phenomenological approach at which he hints to its logical conclusion. Then he would have been able to ground his critique of technology on the lived experience of nature independent of science. Categories such as health and sensual beauty can plausibly guide the reconstruction of important aspects of technology, although their relevance to the scientific conception of nature is questionable at best. In what follows, I will show how this alternative implied in Marcuse's approach might have played out.

The Correlations

The question concerning technology leads in Marcuse to the still deeper question of the relation of nature and culture. This problem arises in the context of the Frankfurt School's critical appropriation of Kant, Hegel, and Marx. Horkheimer, Adorno, and Marcuse have a paradoxical relationship to this tradition. They draw on its discovery of the creative role of the autonomous subject in establishing a world, and yet they resist the radical constructivist conclusion to which the argument tends.[1]

This ambivalence is particularly strong in Marcuse. It is reflected in a theoretical move implicit in much of his later work. I call this move "deconstructive," although not in any orthodox sense. We find him frequently engaged with antinomial opposites he attempts to subvert, playing one off against the other to reach a position that defies the categories of the philosophical tradition. The most important such antinomy divides nature from culture. It reappears in many forms, most notably in the opposition of instinct and socialization, sensation and reality, and facts and values. In what follows I will discuss Marcuse's various approaches to these versions of the antinomy.

The antinomy is a remote consequence of the Kantian construction of experience as a correlation between subject and object. Until Kant most philosophers were realists of one sort or another. They therefore assumed that the unity and coherence of things in the world lay within those things themselves. Kant for the first time demonstrated that this unity and coherence was a result of our concepts rather than a fact of nature. Concepts did not merely correspond with reality, they "synthesized" it. From this insight stems a long line of speculations on the essential correlation between concepts and things, subject and object, mind and world, theory and observation, and so on. But Kant's correlations extruded an alien thing in itself as the other of experience. Nature was doubled into an experienced world and an unknowable transcendence. His successors struggled to eliminate the unwanted offspring of the theory in order to reconceptualize the correlations as guarantors of truth and reconciliation.

Hegel eliminated the thing in itself by interpreting the correlations historically, as a process in which the unmediated opposition of their poles was overcome and reconciled. In the *Phenomenology* that overcoming occurred through "labor," either literally as work or figuratively as cultural creativity. The intelligibility of the world was a result of human activity in a far more concrete sense than for Kant. The Hegelian concept of totality derives directly from this approach. The harmony of subject and object, value and fact that the Greeks found in the world, Hegel finds again in the activity of "spirit." An echo of this conception resounds in the modern concept of culture which attributes a special type of reality to social objects that acquire their existence as such in a relationship to a conscious subject.

Hegel's theme was reconciliation of the contraries through an idealized notion of labor. Ludwig Feuerbach naturalized this Hegelian insight with his interpretation of God as an alienated projection of the community. The early Marx applied Feuerbach's method to nature itself which, like God, now appeared as a human product. But unlike God, nature is not an imaginary entity. Alienation from nature is experienced physically in pain and hunger. The correlation of subject and object, and their reconciliation in a unity now appeared as a demand for revolution against the real disunity capitalism imposes.

Once the unification of the real by concepts was historicized, it mattered whose concepts were doing the unifying. It was not the revolution. With the rise and stabilization of modern industrialism and its totalitarian apotheosis, the humanization of nature came to mean the assimilation of the objective world to the very apparatus of production socialism was supposed to overthrow. A dystopian caricature of Marx's utopian projection prevailed in both the capitalist and communist worlds. The Frankfurt School attempted to reassert the claims of the object, emphasizing nonidentity against the all-conquering rush to bring everything under "concepts" imposed by industry and administration. Nature, as the unassimilated other, was reevaluated positively.

This correction was not intended to rescind the Kantian–Hegelian insight into the ontological role of human activity so much as to moderate its Promethean thrust. After all, the human subject is also an object in the world and has rights and claims as such that must not be ignored by overweening subjectivity. That there is something, a trace however small, not assimilated to subjectivity becomes the article of faith on which the possibility of resistance depends. This trace commands receptivity rather than activity, which has exceeded its mandate with catastrophic consequences. So concludes not only Adorno and Horkheimer, but also Heidegger in his own way.

But the Frankfurt School was unable to develop its insight coherently, or so it appears to me. It is impossible simply to choose between identity and nonidentity, reconciliation and resistance. Regression to pre–Kantian realism is excluded by the whole history of modern philosophy, but the bare assertion of a mysterious dissonance at the core of reality makes no sense in the post–Kantian context. How would such a dissonance enter experience? Under what concept would it be understood? How could it avoid becoming a component in the apparatus of identification, for example, an aesthetic *point d'honneur* legitimating the everyday ugliness and violence of the established order? If it fell under no concept, how would it differ from mental illness as an incoherent breakdown of meaning? The endless oscillation and mutual correction between subject and object, history and nature recommended by Adorno is not so much a solution to the enigma as a method for canceling any solution, most especially of course the bad ones that currently prevail in the societies of "total administration."

This inconclusive search for a resistant core is the background against which Marcuse too develops his theory. Nonidentity is the essential evidence in the age of totalitarianisms, both hard and soft. But under the impact of the New Left, Marcuse's position evolves in a very different direction from Adorno's. The correlation of subject and object is doubled now, and appears both in the guise of one-dimensionality and as a utopian alternative that would reconcile the nonidentical contraries without canceling their difference. The final antinomy thus opposes nonidentity to identity. Marcuse's deconstruction of this opposition aims to resolve the contradiction between activity and receptivity in modern thought.

Marcuse's deconstructions bring him into proximity to phenomenology. Edmund Husserl interprets the correlation of subject and object as a fundamental fact of lived experience. Husserl "suspended" the "natural attitude" in which we understand ourselves and things as existing in objective causal relations in order to focus attention on the flow of experience itself, which he called "pure consciousness." The intelligibility of the world is constituted synthetically in it in some sense that Husserl never clearly explains. From this experiential standpoint, Husserl goes beyond the correlations between cognitively significant features of concepts and things in Kant, and the similar correlation between labor and its products in Hegel and Marx. Correlation now applies to every aspect of the subject and object: the seeing corresponds to the seen, the fear to the fearful, the sense of beauty to the beautiful, the need to the object that fulfills it. The "intentional correlation" of subject and object refers to the essential necessity of these connections.

Marcuse's critique of Husserl and Heidegger in the 1930s was ferocious, but in his late work Marcuse hints at a return to phenomenology with the use of the term "*Lebenswelt*," the Husserlian counter to Heidegger's *In-der-Welt-sein* (being-in-the-world). Elsewhere Marcuse mentions the "existential truth" of nature, and argues that aesthetics identifies "objective values" which must be "materialized" in technology. These locutions suggest a phenomenological notion of intentional correlation between subject and object.

But although Marcuse presupposes something like phenomenology, he no longer articulates its premises. Instead, he goes back to a framework derived from the early Marx. That Marxian framework resembles phenomenology in identifying a broad range of correlations of subject and object, but it suffers from a confusing ambiguity about the ontological status of nature. As a result Marcuse's speculations on the relations of nature and culture are suspended between objectivity and subjectivity, not a comfortable place for a philosophical theory (Feenberg 1999, 164–65).

I will argue that Marcuse could have formulated his late position more convincingly as a modern return to *techné*. To do so, he would have had to reappropriate certain basic Heideggerian themes from the time of his studies in Freiburg. It is no accident that Marcuse's late work recalls this earliest beginning while also repressing it.

If it is possible to save Marcuse's argument in some other way, I have not discovered it. Without a phenomenological notion of being-in-the-world, he seems to be engaged in inflated rhetoric or, worse yet, a naïve metaphysical challenge to the modern scientific understanding of nature. It is clear that this was not his intent, but he failed to find a convincing way of expressing his intuition. After briefly visiting the labyrinth of inappropriate concepts he introduces—instincts, innate ideas, recollection, forms of sensibility—I will follow this phenomenological trail in pursuit of a solution I doubt would have convinced him, but which may be useful to us in our conversation about technology today.

Marcuse's Deconstructions

Nature and Culture

I would like to begin by illustrating Marcuse's deconstructive strategy with his appropriation of Freudian instinct theory. This has confused many commentators who superciliously dismiss Marcuse's "biologism" without the slightest notion of what he was about. Marcuse's Freud interpretation is based on a deconstruction of the reified opposition of nature and culture that first emerged in the sophistic discourse of ancient Greece (we saw it with Callicles), and that continues to this day as a fundamental assumption of modern thought.

Notions like the "libido," the "reality principle," and the "pleasure principle" are thoroughly historicized in Marcuse's application. He claims that needs and qualities that have become so vital they cannot be modified or ignored can be considered as "biological," even "instinctual." Why he uses this vocabulary will be addressed in a moment, but, as Robert Pippin writes, "far from smuggling an *a priori* anthropology into critical theory (as readers of Marcuse sometimes charge), [he] argued that even the instincts should be viewed as historical phenomena" (Pippin 1988, 86). All that can be traced back to a realm prior to history is a primordial life energy that expresses itself in socially constructed forms under the horizon of the society that originally shaped it, and also, under certain conditions, beyond that horizon. Marcuse made this position explicit in a lengthy footnote to *An Essay on Liberation*.

> I use the terms "biological" and "biology" not in the sense of the scien-
> tific discipline, but in order to designate the process and the dimension
> in which inclinations, behavior patterns, and aspirations become vital
> needs which, if not satisfied, would cause dysfunction of the organism.
> Conversely, socially induced needs and aspirations may result in a more
> pleasurable organic behavior. If biological needs are defined as those
> which must be satisfied and for which no adequate substitute can be
> provided, certain cultural needs can "sink down" into the biology of man.
> We could then speak, for example, of the biological need of freedom, or
> of some aesthetic needs as having taken root in the organic structure of
> man, in his "nature," or rather "second nature". (Marcuse 1969a, 10)[2]

Marcuse's notion of biology is thus historically relative. Indeed, it seems that
Marcuse is a thoroughgoing relativist. But note the paradoxical naturalization of
the political and aesthetic ideals in which libidinal energy is sublimated. Just as the
natural instincts are shaped through and through by culture, so the cultural
heritage is rooted in "second nature." Culture is biologically relative.

Yet Marcuse is careful to explain that criteria of social advance are not grounded
on scientific biology but are discovered in historical struggles and artistic and
philosophic works. Despite their social origins, Marcuse argues that they transcend any particular historical period and shed light on human potentialities
generally. Works of art belong to their epoch and yet contain transcending
contents that have validity against the very historical universe in which they arise.
Similarly, the substantive universals of philosophy, such as freedom and happiness,
are not exhausted by the meaning they acquire in their original historical context.
Marcuse is no relativist after all.

One way to interpret these claims would be in terms of a traditional theory of
eternal values. Marcuse seems to hint at such a solution with surprising references
to "innate ideas" and Platonic recollection. This is the usual defense of universalism, but it does not quite fit the case. The universality of the truth revealed in
art and philosophy is a placeholder filled by historically specific content from one
age to the next. The beauty of art and the categories of philosophy interpret the
given world in terms of its negativity, its potentialities. They promise increased
freedom and happiness along a continuum that forms a tradition in which
contemporary thought can seek enlightenment. But there is no definitive transhistorical formulation of the content of this tradition, certainly not in classic
authors such as Plato or Aristotle. As Adorno and Horkheimer once wrote, "The
task to be accomplished is not the conservation of the past, but the redemption
of the hopes of the past" (Adorno and Horkheimer 1972, xv). Interpreting these
hopes is an act in the present. Thus, cultural relativism is rejected but paradoxically not the historical basis of culture.

His new emphasis on "biology" suggests to Marcuse a whole dimension of
Marxism missing from the orthodox accounts. The historically developing

instincts and sensory capacities form a level of social determination below the infrastructure as conventionally understood. The truncated and restricted range of satisfactions possible in societies of scarcity is reflected in the narrowly utilitarian focus of sensory experience and the predominance of the survival instinct. A rich society can afford a richer development of individuality. It can subordinate the struggle for existence to "the laws of beauty" in the early Marx's sense of the term.

What is the outcome of these discussions? Instincts turn out to be historical while political and aesthetic ideals are transhistorical. The biological falls into time and so resembles culture while the cultural transcends time and so resembles nature. The paradox indicates the place of a missing concept.

What Marcuse's supposed biologism really amounts to is the claim that the human body is the bearer of ideals inscribed in nature. But this cannot be the body and nature as objects of scientific knowledge. Which body then? Nature in what sense? What confuses us in reading Marcuse today is his reliance on objectivistic notions drawn from Marx and Freud to signify a dimension of human life he interprets in existential terms. It is as though he were afraid that anything short of the tragic rhetoric of social and psychological determinism would collapse back into superficiality. There is something to this. When the concept of the lifeworld returns in Habermas, it is thinned out to a linguistic phenomenon lacking the compelling force Marcuse senses at the bottom of human existence. The historical interpretation of the instincts is an attempt to get below the superficial levels of language, psychology, and opinion to the basic moving forces of personal existence, the body, identity, self-understanding. At this basic level, the physical and the cultural are encountered together. Here the opposition of nature and culture does not apply.

In the phenomenological tradition Marcuse's insight would be expressed in terms of the lived body, that is, the body insofar as it is experienced as "mine." Heidegger did not apply his notions of facticity and "mineness" (*Jemeinigkeit*) to the body, a lacuna corrected in Jean-Paul Sartre and Maurice Merleau-Ponty. The phenomenological approach to language and tradition, from Heidegger to Merleau-Ponty, complements the theory of the body by directing our attention to the operative significance of meanings and values in the lived experience and activities of individuals and groups. Similarly, phenomenologies of identity analyze the experience in which individuals or groups assume their identity as they live it and as it reveals them in the world. Existential race theory in Sartre and Frantz Fanon, and Simone de Beauvoir's gender theory show the relativity of the nature/culture dichotomy in this domain.

Marcuse read these authors as they published and comments positively on the later Sartre and Fanon (Marcuse 1973a, 189–90). He could have used their ideas in the explanation of his own position. It is regrettable that he did not explore the exciting territory of "existential Marxism" during the period of its heyday.[3] Instead he drew on Freudian instinct theory to bridge the gap between his older Marxist account of social forces and his new existential theory of individual resistance.

The result is an incoherent attempt to transcend the opposition of biology and history from an objectivistic standpoint that presupposes their separation. As we will see in the remainder of this chapter, Marcuse has even greater problems when he applies his deconstructive method to the senses. Once again, he might have found solutions in the phenomenological tradition.

It should be clear in any case that Marcuse avoids the biologism with which he is charged. His position may still be unacceptable to postmoderns convinced (in a sad caricature of Derrida) that history is a superficial "play of signifiers," but postmodern irony misses any sense of the first person experience of participation in history under the pressure of human passions and the unavoidable demands of the present. Some postmodern and feminist discourse introduces that dimension anew through a focus on the body. The problem is still the same as the one Marcuse faced: how to give existential weight to a constructed identity. Marcuse would have found these reflections interesting. For him the existential significance of history was an undeniable aspect of the human condition that had to be conceptualized by any adequate social theory. As he himself said of Freud, so for Marcuse, "'biologism' is social theory in a depth dimension" (Marcuse 1966b, 6). One might reject biological language as inappropriate without losing sight of that dimension.

From 1844 to 1968

If it can be said of aesthetics that it belongs to a naturalized culture, then perhaps the senses can be regarded as part of a culturalized nature. Here we reach the heart of the Marcusian paradox. How can the senses be cultural in their principle when they are the chief means through which nature becomes present and indeed *is* present in the subject? The answer to this question is vital as Marcuse's whole redemptive project depends on it. The concept of a new technology requires the emergence of a new and richer form of perception that reveals its objects in the light of their intrinsic growth potential. Marcuse proposes to discover the second dimension in experience as it is refracted by this new sensibility. With such a perception, nature would not be conquered but brought harmoniously under the aegis of human needs.

Marcuse presents this notion through a daring interpretation of Marx's 1844 *Manuscripts*. This marks a surprising return to a text Marcuse had already analyzed in 1933. His early article, "New Sources on the Foundations of Historical Materialism," belonged to the first reception of the *Manuscripts*, which were only published in 1932.

The discovery of the *Manuscripts* contributed to Marcuse's drift away from Heidegger toward the Marxism of the Frankfurt School he was about to join. Nevertheless, his interpretation of Marx is by no means orthodox and has vaguely phenomenological resonances. Marcuse distinguishes the position of the *Manuscripts* from materialism and emphasizes its roots in Feuerbach and Hegel. In his interpretation, the early Marx innovated an ontology based on sensation and labor. Humanity and nature are one not through mere contemplation as in Feuerbach but through active transformation and objectification as in Hegel. Now, thirty-five years later, Marcuse returns to the elaboration of this ontology in *An Essay on Liberation*. This renewed attention to the *Manuscripts* recalls phenomenological themes from his early studies.

According to the early Marx, the human being is essentially "sensuous," meaning that it belongs to nature through its receptivity and neediness. Note that this is not Lockean empiricism. Locke placed the Cartesian *cogito* in causal relation to the nature of the natural sciences. The empiricist subject-object relation is contingent. Like Feuerbach, Marx emphasizes the essential correlation of human being and the nature encountered in immediate experience. This correlation is evident in the mutual appropriateness of human faculties and their natural objects: the eye belongs with the object of sight, the ear with sound, the hand with the tool, hunger with food, and so on. Marx concludes that "the objects of [man's] drives exist outside himself as objects independent of him, yet they are objects of his needs, essential objects which are indispensable to the exercise and conformation of his faculties" (Marx 1963, 207).

As the argument of the *Manuscripts* unfolds, the correlation of human subject and nature is reinterpreted in terms of the Hegelian notion of objectification through labor. Labor assumes the ontological function of a principle of synthesis of reality. "It is only when objective reality everywhere becomes for man in society the reality of human faculties, human reality, and the reality of his own faculties that all objects become for him the objectification of himself. The objects then confirm and realize his individuality, they are his own objects, i.e., man himself becomes the object" (Marx 1963, 160–61).

This claim of subject-object identity is puzzling since most things cannot possibly be objectifications of human labor. Marx gets around the difficulty by reconceptualizing the senses. They now become "directly theoreticians in practice," acting on their objects as does the worker on his raw materials (Marx 1963, 160). The senses, unlike labor, have traditionally been conceived as a potentially universal mode of reception, relating to all possible (real) objects. The senses can therefore take over where labor leaves off, supporting the assertion of universal identity. Yet in Marx this identity coexists paradoxically with the independent material reality of the moments of which it consists.[4]

In his 1933 essay on the *Manuscripts,* writing still under the influence of Heidegger, Marcuse interprets Marx as a kind of phenomenologist. In Marx as in Husserl and Heidegger, subject and object stand in essential relations of meaning rather than accidental causal relations. Marcuse emphasizes passages that hint at something similar to his theory of the two dimensions. He argues, for example, that Marx's notion of "species being" means that human beings are aware of the "species" of things, the universals under which each particular falls. "Labor, as the specifically human 'life activity,' has its roots in man's nature as a 'species being;'

it presupposes man's ability to relate to the universality in objects and to the *possibilities* contained in it" (Marcuse 1973b, 16, trans. modified). And he interprets Marx's claim that human history is the history of the whole of nature to mean the "furtherance of what exists objectively through once again transcending its current form" (Marcuse 1973b, 24). The human being "can 'confront' any object and exhaust and realize its inner possibilities in his labour. He can produce 'in accordance with the laws of beauty' and not merely in accordance with the standard of his own needs (p. 114)" (Marcuse 1973b, 17).

Marcuse's later retrieval of the *Manuscripts* carries this argument further. He suggests that nature is ultimately, ontologically, just what is experienced in a world no longer obsessed by the struggle for existence. This sounds a bit like phenomenalism but there is a difference. In his later work Marcuse makes much of the passage cited above in which Marx describes "the specifically human faculty to form his environment 'in accordance with the laws of *beauty*'" (Marcuse 2001, 131). Marcuse now emphasizes the role of the senses in their capacity to experience the truth of existence. As "theoreticians in practice" the senses engage with the potentialities of things and bring them to fruition. He asserts "the capacity of the senses to experience not only the 'given' but also the 'hidden' qualities of things which would make for the betterment of life. The radical redefinition of sensibility as 'practical'" desublimates the idea of freedom without abandoning its transcendent content: the senses are not only the basis for the *epistemological* constitution of reality, but also for its *transformation, its subversion* in the interest of liberation" (Marcuse 1972, 71). Here the correlation between the sensuous subject and object is truly essential in the Heideggerian sense that the qualities of the object are revealed in the light of their meaning and require a "besouled being" for their revealing. This is the sense in which values can be considered "objective" (Marcuse 1972, 69).

Marcuse relates the liberation of the senses to the notion of objectification in the early Marx. He argues that in a free society labor both humanizes nature and liberates it to the free development of its own potentialities. Human beings "experience the object-world (including man) not as mere stuff of manipulation and use . . . but rather a human world in which the particular objects embody, in their 'form,' truly human needs and satisfactions, so that, in relating to an object, the senses are the realization of a human being: the individual while being with another, is with himself: the universal in the particular" (Marcuse 2001, 136).

Marcuse practically quotes Hegel in this passage. Human beings in a humanized nature will be "at home in the other as such." This is the very formula of the absolute in which all alienation is transcended. Marcuse wants to preserve the ontological implications of Marx's identity theory of labor while transcending its reduction in traditional Marxism to an idealization of mere work. Despite the dependence of nature on labor, the otherness of the object is preserved: the meaning of the object is not arbitrarily imposed, it is not just raw material for human projects. Nature retains its independence, its truth, even in the process of transformation by human labor. But for this to be possible, there must be "forces in nature which have been distorted and suppressed—forces which could support and enhance the liberation of man" (Marcuse 1969a, 66).[5]

At this point Marcuse appears to re-enchant nature. This outcome results from Marcuse's relatively uncritical appropriation of the *Manuscripts*. Like Marx's theory of the senses as practitioners, Marcuse's aesthetic theory of sensation enlarges the project of humanization of nature. In the process it reveals a fundamental problem. The original Feuerbach–Marx account of human sensuousness appears more plausible than it is because the correlations it posits are so obvious. It is hardly surprising to learn that hunger has food as its essential object, or that labor requires natural objects on which to work. Even when Marx suggests that the human ear achieves fulfillment in hearing the music hidden to the lower animals, we understand easily, at least we think we do. It is tempting to read these correlations non-ontologically, as relevant to human experience but not to nature "in itself," although this is not what Marx had in mind in 1844. In this common sense reading, the link between human beings and nature is anthropologically essential but ontologically contingent.

This common sense Marx is not the author of the *Manuscripts*. Marx's talk of the humanization of nature implies that the correlations are not just social and psychological but apply to reality itself. As Marx puts it, "Man's feelings, passions, etc., are not merely anthropological characteristics in the narrower sense, but are true *ontological* affirmations of being (nature)" (Marx 1963, 189). In what sense, ontological? Marx seems to be saying that human needs and the so-called secondary qualities reveal aspects of reality unknown to the scientific conception of nature. In this more faithful ontological reading, we are in uncharted territory that certainly does not look like Marxism as usually understood. Marcuse forces us to enter that territory by emphasizing that the humanization extends to aesthetic values that reflect inherently benign natural forces. This view contradicts common sense which finds beauty in the eye of the beholder. Marcuse thus brings us face to face with a disturbing ambiguity in Marx's account.

Marx's word "nature" refers at one and the same time to the immediate object of sensory experience, the lived nature contrasted in romanticism with the nature of natural science, and the nature appropriated by labor in the production process. This latter concept of nature evokes not poetry but industry. It is generally understood to be an objective reality independent of the human being and comprehended rationally by natural science. Poetic receptivity to nature and technical transformation of it are opposites referring us to different understandings of the object. What is puzzling is Marx's insistence, against both idealism and naturalistic realism, that nature in this ambiguous sense is essentially correlated with and yet wholly independent of the subject. The pathos of a romantic, pre-phenomenological concept of experience is captured for "material" reality, the reality of the raw materials and products of industry.

Heidegger's Aristotle could have made sense of this. Heidegger's account of *techné* explains technical action from within, phenomenologically. Thus conceived, production does not address the indifferent nature of science and industry but the material correlate of human action. But Marx did not develop such a phenomenological account. Instead he proposes a solution that duplicates the ambiguity at a higher level, the notion that nature is the "inorganic body" of man. Alfred Schmidt interprets this strange notion as a kind of naturalized Hegelianism in which humanity is the self-consciousness of nature.

> The hidden nature speculation in Marx [holds that] the different economic formations of society which have succeeded each other historically have been so many modes of nature's self-mediation. Sundered into two parts, man and material to be worked on, nature is always present to itself in this division. Nature attains self-consciousness in men, and amalgamates with itself by virtue of their theoretical-practical activity. Human participation in something alien and external to them appears at first to be something equally alien and external to nature; but in fact it proves to be a "natural condition of human existence," which is itself a part of nature, and it therefore constitutes nature's self-movement. Only in this way can we speak meaningfully of a "dialectic of nature". (Schmidt 1971, 79)[6]

The fragments of the totality, human beings and nature, are held together here by the mythic identification of the one with mind and the other with body. The solution has a certain charm but it also has a disturbing epistemological consequence: the existing natural sciences are falsified since they address a merely abstract thought-nature and not the "real" nature of lived experience.

Marcuse echoes this notion that the natural sciences must be transformed to accommodate the experience of lived nature. Although he rejects the idea of a "qualitative physics," an ambiguity hangs over his call for a "new science" (Marcuse 1964, 166). The extension of his critique beyond experience to objectivity exposed him to unfair attacks as an irrationalist, a foe of science with a romantic hostility to the modern world. The early Marx offered no help in refuting these attacks since he was an even more plausible target than Marcuse. But Marcuse never distinguished his idea of nature from Marx's. Instead, he tried out a whole series of unsatisfactory explanations for the concept of nature he derived from Marx.

Multiplying Discourses

How does Marcuse explain the harmony of human being and nature? In answering this question Marcuse's argument takes off into the philosophical stratosphere. It is no wonder he did not win many converts with it. In various late books and essays he offers several different explanations loosely derived from Plato, Goethe, Freud, and Kant.

In one unpublished text he sums up his argument that beauty is an "innate idea," claiming that

> "innate ideas" turn out to be repressed claims of the human senses, and their universality, far from being a vague, rather abstract idea of humanity and humanism, would turn out to be a rather material, physiological condition. And the recollection, *Erinnerung* would be a capturing of potentialities of the human senses. And, to push speculation one step further, we may take the translation of Plato's concept literally and say that these potentialities are yet unrealized Forms of things: modes of existence of man and nature (*Dasein*) which would constitute a cosmos of Justice where satisfaction would be in the free human productivity in creating a good world for everyone" (Marcuse 2001, 129; compare, Marcuse 1972, 69–70).

In an implicit reference to Goethe, Marcuse invokes "the ancient theory of knowledge as *recollection*: 'science' as the *re*discovery of the true *Forms* of things, distorted and denied in the established reality" (Marcuse 1972, 69–70; Jay 1984, 229). And Freud takes a bow with the theory of the "erotic cathexis" binding human beings to nature in a harmonious unity (Marcuse 1972, 60).

Elsewhere Marcuse follows a different and more promising line of argument. He claims that "nature is a part of history, an object of history" (Marcuse 1972, 60). By this he means that we encounter nature only in historically given forms, determined by a specific social background. Physical and historical nature "cannot be insulated from each other; the historical aspect can never be eliminated so radically that only the 'absolute' physical layer remains" (Marcuse 1964, 218). Marcuse tries twice to develop this argument in terms of Kant's notion of the synthetic *a priori*. He first suggests the "radical hypothesis" that aesthetic archetypes should be added to the Kantian "pure forms" of sensibility. These are differentiated historically but common to all human beings in their source, reflecting a pre-established harmony between nature and human needs (Marcuse 1969a, 32). This is not much of an improvement on the innate ideas of Plato. The pure forms of sensibility in Kant are twofold: space and time. Neither has a normative content; both are universally shared and present in all perception. How beauty could form a third is hard to say as it is normative and by no means universal either as perceived by individuals or as a criterion applied to objects. This is not to reject the idea of innate aesthetic archetypes as absurd, but it gains no plausibility from Plato and Kant, merely a metaphorical expression.

A more suggestive reference to Kant appears in a later essay: "The senses are not merely passive, receptive: they have their own 'syntheses' to which they subject the primary data of experience" (Marcuse 1972, 63). This sounds like a Kantian thesis and indeed it would be if Marcuse did not go on to argue that Kant was mistaken in limiting the forms of intuition to space and time, overlooking "other syntheses, far more concrete, far more 'material,' which may constitute an empirical (i.e., historical) *a priori* of experience" (Marcuse 1972, 63).[7] We have an idea what these *a priori* principles are from Marcuse's discussion of the difference between experience under capitalism and socialism. Each determines the universal elements of experience in accord with its own requirements. The narrow utilitarian qualities objects acquire in the one system are contrasted with the aesthetically rich qualities available in the other. In the liberated society, "Man" would finally be capable of "finding himself in nature, beyond and this side of alienation" (Marcuse 1972, 60).

But no sooner stated, then Marcuse draws back from this account as it implies a hubristic overemphasis on human activity. The Frankfurt School critique of identity theory takes over. As Marcuse writes, "Nature is not a manifestation of 'spirit' but its essential *limit*" (Marcuse 1972, 69). How does this square with his earlier claim that nature is a part of history? As with the early Marx, so with Marcuse, we are left in doubt about the ontological status of nature.

How seriously did Marcuse take these speculations? There is an undeniable element of provocation in the reference to such outworn concepts as innate ideas and Platonic forms. The Kantian reference makes more sense, but it too is problematic since Marcuse had no intention of reviving transcendental idealism. Surely Marcuse did not expect these speculations to be taken literally! But how are we to take them figuratively? That is by no means obvious. He is engaged in an act of philosophical retrieval, "repeating" the tradition in something like Heidegger's sense of the term. But the exoteric doctrine hides an esoteric one that Marcuse never fully articulated. This is worrisome. Is this the downfall of rational thought in a sentimental re-enchantment of nature? The objection is facile but telling. Marcuse's notion of an aesthetic synthesis of experience deserves a more sympathetic reading, which I will develop in the next section. But I do agree with the critics that he failed to provide a convincing account of his notion of an aesthetic *Lebenswelt*. To do so, he would have had to stick closer—critically, to be sure—to his Heideggerian origins.

A Phenomenological Marcuse?

What is truly innovative in Marcuse's position is the hypothesis that once increasing wealth releases society from the struggle for existence, perception can transcend the given toward unrealized potentialities foreshadowed in art. Art has anticipated the realization of these potentialities in imagination for thousands of years. They "cannot possibly be given in the immediate experience which prevails in repressive societies. They are given rather as the horizon under which the immediately given forms of things appear as 'negative,' as denial of their inherent potentialities, their truth" (Marcuse 1972, 70). In such societies, the aesthetic imagination produces images that serve as the normative context of what is revealed in sensation.[8] Now, in an advanced society, the sheer technical possibility of the realization of these norms destabilizes the structures of class rule and the underlying forms of experience and individuality on which it is based. At this higher stage of economic and technical development, the aesthetic ceases to be a "horizon" of appearance and begins to structure perception itself. The senses take on the aesthetic function in the full sense of the term. With this "new mode of experience," "the imagination [turns] into a meta-political power" (Marcuse 2001, 118).

The earlier Hegelian–Marxist argument that establishes the second dimension theoretically now becomes practical, existential. Sensation itself has a normative aspect inseparable from its truth value. Marcuse writes that the violation of nature "offends against certain objective qualities of nature—qualities which are essential to the enhancement and fulfillment of life. And it is on such objective grounds that the liberation for man to his own humane faculties is linked to the liberation of nature—that 'truth' is attributable to nature not only in a mathematical but also in an existential sense. The emancipation of man involves the recognition of such truth in things, in nature" (Marcuse 1972, 69).

The use of the term existential here, like Marcuse's references to the *Lebenswelt*, invites a phenomenological interpretation he does not elaborate. Instead, he leaves us in suspense, wondering precisely what he means. Clearly, the existential truth is not rationally validated in scientific research ("mathematically"). What makes it an *existential* truth must be its experiential character. Marcuse seems to intend a truth that is revealed in experience rather than one that is proven by experience. But in what modern philosophical framework other than phenomenology does this make sense?

Because Marcuse did not return to phenomenology, but insisted to the end that he could reconcile his theoretical innovations with Marxism, his interpreters and critics have had a hard time knowing what to do with him. In his later work Marcuse appears to waver between a Hegelian–Marxist historicism and a Heideggerian phenomenology. Most interpreters sympathetic to Marcuse prefer the first option, while his critics accuse him of the second (Schmidt 1988). But neither approach seems exactly to describe his position.

Marcuse's deconstructive strategy plays the one off against the other. "Nature," as he uses the term, is known in its truth from the standpoint of a historical dialectic, but it is also experienced in its truth bodily in sensation and action. And what of the nature of natural science? It appears in Marcuse's theory as a theoretical construct specific to the world of modern class society. Its truth value is not in question but Marcuse denies that it can explain either the history from which it originates and in which it will someday be refuted, or the sensory world that grounds its concepts. Science prevails in a limited domain that reflects the limits of class society. This is undoubtedly a controversial thesis, but it is clear that Marcuse is attempting to distinguish the experience of lived nature from the various theories in which nature is explained, both historically and scientifically. He is not proposing to collapse these all important distinctions in a way that would reverse the achievements of Enlightenment and return us to an anthropomorphic worldview.

Phenomenology does a better job than any of Marcuse's multiple discourses at avoiding confusion between the nature of lived experience and the objective nature of the historical and natural sciences. Husserl and Heidegger argue that the concepts through which we understand objective reality are founded in lived experience. Scientific ideas of space, time, causality, and so on, are grounded in corresponding experiences in everyday life. This sounds like empiricism, but the phenomenological concept of experience differs by its emphasis on the ontological significance of the first person perspective. Our experience of the world in the first person, as an embodied "I," has specific characteristics that distinguish it from the common sensical third-person perspective of objectivistic thinking.[9] These characteristics include the immediate relation of perception to meanings, including the meanings embodied in the second dimension as Marcuse describes it. Here Marcuse could have found a model of a theory of sensation in which the "ideal forms" come down to earth as structures of experience without suffering an instantaneous devaluation at the hands of scientific naturalism.

Heidegger rejected Husserl's idea of consciousness and turned to everyday activity as the fundamental domain of experience. Like action itself, phenomenology engages with the world as a unified whole. Thus, phenomenologically considered, beauty inheres in the person or the thing, and is no "investment" of a subjective preference in a value neutral fact (Heidegger 1962, 132). In this framework, sensation and the practice that accompanies it are not objects in the world, not the result of a causal interaction of two things, sense organs and nature. Nor is the object split up into a thing in itself and humanly imposed secondary qualities. Rather, the analysis follows prereflexive experience in which subject and object are correlated without dissolving one into the other.

On this basis Heidegger developed a consistent analysis of production (*techné*) in which nature is grasped as the essential object of the producing subject. In that scheme the object is not indifferent to its transformation by craft but is appropriate to its finished form in which its own potential is realized. Form is not a fact in the world on the same terms as a thing, nor is it simply the realization of the maker's will. A reciprocal interaction and exchange takes place joining maker and materials in a unity in diversity, a totality. It is at this level that activity and receptivity complement each other rather than appearing as alternatives, that the subject is in harmony with the object it transforms without wholly suppressing its independence, that identity and nonidentity are reconciled. The object belongs to a human lifeworld as a subject with its own potentialities.

Marcuse's notion of an existential truth of nature makes sense in this context. Recall Heidegger's claim in his study of Aristotle that the *eidos* is only fully real in the craft work itself (Heidegger 1998, 210). The craftsman engages with his materials in accordance with the *logos*, the "objective value," embodied in the *eidos*. But the *eidos* is not primarily an idea in our modern sense of the term, a content of thought, but rather a living guide to practice, embodied in sensation and action. The tension between the good formulated in the technical *logos* and its corresponding privations shapes the sensibility and movements of the artist or craftsman. Marcuse's notion of liberated sensation can be interpreted in these terms: the skilled craftsman sees in the object not only its present form but the formlessness it must lose in the work. This seeing is experiential, not intellectual. A liberated aesthetic sensibility would relate to the social world as a whole in a similar manner.

The normative patterning of perception and structuring of action is obvious. We are well aware that some people see the glass as "half full" and others "half empty." Phenomenologically considered, each perception is adequate to its object. Norms such as "appropriate" or "inappropriate," "helpful" or "harmful," "healthy" or "unhealthy" routinely appear in our perceptions and shape our prereflective behavior, not just our judgments. Marcuse proposes that social critical standards would become similarly available as structures of perception and action. In a free society the universal element involved in all perception, the "concept" under which a "manifold" is unified, would incorporate an immediate awareness of the potentialities of the object. The object would be perceived through its concept, as it is today, but that concept would include a sense of "where the object is going," what it can become. The object to which these qualities are attributed is not the object of science. It is the lived experience of the world in which the perceived incompleteness and imperfection of things drives action forward.

The reified distinction of value and fact is the product of reflection and theory and presupposes a prior disclosure of the world. That disclosure makes no such distinction. Phenomenology treats experience as ontologically fundamental.[10] But the grounding of objectivity in experience does not devalue science as an explanation of nature. Rather, phenomenology affirms the legitimacy and truth of science in its own sphere, while stripping it of ultimate ontological significance. There is no better explanation of objective things than science. But objective things are not fundamental. At the most basic level, the problem is understanding the presence of a meaningful world, and *that* is something science presupposes but cannot explain.

Phenomenology thus proposes a kind of "doctrine of double truth." The world is given twice: once as a system of meanings in act, revealed to each of us individually in lived experience; and a second time as existence given objectively to all of us and comprehended in various ways, none of which exhaust its significance. Natural science and historical dialectics represent two approaches to understanding existence, the one explaining the first dimension, the other articulating the second dimension which science enters as an object rather than a subject. Marcuse hints at a possible transcendence of this methodological dualism, but he has no concrete idea how it would take place and what it would yield. Although there will surely be a different science someday, the project of a "new science," unlike the demand for a new technology, is theoretically incoherent (Feenberg 2002, 170ff). The real "mystery" is not at the epistemological level, but is rather the irresolvable duality between experience and objectivity in all its forms. This duality results from a resolutely finite ontology in which no god or *cogito* or neuroscience can survey the world from "nowhere" and explain its meaningfulness in experience on the same terms as its objective existence for thought.

This argument has practical implications. Marcuse emphasizes that reason is bound to civilizational projects but he cannot explain concretely how this actually plays out because he confuses two very different levels of rationality. The level of natural scientific abstractions must be distinguished from the concrete technical disciplines through which those abstractions become historically active. These disciplines respond to both the nature of lived experience and scientific nature, merging them seamlessly in a practical unity that guides action. In so doing, they embody social forces in technically valid forms.[11]

The place to look for transformation is at this level, not the level of the scientific abstractions. After all, even Socrates' *techné* must have incorporated basic mathematics without thereby conceding the field to Callicles. This is not to deny the unique availability of the modern scientific conception of nature for the sort of applications Marcuse condemns, but modern science can also serve the affirmation of life in Marcuse's sense, an obvious point he nowhere denies. The ambivalence of science, like the ambivalence of many other social institutions that have developed under capitalism is essential to any credible conception of socialism (Feenberg 2002, chap. 2).

Could Marcuse have developed an explicit phenomenological Marxism to explain his theory of potentialities? His early Hegel interpretation could have provided a starting point. Recall that in *Hegel's Ontology*, life is not primarily an epistemological category but a category of practical relatedness. In the Marcusian phenomenology that might have followed *Hegel's Ontology*, the structures of perception would be relative to the practical relations established in the labor process. They would not be fixed permanently, as in Kant, but would change with the historical development of humanity. The later work goes beyond this conception with the introduction of the aesthetic. But the aesthetic is not opposed to labor; it will inform the world of work by transforming technology in accordance with "the laws of beauty." A phenomenology of the aesthetic *Lebenswelt* could have been developed to explain the anticipated transcendence of affirmative culture. Marcuse did not develop such an approach but remained caught in the ambiguities of his source in the early Marx.

As a result, his argument fell below the level of the current debates in philosophy. It was not clear how he could refute naturalism and defend his normative stance against relativism and value nihilism. Had Marcuse conceded that he was not talking ontology but ethics, he would have had to face the challenge of

Habermas, whose theory offered an otherwise powerful grounding than Marcuse's notion of potentiality. The claims Marcuse made in the name of "life" could be seen as psychological rather than philosophical, but then they would have been no more persuasive than their Freudian basis, which lost favor during the late 20th century. One sees why Adorno's work has survived better, but it takes no risks and offers no prospects. Marcuse refused to give up on the idea of an existential politics and this is his vulnerability and his greatness.

Chapter 7
Conclusion
The Path to Authenticity

I would like to conclude by summarizing our trajectory and considering where it has led us. We have seen that the idea of *techné* in Plato and Aristotle implies an understanding of experience that is radically different from our modern view. While we tend to separate subject and object, values and facts, the Greeks treated them as a harmonious continuum. Their technical action was not the arbitrary imposition of subjective intentions on mere raw materials, but a mutual engagement with a world rich in useful potentialities awaiting the facilitating intervention of craft to show themselves. The implicit ontology of ancient craft corresponds to the everyday experience of the world as phenomenology analyzes it. The indifferent nature recognized by scientific reason and manipulated by modern technology belongs to a different and derivative dispensation.

Heidegger's construction of this contrast is powerful and interesting. He explains that the Greeks imposed a limited horizon on the world without superstition or anthropomorphism. They understood things in terms of their potentialities in the framework of human action, specifically production. Their world was thus confined within the parameters of phenomenologically interpreted everydayness. Yet they were able to articulate this experience of the world in theoretical terms. What we interpret as their "teleological" standpoint and dismiss for lack of experimental evidence of purpose in things, was in fact their objectivistic way of signifying the necessary bond between human being and being, the intrinsic relation between action and world. That they could recognize this bond and this relation while also innovating a scientific reason directed at the objective properties of things was the founding miracle of the West. For us such a paradoxical combination is impossible since we immediately dismiss the bond and the relation in affirming science and objectivity. But they held these apparent contraries together and this made it possible for them to treat things with respect as partners in technical making while also creating the sciences.—This is the lost Eden of reason to which we cannot return.

For us the human is the subjective, and our everyday relation to reality an accident of culture and biology from which we must abstract to achieve scientific objectivity. For the Greeks, on the contrary, the contingency of human making and purpose in any given instance could be understood in the light of a general ontological necessity. Differences from one instance to another, for example, in the customs of different cities or the political opinions of different citizens, could be related to more fundamental principles or resolved by argument, as Socrates refuted Callicles. However, Socrates' victory was bound to a pregiven, unhistorical ideal of the good. Modern freedom is also freedom from any such ideal. But once the bond of human being and being is broken, the whole Greek construction collapses. A bifurcated subject and object confront each other across an unbridgeable gulf. Technology is the new form which technical action takes in this bifurcated world.

In Hegel Marcuse found a way of squaring the circle of modernity. We are cast out of Eden but we can build a second garden by founding objectivity on life. Dialectics now establishes the ontological priority of what Heidegger analyzed as everydayness but it does so in the more complex form of the living and working community, alienating itself and returning to itself in the course of history. The underlying totality of human beings and things the Greeks discovered in the objective structure of the world now depends on the human being as the principle of world creation. Subjectivity again relates to its world with the intrinsic necessity of the Greeks but without the narrowness of the Greek vision. With Hegel the modern principle of creativity is affirmed, while the dialectic avoids the mere "arbitrariness" of romanticism.

But this affirmation is not a task for theory alone. Simply to know that subject and object are bound together in an underlying totality from out of which modern reason springs is insufficient to transform that reason into an instrument of peace and freedom. Marxism finds liberating knowledge not in absolute science but in the proletariat which, as Lukács argued, can transform society in becoming conscious of its role as creative subject of the labor of historical construction. The essential potentialities the Greeks found in things return here as human potentialities. But since the world is a human creation in some sense, things too are restored in their rights and claims along with the human beings who created them. Exactly in what sense it is possible to argue that labor creates the world and exactly how the rights and claims of things are to be recognized is certainly unclear in the early Lukács and Marcuse. Marcuse's later work comes closer to a workable theory. He affirms things as "subjects" through a revised concept of technology that has a strong resemblance to Greek *techné*.

In his early Heideggerian period, Marcuse believed he could found Marxism theoretically in the Hegelian dialectic but he presupposed Marxism itself. The Marxist confidence in a revolutionary alternative was predicated on the notion that workers' pursuit of economic self-interest would transform them into individuals capable of appropriating and acting on the scientific critique of capitalism. This transformation would of course involve more than narrow economic interests and would promote mental independence and social solidarity. But Marx believed that the economic struggle would create the opportunity for such self-development. What happens when economic self-interest is no longer allied with critique but with conformism instead? At that point the revolutionary can turn to irrational sources of change such as nationalism or "new gods," as does Heidegger, or revise the concept of self-interest to enlarge its range beyond the economic sense it has in Marx. Marcuse exemplifies the latter alternative which he pursues by restoring the claims of the aesthetic imagination to a share in the rational comprehension of reality.

Now, aesthetics is surely a strange place to look for a solution to the problems of modernity. Aesthetic experience is marginalized today, put out of action when it comes to matters of importance such as technical mastery of the environment. Still, the perception of social reality as "beautiful" or "ugly" is commonplace, and Marcuse frequently refers to contemporary instances illustrating his thesis that aesthetics is a fundamental category of social experience and not confined to the realm of art. He argues that in a liberated society images of harmony preserved in the imaginary world of art during millennia of scarcity and strife would serve as criteria for judging everyday objects and activities. Perception itself would incorporate aesthetic criteria and inspire a very different attitude toward the world. The *theory* of social potentialities would enter *practice* at the most fundamental level. As a consequence, aesthetic judgments would be systematically considered in political and technical decisions. Beyond interests, which can be accommodated to an oppressive society, beyond ethics, which does not define a concrete way of life, aesthetics would support a constructive engagement with political and technical possibilities that might be realized in alternative configurations of social reality.

Marcuse argues that a new technology based on aesthetically informed sensation would respect humans and nature rather than destroying them. The creation of this technology would require not merely a political and social revolution but the end of the *Gestell,* Heidegger's technological age, since it would replace the "standing reserve" with a living world once again. Heidegger's patient attendance on the coming of new gods, Adorno's dismal complaint that life is unlivable, Habermas's cautious reformism, all thrown to the winds. One has to admire the nerve with which Marcuse challenged common sense and the future; this was an act of fidelity to a revolutionary experience that began in youth and shaped his whole intellectual career. But what are we to make of it today?

I have attempted to think through some of his most daring probes with sympathy if not literalness. Retrieving Marcuse is more than a theoretical exercise.

It is one test of whether we can still justify the pursuit of a radical argument with our time. But we suffer from a serious handicap in evaluating his conception of liberation. Heidegger and Marcuse wrote out of a sense of crisis we do not share. World War I, the rise of fascism and communism, the great depression formed an apocalyptic repertoire that discredited the Enlightenment and its liberal democratic succession. Vast civilizational transformations appeared necessary and imminent. The philosopher was situated on the border between worlds and could speak in the name of a future about to be realized through heroic affirmation amidst cataclysmic events. At the deepest level the crisis involved reason itself, which was revealed in its irrationality in the technological slaughter in the trenches. As Paul Valéry wrote at the time, "We late civilizations . . . we too now know that we are mortal" (Valéry 1977, 94). World War II confirmed the diagnosis for those inclined to judge reason by its fruits rather than its promise.

These experiences do not resonate with the current mood in the advanced societies. Free market ideology and the Internet have so captured the imagination that there is none of the sense of civilizational crisis that preoccupied Heidegger and Marcuse. Yet how much safer is our world in reality? Genocide, the AIDS epidemic, nuclear proliferation, wars of conquest continue. While earnest tomes on political philosophy and communication theory present a picture of a basically pacified society that can be improved with a small dose of reform, for millions of people around the world conditions are quite as catastrophic as anything experienced by the generation of Heidegger and his students. There is little more reason today than in 1930 to believe that a civilization based on the current scientific-technical rationality and capitalist economics can solve the riddle of history.

Marcuse saw the first intimations of a solution in the New Left. The New Left was inspired by a renewed perception of social crisis. It showed *that* and *how* crisis could be *experienced* once again in the unprecedented situation of the "affluent society" that was supposed to have surpassed all such threats. Marcuse revised revolutionary theory on this basis. Should he, instead, have followed most academics (including his Frankfurt School colleagues), in criticizing the juvenile excesses of the New Left? After all, weren't things improving in many ways—the Nazis defeated, democracy restored in Europe, a car in every American garage, a "Great Society" proclaimed? No doubt his good judgment would be celebrated today had he joined the chorus. But from Marcuse's standpoint there has never been a time when a radical refusal of society, such as that of the New Left, was not justified. The miracle was the emergence of a sensibility adequate to the real horror and possibilities. To have missed this encounter with history would have been a shame. It is astonishing that today Marcuse's courage in rising to the occasion sheds no reflected glow on his work and is even compared unfavorably with the panicky prissiness in their late years of his old friends Adorno and Horkheimer. But neither should Marcuse be read as the prophet of a failed revolution. He made no predictions and promised no shining tomorrows.

In the absence of realistic political prospects, what was the significance of his utopian speculations? To make sense of his radicalism we need to go back to the concept of authenticity that so attracted Marcuse in his youth even before his encounter with Heidegger. Achieving individuality is problematic in new ways in the 20th century. It is no longer enough to "think for oneself" and "stand up to authority." That was the old formula for individuality which operationally meant little more than reading the newspapers and looking out for one's interests, be they investments or a union wage. Where the thoughts are supplied by "*das Man*" or manipulated by the media, and the ultimate authority is no person but the "facts of (corporate) life," what looked like daring self-assertion in an earlier generation becomes the new conformism. Authentic individuality now depends on not going along (*nicht mitmachen)*, resisting at least inwardly complicity with the system. And this is not merely a matter of words.

For Marcuse, authenticity involves a confrontation with one's own time and its possibilities. Individuality is inseparable from critical consciousness and revolt. Thus, individual and society, present and future are connected. The idea of authenticity, as he formulated it, reflects these inescapable connections which are occluded in the ordinary course of daily life. To bring the connections to the surface and live accordingly is to achieve the higher level of mental independence required in a modern society that knows how to erase the very individuality it pretends to foster.

The emptiness of the existential idea of authenticity which has been criticized over and over, not least by Marcuse himself, is easy to see. Its incoherence was already clear from the diametrically opposed ideological choices with which it was given content by Heidegger and Marcuse in the 1930s. Nevertheless, there is something compelling about it which shows up in Marcuse's later work despite his best efforts to transpose his allegiance from existentialism to Marxism. At the end of the 1960s he returned to the early Marx for concepts with which to interpret the New Left. The result is a renewed interest in the idea of the individual "who, no matter how much he may be 'socialized,' can never be 'dissolved' into an aliquot part of a class: his concreteness resists abstract generalization" (Marcuse 2001, 127). To defend that concreteness now becomes the main task of philosophy.

But individuality can no longer be based on a return to nature, either literally or in the form of those "natural rights" invoked by the Enlightenment. The nature of modern reason has been stripped bare of substantive normative implications to become little more than the scene of technical action. We must go "forward to nature," to an imagined future in which critical consciousness will inform the schemata of an enriched perception, revealing aspects of reality obscured today. Marcuse certainly believed this might happen, so severe is the underlying crisis of advanced industrial society, and so great its potential. But the question for him was never whether this was a near or a probable future. More important is the present function of this projection: to validate critical consciousness under impossible conditions. As Marcuse once explained, "obstinacy [is] a genuine quality of philosophical thought" (Marcuse 1968, 143). This was a quality he displayed with tremendous vigor to the very end. Holding open the possibility of critique in a society with so many resources for disarming it requires no less.

Notes

Preface

1. W.H. Auden's poem on this painting and a reproduction of it can be found at http://www.tasc.ac.uk/depart/media/staff/ls/Modules/MED1110/Narrative/WHAuden.htm
2. A term Marcuse used in a famous article in the 1930s referring to bourgeois art (Marcuse 1968, 88ff).
3. This and subsequent quotations from Marcuse's essays "Contribution to a Phenomenology of Historical Materialism," "On the Problem of the Dialectic" and "On Concrete Philosophy" are cited in the original German but the translations are taken from Abromeit and Wolin (forthcoming, 2004).
4. For a comparison of Heidegger and Marcuse on technology that develops this point further, see Zimmerman (1979). A number of Heideggerians have tried to extract a politics from his work. Dreyfus (1995) even considers Woodstock as an example of a new dispensation. This is surely the most fanciful attempt. Schürmann is more accurate (although lacking in irony) in conceding that "One would especially like Heidegger to have been more specific about the precise actions that are to allow for an entry into the event" (1990, 244). The interpretation of Marcuse offered here responds to Schürmann's objections to the Frankfurt School. See (1990, 368-69).
5. For accounts of Heidegger's early productionism, see Prauss (1977) and Zimmerman (1990, chap. 10).
6. There is a relevant exchange of letters between Heidegger and Marcuse shortly after World War II. See Wolin (1993, 152ff). For Marcuse's final view of Heidegger, see Olafson (1988).

Chapter 1. *Techné*: Prologue with Plato and Aristotle

1. For a full account of the relations between these students and Heidegger, see Wolin (2001). For accounts of Marcuse's early work and his relation to Heidegger, see Kellner (1984), Katz (1982), Reitz (2000), Wolin (2001), and Abromeit (2003).
2. For good accounts see Sadler (1996) and Kisiel (1993).
3. As Heidegger's assistant, Marcuse had access to many unpublished lectures and course transcripts, some of which he made himself. The transcript of this lecture is found among his papers in the Marcuse archive in Frankfurt. For a list of these documents, see Regehly (1991).
4. In this passage and throughout this book, italics are found in the original.
5. I realize that Heidegger calls *physis* a form of *poiésis* (Heidegger 1977, 10), but I cannot find anything justifying this usage in my Greek grammar. Whether or not he is on to something here, eliding the contrast is so confusing I will stick a bit more closely to the conventional definitions.
6. For an interpretation of the relation of essence and existence in terms of Heidegger's concept of ontotheology, see Thomson (2000). I think production is the source of the

duality in ontotheology as between that which all beings have in common that makes them beings, and the highest being that founds them in being. Iain Thomson's illuminating discussion of this theme might be taken further along these lines. For the centrality of production in Heidegger's conception of metaphysics, see Bernasconi (1986).

7. As I write this I realize that these are practically the words of Callicles who admits he finds Socrates' arguments attractive but concludes, "You can't quite convince me" (Plato 1952, 90).

8. Are we still moderns? I think the answer is obvious. So-called postmodernity is a variation on modern themes as the shrewder postmodernists admit. It succeeds in distinguishing itself as a new era only by creating straw men out of figures such as Descartes. I find it hard to believe that a new era has opened in a time as mediocre as this. The last epochal change in Western thought occurred a century ago and it was not postmodern but modernist.

9. Is this an idealistic regression to what Adorno condemned as "identity" thinking? I do not believe so. The Marcusian universals signify precisely the non-identical, that which resists the forms of the existing society. For example, the "ideal" of freedom, understood as free development of an autonomous subject, simply validates the striving to realize potentialities, if necessary, against the established forms, i.e., the identical.

Chapter 2. The Question Concerning *Techné*

1. For a thorough study of Heidegger on essence, see Grieder (1988).
2. Heidegger understands "*alétheia*" to mean "truth" in the sense of unveiling, revealing.
3. Robert Bernasconi makes the interesting suggestion that "The annihilation of the thing in the age of technology functions somewhat like the default of equipment in Section 16 of *Being and Time* and, as the latter revealed what was called the worldhood of the world, the former shows 'the innermost indestructible belongingness of man within granting'" (Bernasconi 1986, 122).
4. For a good explanation of the concept of "*Verwindung*" that also reveals its political emptiness, see Gianni Vattimo (1991, 171ff).
5. John Caputo denies that this is possible for Heidegger (Caputo 1993, 16); but I think Reiner Schürmann and David Kolb are correct to argue that it is at least a possibility (Schürmann 1990, 207–8; Kolb 1986, 191–93).
6. That impulse is actually quite interesting. See May (1996) and Parkes (1987).

Chapter 3. The Dialectic of Life

1. See Seyla Benhabib's introduction to Marcuse (1987) and Pippin (1988) for exceptions. I stick close to Marcuse's text in this chapter to make a case for its theoretical significance.
2. As Douglas Kellner writes, "Lukács's importance for Marcuse and other radicalized intellectuals of his generation can hardly be exaggerated" (Kellner, 1984, 381). See also Wolin (2001, 145–47).
3. Jacques Taminiaux contests Heidegger's self-interpretation in a discussion that brings him closer to Marcuse as I interpret him here (Taminiaux 1995, 207–10).
4. Nancy Holland discusses Heidegger's interpretation of the passage on the Megarians in Heidegger's lecture course of 1931 as a preliminary hint at the later critique of modern technology (Holland 1999, 412). She argues that it grounds a Heideggerian ecology. See also Bruce Foltz (1995) for an ecological reading of Heidegger.
5. Marcuse could not know that Marx had drawn the same conclusion from Hegel in the still unpublished *Grundrisse*, where he writes that under communism the human being "Strives not to remain something he has become, but is in the absolute movement of becoming" (Marx 1973, 488).
6. I have discussed the concept of nonduality implied in this position in Feenberg (1995, 198–200).

Chapter 4. Interlude with Lukács

1. For more on Lukács's early Marxism, see Feenberg (1986).
2. It is a weak echo as Martin Jay points out (Jay 1984, chap. 6).
3. I develop this argument in Feenberg (1999, chap. 7).

4. Compare Lukács: "Nature is a societal category. That is to say, whatever is held to be natural at any given stage of social development, however this nature is related to man and whatever form his involvement with it takes, i.e., nature's form, its content, its range and its objectivity are all socially conditioned" (Lukács 1971, 234).

Chapter 5. Aesthetic Redemption

1. The whole miserable story is told in Rolf Wiggershaus (1994, 609ff). For a discussion of Habermas's complex position, see Martin Matuštík (2001, 48ff).
2. This is not to say that Heidegger denies the notion of potential in this sense. See, for example, Heidegger (1962, 287–88) and Heidegger (1966, 149).
3. On the refusal of utopian thinking in the Frankfurt School see Jay 1973, 60–61.
4. It should not be forgotten that the Platonic Socrates was also an early critic of the arrogance of expertise. Of the craftsmen of this day, he said: "Each of them believed himself to be extremely wise in matters of the greatest importance because he was skillful in his own art: and this presumption of theirs obscured their real wisdom" (Plato 1956, 27).
5. Richard Wolin, whose fine work as a historian I have relied on in this book, does not always get it right. He gives a truly awful example of a tendentious reading of Marcuse in Wolin (2002). He cites the same remark from *Eros and Civilization* I have quoted in full above, but stops after the first sentence leaving the impression that Marcuse favored educational dictatorship today (Wolin 2002, 85). He quotes Marcuse as approving of "a dictatorship of the intellectuals" in "Repressive Tolerance" although Marcuse puts the phrase in the mouth of those who "denounce" "radical critics" (Wolin 2002, 85; Marcuse 1969b, 121). Finally, he fails to cite Marcuse's comment in the same essay that "the alternative to the established semi-democratic process is *not* a dictatorship or elite, no matter how intellectual and intelligent, but the struggle for a real democracy" (Marcuse 1969b, 122; italics in original).
6. For a powerful but unsympathetic reading of this tradition, see Terry Eagleton (1997).
7. For more on this subject, see Peter Bürger (1984).
8. For critiques of Marcuse's aesthetics, see Bronner (1988), Lukes (1985), and Reitz (2000).
9. The correlation is essential: the imagination is a transcendental faculty that shapes objects as well as the knowledge of objects. Marcuse's theory of the imagination resembles Heidegger's early *Kant and Problem of Metaphysics*, an innovative work in which Heidegger for the first time analyzed the central role of the imagination in Kant. There is a universal aspect to the perception of particulars which is the work of what Kant called the "schematism." Heidegger's Kant interpretation drew attention to the dependence of schematization on the imagination, which bridges the gap between concept and object. The theory of significance in *Being and Time* is a revision of this Kantian doctrine. The schemata, understood in terms of the care structure of *Dasein*, form the framework within which sensed objects are interpreted and given a meaning. Recall that Heidegger proposed something similar in connection with Aristotle. In a sense, the Kantian imagination carries out the work of the *eidos* in Heidegger's earlier analysis, making it possible to perceive and know the object *as* something. The *eidos* returns in this new guise, granting the meanings of beings. It binds the general and the particular together in the specific type of each thing at the level of the revealing, which is more basic than either perception or thought taken separately.
10. For my response to Habermas's interpretation, see Feenberg (1999, chap. 7). See also Gandesha (2004).
11. For an explanation of this reticence, see Wiggershaus (1994, 503–7).
12. For a recent volume offering a wide variety of social approaches to technology, see Misa, et al. (2003).
13. This is not the place to carry on an argument with empiricism in science and technology studies. I have explained my position elsewhere. See Feenberg (2003).
14. Quoted in Merleau-Ponty (1960, 201).
15. I have developed this approach in my instrumentalization theory. See Feenberg (1999, 202ff.)
16. See Böhme (1992) for an important contribution to reviving the aesthetics of nature.
17. Albert Borgmann is the one communitarian who has squarely faced the problem. His thought owes much to Heidegger but usefully avoids the worst problems in Heidegger's evaluation of modernity. His communitarian conclusion comes up against the very forces of the technological consensus he so tellingly analyzes (Borgmann 1984). His central concept of "focal things" is an insightful reformulation of a Heideggerian theme that deserves application in a wider variety of contexts than

Borgmann's communitarianism allows. For my critical discussion of Borgmann, see Feenberg (1999, chap. 8). Borgmann replies in Higgs, et al. (2000, chap. 18).
18. Löwy and Sayre (2001) analyze the history of this critique as romanticism.

Chapter 6. The Question Concerning Nature

1. For a treatment of this problem, see Vogel (1996).
2. It is worth noting that Marcuse rejects the normalizing interpretation of Freud's theory of sexuality and actually valorizes the so-called "perversions": "In a repressive order, which enforces the equation between normal, socially useful, and good, the manifestations of pleasure for its own sake must appear as *fleurs de mal*" (Marcuse 1966b, 50).
3. See Poster (1975).
4. For more on subject-object identity in the early Marx, see Feenberg (1986, chaps. 2 and 7).
5. This speculation brings Marcuse closer to Ernst Bloch than either Heidegger or the Frankfurt School. Bloch writes, "The current of nature as a friend, technology as the delivery and mediation of the creations slumbering the womb of nature, this belongs to the most concrete aspect of concrete utopia" (Bloch 1996, II, 695).
7. See Bernard Yack's interesting response to Schmidt (Yack 1992, 294ff).
8. Compare Heidegger's criticism of Kant for having narrowly defined the thing in terms of the mathematization of space–time in the natural sciences. "Only the mathematical starting point effected a favorable hearing for a corresponding theory of sensation. Kant also remains at the level of this starting point. Like the tradition before and after him, he skips that sphere of things in which we know ourselves immediately at home, i.e., things as the artist depicts them for us, such as Van Gogh's simple chair with the tobacco pipe which was just put down or forgotten there" (Heidegger 1967, 211).
9. It is odd that Marcuse does not discuss the religious horizon of experience which would seem to have a similar function. This was Walter Benjamin's theme and must have been well known to Marcuse.
10. The first person perspective is not necessarily "subjective" in the pejorative sense of the term. For an account in terms of the irreducibility of indexicals, see Olafson (1987, 36ff.)
11. For a current example of phenomenology of technology, see Ihde (1990). Don Idhe has shown the fruitfulness of this approach, however, he does not engage with Marcuse's central concern, value conflict in advanced societies as it impacts the understanding and the future of technology. Ihde mentions differences in values as between national cultures and the effect of those differences on technology, but not the clash of values in the same society. Politics is not a theme he pursues with the resources of phenomenology.
12. Has this distinction between scientific knowledge and technical disciplines been outmoded by the emergence of "technoscience"? Heidegger would no doubt agree with the currently fashionable identification of science and technology. But the distinction is not entirely effaced as some students of science and technology now claim. I think it is obvious that there are both intimate connections and significant differences. For more on my position, see Feenberg (2002, 170ff).

Bibliography

Abromeit, John. "Herbert Marcuse's Critical Encounter with Martin Heidegger: 1927–1933." In J. Abromeit and W. M. Cobb, eds., *Herbert Marcuse: A Critical Reader.* New York: Routledge, 2004.

Abromeit, John and Richard Wolin, eds. *Herbert Marcuse: Heideggerian Marxism.* Lincoln, Nebraska: University of Nebraska Press, 2004 (in press).

Adorno, Theodor. *Minima Moralia.* E. F. N. Jephcott trans. London: Verso, 1974.

Adorno, Theodor and Max Horkheimer. *Dialectic of Enlightenment.* J. Cummings, trans. New York: Herder and Herder, 1972.

Alford, C. Fred. *Science and the Revenge of Nature.* Tampa: University of Florida Press, 1985.

Arendt, Hannah. *Lectures on Kant's Political Philosophy.* Chicago: University of Chicago Press, 1982.

Auden, W. H. "Musée des Beaux Arts." Available at: http://www.tasc.ac.uk/depart/media/staff/l s/Modules/MED1110/Narrative/WHAuden.htm (accessed Feb. 9, 2004)

Benjamin, Walter. "Theories of German Fascism: On the Collection of Essays War and Warrior, ed. Ernst Jünger," *New German Critique*, no. 17, 1979.

Bernasconi, Robert. "The Fate of the Distinction between *Praxis* and *Poesis*," *Heidegger Studies*, II, 1986.

Bijker, Wiebe, Thomas Hughes, and Trevor Pinch. *The Social Construction of Technological Systems.* Cambridge, MA: MIT Press, 1987.

Bloch, Ernst. *The Principle of Hope.* N. Plaice, S. Plaice, and P. Knight, trans. Cambridge, MA: MIT Press, 1996.

Böhme, Gernot. *Natürlich Natur: Über Natur im Zeitalter ihrer technischen Reproduzierbarkeit.* Frankfurt: Suhrkamp, 1992.

Borgmann, Albert. *Technology and the Character of Contemporary Life.* Chicago: University of Chicago Press, 1984.

Bronner, Steven. "Between Art and Utopia: Reconsidering the Aesthetic Theory of Herbert Marcuse." In R. Pippin, A. Feenberg, and C. Webel, eds., *Marcuse: Critical Theory and the Promise of Utopia.* South Hadley: Bergin & Garvey, 1988.

Butler, Eliza M. *The Tyranny of Greece over Germany.* Cambridge: Cambridge University Press, 1935.

Bürger, Peter. *Theory of the Avant-Garde.* M. Shaw, trans. Minneapolis: University of Minnesota Press, 1984.

Caputo, John. *Demythologizing Heidegger.* Bloomington and Indianapolis: Indiana University Press, 1993.

Descartes, René. *Philosophical Works of Descartes.* E. Haldane and G.R.T. Ross, trans. New York: Dover, 1955.

Dreyfus, Hubert. "Heidegger on Gaining a Free Relation to Technology." In A. Hannay and A. Feenberg, eds., *Technology and the Politics of Knowledge.* Bloomington and Indianapolis: Indiana University Press, 1995.

Dodds, E. R. *Plato's Gorgias.* Oxford: Oxford University Press, 1959.

Dumouchel, Paul. "Systèmes sociaux et cognition." In D. Andler, ed., *Introduction aux sciences cognitives.* Paris: Gallimard, 1991.

Eagleton, Terry. *The Ideology of the Aesthetic.* Oxford: Blackwell, 1997.

Feenberg, Andrew. *Lukács, Marx, and the Sources of Critical Theory.* New York: Oxford University Press, 1986.

———. *Alternative Modernity: The Technical Turn in Philosophy and Social Theory.* Berkeley and Los Angeles: University of California Press, 1995.

———. *Questioning Technology.* New York: Routledge, 1999.

———. *Transforming Technology.* New York: Oxford University Press, 2002.

———. "Modernity Theory and Technology Studies: Reflections on Bridging the Gap." In Misa, P. Brey, and A. Feenberg, eds., *Modernity and Technology.* Cambridge, MA: MIT Press, 2003.

Feenberg, Andrew and Jim Freedman. *When Poetry Ruled the Streets: The French May Events of 1968.* Albany: State University of New York Press, 2001.

Foltz, Bruce. *Inhabiting the Earth.* Atlantic Highlands, NJ: Humanities Press, 1995.

Gadamer, Hans-Georg. "Heideggers 'theologische' Jugendschrift." In M. Heidegger, *Interprétations Phénoménologiques d'Aristote.* Mauvezin: Trans-Europ-Repress, 1992.

Gandesha, Samir. "Marcuse, Habermas, and the Critique of Technology." J. Abromeit and W. M. Cobb, eds., *Herbert Marcuse: A Critical Reader.* New York: Routledge, 2004.

Goldmann, Lucien. *Lukács et Heidegger.* Paris: Gonthier, 1973.

Grieder, Alfons. "What Did Heidegger Mean by 'Essence'?", *British Journal of Phenomenology,* 19, 1988.

Habermas, Jürgen. "Technology and Science as Ideology." In *Toward a Rational Society,* J. Shapiro, trans. Boston: Beacon Press, 1970.

———. *The Theory of Communicative Action.* Boston: Beacon Press, 1984.

Heidegger, Martin. *An Introduction to Metaphysics.* R. Manheim, trans. New York: Anchor, 1959.

———. *Being and Time.* J. Macquarrie and E. Robinson, trans. New York: Harper & Row, 1962.

———. *Discourse on Thinking.* J. Anderson, trans. New York: Harper & Row, 1966.

———. *What Is a Thing?* W. B. Barton and V. Deutsch, trans. Chicago: Henry Regnery, 1967.

———. "The Way Back into the Ground of Metaphysics." In W. Kaufman, ed., *Existentialism from Dostoevsky to Sartre.* Cleveland and New York: Meridian Books, 1968.

———. *Poetry, Language, and Thought,* A. Hofstadter, ed. and trans. New York: Harper & Row, 1971.

———. *The Question Concerning Technology.* W. Lovitt, trans. New York: Harper & Row, 1977.

———. *Basic Problems of Phenomenology.* A. Hofstadter, trans. Bloomington: Indiana University Press, 1982.

———. *Hegel's Phenomenology of Spirit.* P. Emad and K. Maly, trans. Bloomington: Indiana University Press, 1984.

———. *Basic Questions of Philosophy.* R. Rojcewicz and A. Schuwer, trans. Bloomington and Indianapolis: Indiana University Press, 1994.

———. *Aristotle's Metaphysics* θ *1–3: On the Essence and Actuality of Force.* W. Brogan and P. Warnek, trans. Bloomington and Indianapolis: Indiana University Press, 1995a.

———. *The Fundamental Concepts of Metaphysics.* W. McNeill and N. Walker trans. Bloomington and Indianapolis: Indiana University Press, 1995b.

———. *Kant and the Problem of Metaphysics.* R. Taft, trans. Bloomington and Indianapolis: Indiana University Press, 1997.

———. "On the Essence and Concept of *physis* in Aristotle's *Physics* B, I." In W. McNeill, ed. and trans., *Pathmarks.* Cambridge: Cambridge University Press, 1998.

———. "Phenomenological Interpretations in Connection with Aristotle." In J. Van Buren, ed. and trans., *Supplements.* Albany: State University of New York Press, 2002.

———. *Four Seminars.* A. Mitchell and F. Raffoul, trans. Bloomington and Indianapolis: Indiana University Press, 2003.

Herf, Jeffrey. *Reactionary Modernism: Technology, Culture, and Politics in Weimar and the Third Reich.* Cambridge: Cambridge University Press, 1984.

Hickman, Larry. *Johns Dewey's Pragmatic Technology.* Indianapolis: Indiana University Press, 1990.

Higgs, Eric, Andrew Light, and David Strong. *Technology and the Good Life?* Chicago: University of Chicago Press, 2000.

Holland, Nancy. "Rethinking Ecology in the Western Philosophical Tradition: Heidegger and/on Aristotle." *Continental Philosophy Review,* 32, no. 4, 1999.

Horkheimer, Max. *Eclipse of Reason.* New York: Seabury Press, 1947.

———. "Traditional and Critical Theory." In *Critical Theory.* M. O'Connell, trans. New York: Herder and Herder, 1972.

Hughes, Thomas. "The Evolution of Large Technological Systems." In T. Pinch, T. Hughes, and W. Bijker, eds., *The Social Construction of Technological Systems.* Cambridge, MA: MIT Press, 1989.

Ihde, Don. *Technology and the Lifeworld.* Bloomington and Indianapolis, Indiana University Press, 1990.

Jay, Martin. *The Dialectical Imagination.* Boston: Little, Brown, & Co., 1973.

———. *Marxism and Totality: The Adventures of a Concept from Lukács to Habermas.* Berkeley: University of California Press, 1984.

———. "'The Aesthetic Ideology' as Ideology: Or What Does it Mean to Aestheticize Politics?" In *Force Fields: Between Intellectual History and Cultural Critique.* New York: Routledge, 1993.

Katz, Barry. *Herbert Marcuse and the Art of Liberation.* London: Verso, 1982.

Kellner, Douglas. *Herbert Marcuse and the Crisis of Marxism.* Berkeley: University of California, 1984.

Kisiel, Theodore. *The Genesis of Heidegger's Being and Time.* Berkeley: University of California Press, 1993.

Kolb, David. *The Critique of Pure Modernity: Hegel, Heidegger and After.* Chicago: University of Chicago Press, 1986.

Latour, Bruno. "Where Are the Missing Masses? The Sociology of a Few Mundane Artifacts." In W. Bijker and J. Law, eds., *Shaping Technology/Building Society: Studies in Sociotechnical Change.* Cambridge, MA: MIT Press, 1992.

————. *Pandora's Hope.* Cambridge, MA: Harvard University Press, 1999.

Loscerbo, John. *Being and Technology.* The Hague: Martinus Nijhoff, 1981.

Lovitt, William. "Techné and Technology." *Philosophy Today,* Spring, 1980.

Löwy, Michael and Robert Sayre. *Romanticism Against the Tide of Modernity.* C. Porter, trans. Durham: Duke University Press, 2001.

Lukács, George. *The Theory of the Novel.* A. Bostock, trans. Cambridge, MA: MIT Press, 1968.

————. *History and Class Consciousness.* R. Livingstone, trans. Cambridge, MA: MIT Press, 1971.

Lukes, Timothy. *The Flight into Inwardness.* Cranbury: Associated University Presses, 1985.

Marcuse, Herbert. *Reason and Revolution: Hegel and the Rise of Social Theory.* New York: Humanities Press, 1963.

————. *One-Dimensional Man.* Boston: Beacon Press, 1964.

————. "The Individual in the Great Society." *Alternatives Magazine,* March-April, 1966a.

————. *Eros and Civilization.* Boston: Beacon Press, 1966b.

————. *Negations,* trans., J. Shapiro. Boston: Beacon Press, 1968.

————. *An Essay on Liberation.* Boston: Beacon Press, 1969a.

————. "Repressive Tolerance." In R. P. Wolff, B. Moore, Jr., H. Marcuse, eds., *A Critique of Pure Tolerance.* Boston: Beacon Press, 1969b.

————. *Counter-Revolution and Revolt.* Boston: Beacon Press, 1972.

————. "Sartre's Existentialism." In *Studies in Critical Philosophy.* Boston: Beacon Press, 1973a.

————. "The Foundation of Historical Materialism." In *Studies in Critical Philosophy.* Boston: Beacon Press, 1973b.

————. "Marxism and Feminism." *Women's Studies,* vol. 2, 1974.

————. "Uber Konkete Philosophie." In Marcuse, *Herbert Marcuse Schriften: Band I.* Frankfurt: Suhrkamp Verlag, 1978a.

————. "Zum Problem der Dialektic I and II." In Marcuse, *Herbert Marcuse Schriften: Band I.* Frankfurt: Suhrkamp Verlag, 1978b.

————. "Beiträge zu einer Phänomenologie des Historischen Materialismus." In *Herbert Marcuse Schriften: Band I.* Frankfurt: Suhrkamp Verlag, 1978c.

————. *Hegel's Ontology and the Theory of Historicity.* S. Benhabib, trans. Cambridge, MA: MIT Press, 1987.

————. "From Ontology to Technology: Fundamental Tendencies of Industrial Society" In E. Bronner and D. Kellner, eds., *Critical Theory and Society: A Reader.* New York: Routledge, 1989.

————. "Ecology and the Critique of Modern Society." *Capitalism, Nature, Socialism,* 3(3), September 1992.

————. *Towards a Critical Theory of Society*. New York: Routledge, 2001.

Marx, Karl. *Karl Marx: Early Writings*. T. B. Bottomore, ed. London: C.A. Watts, 1963.

————. *Grundrisse*. Baltimore: Penguin, 1973.

Matuštík, Martin. *Jürgen Habermas: A Philosophical-Political Profile*. Lanham, MD: Rowman and Littlefield, 2001.

May, Reinhard. *Heidegger's Hidden Sources*. G. Parkes, trans. London and New York: Routledge, 1996.

Maurer, Reinhart. "Die angewandte Heidegger: Herbert Marcuse und das akademische Proletariat." *Philosophisches Jahrbuch* 77, no. 2, 1970.

Merleau-Ponty, Maurice. *Signes*. Paris: Gallimard, 1960.

Misa, Tom, Philip Brey, and Andrew Feenberg, eds. *Modernity and Technology*. Cambridge, MA: MIT Press, 2003.

Murray, Patrick. "The Frankfurt School Critique of Technology." *Research in Philosophy & Technology*, 5, 1982.

Olafson, Frederick. *Heidegger and Philosophy of Mind*. New Haven: Yale University Press, 1987.

————. "Heidegger's Politics: An Interview with Herbert Marcuse." In R. Pippin, A. Feenberg, and C. Webel, eds. *Marcuse: Critical Theory and the Promise of Utopia*. South Hadley: Bergin & Garvey, 1988.

Parkes, Graham, ed. *Heidegger and Asian Thought*. Honolulu: University of Hawaii Press, 1987.

Pinch, Trevor and Wiebe Bijker. "The Social Construction of Facts and Artefacts." In T. Hughes, T. Pinch, and W. Bijker, eds., *The Social Construction of Technological Systems*. Cambridge, MA: MIT Press, 1987.

Pippin, Robert. "Marcuse on Hegel and Historicity." In R. Pippin, A. Feenberg, C. Webel, eds., *Marcuse: Critical Theory and the Promise of Utopia*. South Hadley: Bergin & Garvey, 1988.

Plato. *Gorgias*, trans. W.C. Helmbold. Indianapolis: Bobbs-Merrill, 1952.

————. *Euthyphro, Apology and Crito*. F. J. Church, trans. Indianapolis: Bobbs-Merrill, 1956.

Polt, Richard. "Potentiality, Energy and Sway: From Aristotelian to Modern to Heideggerian Physics?" *Existentia*, XI, 2001.

Poster, Mark. *Existential Marxism in Postwar France: From Sartre to Althusser*. Princeton: Princeton University Press, 1975.

Prauss, Gerold. *Erkennen und Handeln in Heidegger's 'Sein und Zeit'*. Freiburg: Verlag Karl Alber, 1977.

Regehly, Thomas. "Uebersicht ueber die 'Heideggeriana' im Herbert Marcuse-Archiv der Stadt- und Universtitaetsbibliothek in Frankfurt am Main." *Heidegger Studies*, vol. 7, 1991.

Reitz, Charles. *Art, Alienation and the Humanities*. Albany: State University of New York Press, 2000.

Sadler, Ted. *Heidegger and Aristotle: The Question of Being*. London and Atlantic Highlands, NJ: Athlone, 1996.

Schluchter, Wolfgang. The Rise of Western Rationalism: Marx Weber's Developmental History, trans. G. Roth. Berkeley: University of California, 1979.

Schmidt, Alfred. *Marx's Concept of Nature*. B. Fowkes, trans. London: New Left Books, 1971.

————. "Existential Ontology and Historical Materialism in the Work of Herbert Marcuse." In R. Pippin, A. Feenberg, C. Webel, eds., *Marcuse: Critical Theory and the Promise of Utopia*. South Hadley: Bergin & Garvey, 1988.

Schürmann, Reiner. *Heidegger on Being and Acting: From Principles to Anarchy.* Bloomington and Indianapolis: Indiana University Press, 1990.

Sluga, Hans. *Heidegger's Crisis: Philosophy and Politics in Nazi Germany.* Cambridge, MA: Harvard University Press, 1993.

Taminiaux, Jacques. *Lectures de l'ontologie fondamentale.* Grenoble: Editions Jérome Millon, 1995.

Thomson, Iain. "Ontotheology? Understanding Heidegger's *Destruktion* of Metaphysics," *International Journal of Philosophical Studies,* 8, no. 3, 2000.

Valéry, Paul. *Paul Valéry: An Anthology.* J. Matthews, ed. Princeton: Princeton University Press, 1977.

Vattimo, Gianni. *The End of Modernity.* J. Snyder, trans. Baltimore: Johns Hopkins University Press, 1991.

Vogel, Steven. *Against Nature.* Albany: State University of New York Press Press, 1996.

Weber, Max. *The Methodology of the Social Sciences.* E. Shils and H. Finch, trans. New York: The Free Press, 1949.

Wiggershaus, Rolf. *The Frankfurt School: Its History, Theories, and Political Significance.* M. Robertson, trans. Cambridge, MA: MIT Press, 1994.

Wolin, Richard. *The Heidegger Controversy: A Critical Reader.* Cambridge, MA: MIT Press, 1993.

———. *Heidegger's Children: Hannah Arendt, Karl Löwith, Hans Jonas, and Herbert Marcuse.* Princeton: Princeton University Press, 2001.

———. "Herbert Marcuse: A Critical Retrospective from Berlin to Berkeley." In J. McCormick, ed., *Confronting MA Democracy and Industrial Technology: Political and Social Theory from Nietzsche to Habermas.* Durham and London: Duke University Press, 2002.

Yack, Bernard. *The Longing for Total Revolution.* Berkeley and Los Angeles: University of California Press, 1992.

Zimmerman, Michael. "Heidegger and Marcuse: Technology as Ideology," *Research in Philosophy & Technology,* 2, 1979.

———. *Heidegger's Confrontation with Modernity: Technology, Politics, Art.* Bloomington: Indiana University Press, 1990.

Index